CONTINENTAL CONNECTIONS
EXPLORING CROSS-CHANNEL RELATIONSHIPS
FROM THE MESOLITHIC TO THE IRON AGE

edited by

Hugo Anderson-Whymark,
Duncan Garrow and Fraser Sturt

Oxbow Books
Oxford & Philadelphia

Published in the United Kingdom in 2015 by
OXBOW BOOKS
10 Hythe Bridge Street, Oxford OX1 2EW

and in the United States by
OXBOW BOOKS
908 Darby Road, Havertown, PA 19083

© Oxbow Books and the individual contributors 2015

Paperback Edition: ISBN 978-1-78297-809-1
Digital Edition: ISBN 978-1-78297-810-7

A CIP record for this book is available from the British Library

Printed in the United Kingdom by Hobbs the Printers, Totton, Hampshire

For a complete list of Oxbow titles, please contact:

UNITED KINGDOM
Oxbow Books
Telephone (01865) 241249, Fax (01865) 794449
Email: oxbow@oxbowbooks.com
www.oxbowbooks.com

UNITED STATES OF AMERICA
Oxbow Books
Telephone (800) 791-9354, Fax (610) 853-9146
Email: queries@casemateacademic.com
www.casemateacademic.com/oxbow

Oxbow Books is part of the Casemate Group

Cover photo: Satellite image of the Channel, taken on March 14th 2001. Courtesy NASA/JPL-Caltec (NASA/GSFC/METI/ERSDAC/JAROS and U.S./Japan ASTER Science Team).

CONTENTS

LIST OF CONTRIBUTORS

HUGO ANDERSON-WHYMARK
Department of Archaeology
University of York
The King's Manor
York Y01 7EP

DUNCAN GARROW
Department of Archaeology
University of Reading
Whiteknights Box 227
Reading RG6 6AB

JODY JOY
Museum of Archaeology and Anthropology
University of Cambridge
Downing Street
Cambridge CB2 3DZ

CHRIS SCARRE
Department of Archaeology
Durham University
Dawson Building
South Road
Durham DH1 3LE

FRASER STURT
Archaeology
University of Southampton
Avenue Campus
Highfield
Southampton SO17 1BF

ROBERT VAN DE NOORT
University of Reading
Whiteknights Box 227
Reading RG6 6AB

MARC VANDER LINDEN
Institute of Archaeology
University College London
31-34 Gordon Square
London WC1H 0PY

GRAEME WARREN
School of Archaeology
University College Dublin
Newman Building
Belfield
Dublin 4

LEO WEBLEY
Department of Archaeology and Anthropology
University of Bristol
43 Woodland Road
Bristol BS8 1UU

NEIL WILKIN
Department of Britain, Europe and Prehistory
The British Museum
Great Russell Street
London WC1B 3DG

1

Continental connections: introduction

Duncan Garrow & Fraser Sturt

The prehistories of Britain and Ireland are inescapably entwined with continental European narratives. As its subtitle suggests, our primary aim within this volume is to explore 'cross-Channel' relationships throughout later prehistory, investigating the archaeological links (material, social, cultural) between the areas we now call Britain and Ireland, and continental Europe, from the Mesolithic through to the end of the Iron Age. For long periods, this present-day archipelago was of course connected by land to the rest of Europe, allowing people and ideas to flow freely, glaciers permitting. However, with rising sea levels, the island of Ireland formed c. 18,000–14,000 BC, and Britain became fully separated from the European mainland around 6,000 BC (Edwards and Brooks 2008; Sturt, this volume).

The island nature of both Britain and Ireland has subsequently been seen as central to many aspects of life within them, helping to define their senses of identity, and forming a crucial part of their neighbourly relationship with continental Europe and each other. However, it is important to remind ourselves that the surrounding seaways have often served to connect as well as to separate these islands from the continent. In approaching the subject of 'continental connections' in the long-term, and by bringing a variety of very different perspectives (associated with different periods) to bear on it, we hope to provide a new synthesis of the ebbs and flows of the cross-Channel relationship, enabling fresh understandings and new insights about the intimately linked trajectories of change in both regions to emerge.

In this short introduction to the volume, it is our intention to alert the reader to a few of the issues that we see as pertaining to a book addressing the theme of 'continental connections'. We also summarise very briefly the content of each contribution, highlighting the key topics that each of the authors chose to raise within their chapter. The papers follow. In the concluding discussion, we revisit the volume as a whole, picking out some of the key themes that characterise cross-Channel relationships in the past, as well as our archaeological understanding of these in the present.

A Channel apart?

The very act of defining a book as one which seeks to investigate the relationship between

Britain and Ireland on the one hand, and continental Europe on the other, sets up a particular dynamic from the start. As mentioned above, for much of prehistory, these modern-day regions were not separated by the sea at all. However, even after Ireland and Britain became islands after the last glaciation, their definition as entities separate to continental Europe is open to critique. A view of the sea as something which divides regions, making contact problematic, is very much a modern one; the product of recent political boundaries, and of the fact that the vast majority of people living on those islands today are more familiar with land transport than marine travel. In the prehistoric past, things would have been very different – much of the land would have been heavily wooded, and of course would have lacked the roads and railways that make terrestrial communication so easy today. Marine travel, even in the small-scale (and to our minds fragile) boats constructed in prehistory (see Van de Noort, this volume), may well have been quicker and easier than terrestrial movement, especially over long distances. Consequently, connections between, for example, Hampshire and Haut-Normandy, and the social relationships that accompanied them, may well have easier to maintain and more common than those between Hampshire and Herefordshire. Under these circumstances, and in the absence of the modern national boundaries which influence such connections today, an investigation of cross-Channel connections can arguably be viewed as somewhat anachronistic. However, despite this, we argue that it is still worth investigating the nature of continental connections nonetheless. As with period divisions such as 'the Neolithic' or 'the Bronze Age' (which also would not have been relevant to people in the prehistoric past), they provide us with a framework of investigation to work with and around. As will become clear throughout the rest of this volume, the process of dividing Britain/Ireland and continental Europe into separate units can actually help us to see the connections between them.

Bridge or barrier?

A second issue, that relates directly to the one just discussed, is how we choose to characterise the sea itself. In the past, the sea has all too often been characterised somewhat straightforwardly as either a barrier (preventing connections) or a bridge (enabling them). One of the aims of this volume is to move beyond this simple, dualistic understanding of communication across the sea, towards a more nuanced appreciation of maritime connectivity. It is vital that we understand the sea as textured space, which can vary dependent on a wide range of factors, across a variety of temporal and spatial scales. Similarly, it is also important not to focus too singularly on the extremes of sea level change. The large-scale transformations of the Channel we see during the Palaeolithic appear very dramatic. However, that is not to say that later, less extreme changes were actually experienced by people as any less significant in terms of their daily lives. Similarly, as we have argued elsewhere (Sturt *et al.* 2013), whilst the inundation of large landmasses such as Doggerland may appear dramatic to us, especially given the temporal scales we usually investigate it at, people's experiences of that process may have been no more dramatic than those of others elsewhere, where smaller sea level rises would have had, relatively, a very significant impact (e.g. the transformation of the Isles of Scilly from one island into many, or the creation of the island of Jersey which had for several thousand years previously been connected to mainland France by a peninsular).

Material connections

The final issue we want to raise at this early stage in the volume is the relationship between social interaction/isolation and material culture similarities/differences. An understanding of this relationship is arguably the most crucial archaeological issue to confront when investigating 'continental connections'. It is certainly a subject often raised by the authors of the papers which follow. As archaeologists, our primary medium of investigation is material culture. Consequently, our main means of assessing the cross-Channel social relationships that we are interested in here is through comparison of objects on either side of the sea. Yet, in numerous ways, this is an unsatisfactory and extremely partial method of investigation.

The relationship between the material and the social is one which archaeologists have been wrestling with for centuries, particularly so since at least the early twentieth century and the heyday of culture-historical archaeology (see Anderson-Whymark and Garrow, this volume). Nonetheless, the same central question remains today: how exactly should we interpret material similarities/differences in the archaeological record? Do similarities in the forms of objects necessarily indicate strong social relations between the groups using them? Can we really view differences in object styles as implying social divisions or distance? How are we to understand Assemblage A when it has some clear stylistic similarities with Assemblage B, but also many differences as well? As generations of archaeologists have discussed, there are, of course, no straightforward answers to these questions.

In recent years, archaeology has to an extent been able to move beyond typological considerations such as these when discussing mobility. Advances in genetic research and especially in isotopic analysis have begun to make a very significant contribution to the debate as well, allowing us to trace particular individuals across the Channel (and beyond) throughout their life courses (e.g. Fitzpatrick 2011). Nonetheless, these new scientific techniques are unlikely to supersede conventional discussions of material culture any time soon. As will become clear from many of the papers, we still rely predominantly on material similarities and differences when discussing the nature and meaning of continental connections.

It is hoped that this volume, at least to some extent, moves discussion on beyond the simplicity of even some recent debates – where pots in one place that look similar to pots in another have been viewed as straightforward evidence for unidirectional population movement, for example. Equally, a number of papers within the volume question the meaningfulness of material culture *differences*, asking whether a lack of similarity in terms of object styles should necessarily be taken as evidence for a lack of social contact between the groups making and using those objects. As we discuss in more detail within the final chapter, what many authors ultimately describe is an ebbing and flowing of cross-Channel social contact, that must be understood in combination with, *but also as separate from*, comparable ebbs and flows of material culture styles. The two – the social and the material – cannot simply be equated.

An introduction to the papers

The volume begins with two scene-setting overviews. Fraser Sturt's paper 'From land to sea and back again' outlines the shifting character of Europe's landscapes and seascapes over the last million years, charting the ebbs and flows of connection and separation between the land now known as 'Britain and Ireland' and the 'European mainland'. As well as highlighting all of the key changes seen in the palaeogeography of north-west Europe over that time, Sturt also provides a brief history of archaeological engagement with and research on the sea, reminding us just how recently our present-day academic understanding of those past landscapes was formed. He also looks at the practicalities of seafaring through time, and how changing landscapes would have necessitated different kinds of connection and means of travel. As discussed above, Sturt argues that it is not enough to view the sea as simply a connector or a divider, urging us to think about the subtler textures and nuances of cross-Channel connectivity that would have been involved from the Palaeolithic through to the Iron Age.

Robert Van de Noort's paper 'attitudes and latitudes to seafaring' outlines our current state of knowledge about the kinds of boat, and in a much broader sense the kinds of sea travel, we are talking about in prehistory. He neatly summarises all of the evidence we have, in turn, for hide/skin, log and plank-built boats, before going on to summarise the information and insights gleaned from his own very recent project of constructing *Morgawr*, a replica Bronze Age plank-built boat. Van de Noort charts the development of archaeology's perceptions of sea travel and connectivity over the past century. In doing so, he also comes to argue that it is vital to think beyond any straightforward view of the sea as bridge/barrier. He urges us to consider past perceptions of maritime travel that would have been quite different to our own, using that the notion of liminality to explore these.

Graeme Warren's paper, 'Britain and Ireland inside Mesolithic Europe', borrows its title and central theme from an earlier paper by Jacobi (1976), which first investigated the effects of the Channel's formation on connections between Britain and Ireland, and the near continent. Warren begins by reminding the reader that the Mesolithic especially is crucial in terms of our archaeological understanding of continental connections because it was during this period that Britain and Ireland most recently became islands. He outlines briefly the changing nature of the sea and sea travel at that time, before going on to place the cross-Channel developments that occur in the context of much wider long-distance connections right around north-western Europe. Warren suggests that the Mesolithic of Britain and Ireland must be considered simply as *part of* the Mesolithic of Europe, rather than being either 'inside' or 'outside' it, as many of the changes seen at home can often be linked in to historical processes being played out at a much broader scale.

Hugo Anderson-Whymark and Duncan Garrow's paper, 'Seaways and shared ways' investigates the different ways in which archaeologists have imagined and imaged the movement of people, objects and ideas over the course of the Mesolithic–Neolithic transition, *c.* 5,000–3,500 BC. They argue that modern debates about connectivity at that time are in fact still wrestling with issues which were first debated in the heyday of culture-history. In order to contextualise these recent discussions in relation to that older research, they re-visit narratives of Neolithic 'culture change' from the earlier part of the twentieth century. They then go on to summarise the current evidence we have for cross-Channel connectivity in the centuries around 4,000 BC. One of the main conclusions reached is that the material culture associated with the arrival of the Neolithic in Britain and Ireland has *always* been archaeologically confusing. Consequently, they suggest, it is possible that archaeologists have perhaps been trying to imagine – and 'image' (diagrammatically) – this complex set of processes too simply. Rather than depicting the arrival of the Neolithic as a unidirectional process, they argue that we would perhaps be better off embracing the complexity of the record, imagining varied spheres of cultural interaction, with things moving in many directions and differently at different times.

Chris Scarre's paper 'Parallel lives?' investigates the character of continental connections as made manifest through the funerary monuments on either side of the Channel during the Neolithic. He begins by considering the centrality of funerary monuments to our conceptualisations of the Neolithic, discussing how they have generally been considered to have arrived in Britain along with many of that period's other cultural characteristics. Although recent dating programmes have suggested that monuments were not necessarily part of the very earliest Neolithic in Britain, Scarre points out that it is still important to understand how and why they arrived from the continent as part of this broader suit of transformations. He explains that, at a general level, it is relatively easy to see the idea of building funerary monuments arriving in England. However, he then goes on to argue that, once you look in detail at the styles and dates of monuments on either side of the Channel, the comparisons become harder to make. He suggests that, despite these initial (superficial?) similarities, during the later 4th and 3rd millennia Britain and France witness quite different trajectories of monumental architecture and practice. He ends up by suggesting that, in fact, there are more points of divergence than convergence once the records on either side of the Channel are compared. As a result, he suggests that we might helpfully conceptualise continental connections as involving both 'transmission' and 'translation' of practices across the Channel. As we discuss in the final chapter of the volume, this pair of concepts is arguably a very helpful one in terms of thinking through change throughout prehistory much more generally as well.

Neil Wilkin and Marc Vander Linden's paper 'What was and what would never be' looks at the changing patterns of interaction and archaeological visibility across north-west Europe from 2,500–1,500 BC. The central focus of their paper is what they term the Bell Beaker 'phenomenon', the unusually uniform and widespread nature of which, they suggest, cannot be stressed enough. The Bell Beaker period, they argue, represents one of heightened connectivity across Europe at a variety of different levels. They take care to situate the Beaker phase within its broader temporal context, highlighting the rather more varied or 'fragmented' character of the archaeological record around western Europe on either side of the Bell Beaker period. In bringing out these contrasts, they are however careful to stress the variable nature of the evidence we have to deal with, highlighting the fact that the archaeological *visibility* of certain practices can vary enormously, potentially masking actual similarities or differences that may have existed.

Leo Webley's paper rethinks Iron Age connections across the Channel and the North Sea. He begins by suggesting that traditional narratives of the Iron Age, which see continental connections as largely having diminished at the end of the Bronze Age, are misplaced, based on a very narrow and partial view of the archaeological record. He goes on to suggest that it is time to discard the notion that contacts between Britain and the Continent were meagre before the closing stages of the Iron Age. Throughout the paper, he argues that when a broader range of evidence – including everyday (as opposed to elite) artefacts, settlement patterns, ritual practices and the treatment of the dead – is considered, cross-Channel connections are abundantly apparent, with innovations travelling in both directions. He ends by stressing that, even when expressing their distinctiveness, British communities can paradoxically be seen as following wider European trends. The most interesting narratives to be told, he argues, are about the interplay between similarities and differences on either side of the Channel.

Jody Joy's paper investigates 'connections and separation', focusing especially on Iron Age 'Celtic' art from *c.* 400 BC to the early Roman period. Joy questions many of the long-held assumptions about Celtic art, suggesting that the development of the 'insular' style *c.* 300–100 BC may not in fact reflect Britain and Ireland's isolation from the continent. He agrees with Webley that, in many other spheres of Iron Age life, comparisons can be made, also suggesting that differential patterns of deposition on either side of the Channel may have hidden the visibility of similarities in decorated metalwork styles. Finally, focusing in on a number of recently discovered artefacts, Joy emphasises the continental connections that are in fact visible throughout this period. He concludes by suggesting that Celtic art should always be viewed in light of broader contextual evidence, and that the apparently special objects he mentions should be viewed as the product of complex cross-Channel social networks and more mundane trade relationships.

References

Edwards, R. and Brooks, A. 2008. The island of Ireland: drowning the myth of an Irish land-bridge? In J. Davenport, D. Sleeman, and P. Woodman (eds) *Mind the Gap: Postglacial Colonisation of Ireland*, 19–34. Special Supplement to *The Irish Naturalists' Journal*.

Fitzpatrick, A. 2011. *The Amesbury archer and the Boscombe bowmen: Volume 1. Early Bell Beaker burials at Boscombe Down, Wiltshire, Great Britain*. Salisbury: Wessex Archaeology.

Jacobi, R. 1976. Britain inside and outside Mesolithic Europe. *Proceedings of the Prehistoric Society* 42, 67–84.

Sturt, F., Garrow, D. and Bradley, S. 2013. New models of North West European Holocene palaeogeography and inundation. *Journal of Archaeological Science* 40, 3963–3976. http://dx.doi.org/10.1016/j.jas.2013.05.023.

2

From sea to land and back again: understanding the shifting character of Europe's landscapes and seascapes over the last million years

Fraser Sturt

Introduction

The palaeogeography of the north-west margin of Europe has changed markedly, and regularly, since humans first occupied the region around one million years ago (Parfitt *et al.* 2010; Cohen *et al.* 2014). Britain as we know it today has morphed from peninsula to island and back again in response to glacial cycles on at least five occasions over this period. Understanding the timing, nature and extent of these changes is fundamental to appreciating the context within which archaeologically attested activity occurred. That being said, it is argued here that rather than just providing an environmental backdrop to a well-known story, knowledge of the rate, pace and degree of change can provide a secure vantage point from which to reconsider a range of key questions concerning connectivity and social change throughout prehistory.

With advances in computational approaches to landscape reconstruction and increasing knowledge of offshore geology (Cohen *et al.* 2012; 2014; Hijma *et al.* 2012) it is now possible to do more than just note the island or peninsula status of Britain. Through combination of bathymetric (elevation of the seafloor) and topographic data with outputs from glacial isotactic adjustment (GIA) models (which account for changes in the altitude of the earth's crust due to differential loading and unloading by ice sheets, along with variation in the volume of water in the world's oceans and seas) within geographical information systems (GIS), we can begin to consider land and seascape change at ever finer temporal and spatial resolutions for the late Pleistocene and Holocene.

The insights we gain from these outputs can in turn allow us to reconsider changes seen in the deeper past as well, helping us move away from a focus on terrestrial connections alone, to an appreciation of Pleistocene Europe's changing seas and costal landscapes. This is productive as it stymies traditional discourse of 'bridges' and 'barriers', and forces a focus on the dynamics of and potential for communication. In addition, through taking this wider view of connectivity and physical space, it encourages us to engage with additional problems we create through application of archaeological terminology. When looking at north-west Europe in this fashion it becomes apparent that we cannot always split time and space neatly into categories such as Mesolithic, Neolithic or Bronze Age due to the time transgressive nature of human activity coming under each heading in different, but spatially abutting, regions; with the Neolithic in one area corresponding with contemporary Mesolithic activity in another. As such, the sections below consider the changes that were occurring across space and time with regard to more arbitrary, but perhaps in this context more helpful, chronological divisions. This in turn helps us to re-evaluate how we conceive of connectivity, and what we hope to gain from singling it out as a topic for consideration.

Figure 2.1. Clement Reid's (1913, 40) map of his hypothesised extent on the one-time extent of land based on the recovery of submerged peat from the North Sea.

Recognising change

Archaeologists and antiquarians have had a defined interested in the changing palaeogeography of Europe for at least one hundred years. Reid's (1913, 40) publication of a map showing the hypothetical extent of now submerged dry land in the North Sea (Figure 2.1) triggered a wave of interest across Europe, and in particular in England (Clark 1936; Crawford 1936). Clark (1936) seized upon the significance of the recovery of an antler harpoon from the Leman and Ower banks in 1931, determining that the archaeology of the North Sea basin may prove pivotal to our comprehension of the European Palaeolithic and Mesolithic. Fagan (2001) notes that for Clark this discovery sparked a transformation in his archaeological understanding and published outputs. Where previously there were rather staid accounts of cultural groups defined by current distributions of finds divided by the sea, now Clark engaged with the interstitial qualities of the record, considering how these blue blank spaces on maps were once populated and connected parts of Europe.

However, as Coles (1998, 50) notes, following this early rush of enthusiasm, archaeological consideration of submerged landscapes diminished. Instead of viewing this space as the lived landscape that Reid (1913, 8) and Clark (1936) depicted, discussion moved to one of land-bridges and corridors. As Gaffney *et al.* (2007; 2009, 29) argue, this served to diminish the perceived value of offshore deposits; they became a transition space to be described broadly, rather than an area worthy of detailed investigation. Thus while archaeologists working in the Baltic continued to demonstrate the wealth of material that could be recovered from such contexts (Andersen 1980; 2013), wider discourse largely failed to extrapolate this potential for other regions.

It is for this reason that research done by Louwe Kooijmans' (1971), Jacobi (1976) and Wymer and Robbins (1994) documenting finds from the North Sea region (directly indicating something of changing land forms and social connectivity) received surprisingly little attention. This was to change with the publication of Coles' (1998) work on Doggerland. Here the variety of data described, the magnitude of changes that occurred and their potential significance for communities living at the time were clearly set out. Through this key and subsequent papers (1999, 2000) Coles re-asserted the significance of this overlooked space to north-west European prehistory. Pioneering work by Gaffney *et al.* (2007, 2009) then helped to add increasing depth to our knowledge of these once terrestrial landscapes, through intricate geophysical mapping, transforming Reid's (1913) hypothetical realm into a three dimensionally viewable landscape.

The impact of Coles' (1998, 45) work was that it forced people to engage with these areas as once lived terrestrial landscapes rather than as simple connectors. While this was significant, and is a theme picked up on again through this paper, it also served to direct attention to the 'dry-land' and its changing form alone. This may well have been at the expense of deeper consideration as to the wider importance of the broader changes being described. How did inundation impact on the nature of the sea, river behaviour, shoreline ecology and resource distribution? The focus on dry-land also led to a preference for discussion of large-scale inundation and land loss. For later prehistory this has meant that the issues of sea-level change, changes in sea behaviour and maritime connectivity have not been as well developed as they might have been. This is despite a raft of work that has focused attention on the importance of engaging with the specifics of maritime space in our accounts of prehistory (Westerdahl 1992; Warren 2006; Rainbird 2007; Needham 2009; Garrow & Sturt 2011; Van de Noort 2011). In essence, through always focusing on the biggest visible impacts we may have overlooked the importance of smaller scale changes in both land and sea forms. As such, in the sections below, this paper attempts to address impact and significance at a range of scales.

Understanding palaeogeographic change

Changes in relative sea-level are the principle factor impacting on palaeography explored in this paper. These changes broadly correspond to three driving forces; glacio-eustacy, glacio-isostacy and crustal uplift/subsidence. Glacio-eustacy relates to the amount of water free to flow in the world's rivers, seas and lakes, as dictated by the quantity locked on land in glaciers. As Ice Ages are entered into, increasingly large amounts of water become captured within the growing ice sheets, reducing the volume in ocean basins. Glacio-isostacy refers to the impact of the weight of these ice sheets on the altitude of the Earth's crust. As glaciers grew they gained weight and depressed the land underneath them. Away from the glacier's margins, land would be forced upwards (the forebulge effect) in response to the area under depression. With the move to an interstadial, ice sheets would melt and the land under the glacier begin to lift and the forebulge collapse.

Crustal uplift/subsidence corresponds to longer-term tectonic processes. These are significant for this paper due to the uncertainty over their exact nature in the North Sea and Channel regions. As Westley *et al.* (2013, 2) explain, the North Sea basin has undergone *c.* 0.4m of subsidence per thousand years over the last 730,000 years. In contrast the Channel is considered to have seen an uplift rate of 0.1m per thousand years (Laggard *et al.* 2003). While these rates may seem small, over the duration of the Palaeolithic the impact on

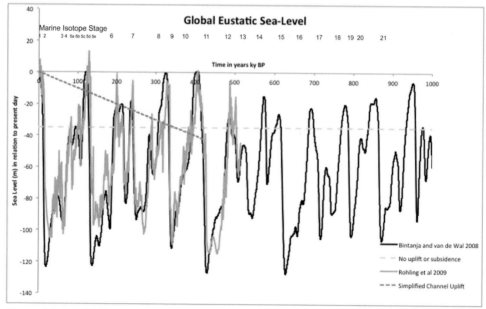

Figure 2.2. Graph showing eustatic sea-level change over the last million years. Data from Bintanja and van de Wall 2008 and Rohling et al. *2009.*

palaeogeography can be substantial. The difficulty comes in understanding if this was a constant rate of change, or one that has had episodes of more rapid adjustment. The way in which this plays out has significance in relation to when Britain becomes separated from the continent during the Pleistocene (Ashton *et al.* 2010; Pettitt and White 2012, 102) and how this may have played a part in changing patterns of hominin occupation.

Figure 2.2 provides data for eustatic sea-level change over the last million years (Bintanja and Van de Wal 2008, Rohling *et al.* 2009). Two lines are given to help explain the elevation that sea-level would have to reach for Britain to become separated from the continent after the initial breach of the Weald-Artois ridge (discussed below, but currently thought to have occurred by MIS12 (*c.* 478–424,000 BP) (Gupta *et al.* 2007; Toucanne *et al.* 2009)). The dashed horizontal line takes a constant depth of -35m as the marker for permanent separation of Britain from the continent based on values gained from modern bathymetry (i.e. this is what it would take to make Britain an island) but not accounting for changes in altitude of the modern sea-floor created through uplift and subsidence (White and Schreve 2000). Above this level the connecting planes of the southern North Sea are thought to have become inundated. The angled dotted line shows the impact of a linear steady expression of uplift for the Channel area over this period based, and the corresponding shift that may have to be considered with regard to depths required for island formation to occur. However, as noted above, it should not be taken for granted that the actual process of uplift played out in this manner, with more punctuated changes being possible. Figure 2.2 makes clear that Britain may have been separated from the continent as many as ten times over this period and a minimum of five (see Pettitt and White (2012, 213) for additional discussion).

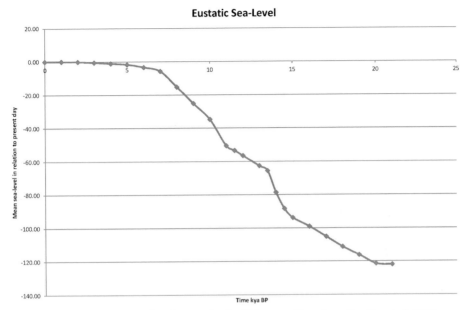

Figure 2.3. Eustatic sea-level curve for the Holocene. Data from Bradley et al. *2011.*

Figure 2.3 gives a more detailed view of eustatic change since the Late Glacial Maximum (LGM), based on Bradley *et al.*'s (2011) recent GIA model. This is the curve used as part of the GIA driven palaeogeographic models for the Holocene discussed by Sturt *et al.* (2013) and illustrated in this paper from Figure 2.8 onwards.

Within this paper models for the changing palaeography of Europe over the last million years are given. These have been created in two different ways. Prior to the last glacial maximum (*c.* 27,000 years ago) the models are generated through plotting mapped sedimentary deposits described in the published literature and matching these to the predicted eustatic elevation of sea-level projected onto current bathymetric data (following Westley *et al*'s 2013 representations). For the LGM onwards into the Holocene, palaeogeographic maps are derived from integration of GIA model outputs with modern bathymetry via GIS for the British Isles. A detailed account of the methodology used for this process can be found in Sturt *et al.* (2013). In addition, a broader region beyond the extent of the GIA model is shown. For this region shorelines are based purely on bathymetric depths taken from the eustatic sea-level curve. The difference between the GIA model extents and those generated in the more simplistic manner point to the degree of uncertainty inherent in the Pleistocene palaeogeographic models. For pre-LGM periods there are not enough surviving direct records of sea-level change and ice sheet behaviour to create a detail GIA. The shorelines given in Figures 2.4 to 2.7 are thus suggestive heuristic devices giving an indicative coastline.

While the GIA driven outputs can be seen to be a marked improvement for post-LGM periods, some caveats still need to be bourn in mind. The models presented here do not account for sedimentation, erosion or progradation through saltmarsh or peat development over the last ten thousand years. In addition, they do not directly depict the changes in tidal patterns caused by coastline reconfiguration and inundation, although an appreciation of this can be gained by viewing them alongside the palaeotidal modelling of Uehara *et al.* (2006) and Neil *et al.* (2010). Thus, while they can be seen as our best regional level understanding of change, detailed archaeological and palaeoenvironmental work will always pick up a more subtle story at the local level. However, they do allow us to infer change in regions where we have no direct record, and to extrapolate through time in a robust manner. Thus rather than invalidating the use of such models, acknowledging these limitations helps frame how we should engage with them.

The Pleistocene

As noted above, reconstructing Pleistocene palaeogeography is complicated due to the reduced resolution of supporting data relating to relative sea-level change and the impact of crustal subsidence and uplift. However, as Westley and Bailey (2013, 18) argue, the data we do have from sedimentary deposits, raised beaches and global eustatic sea-level indicators

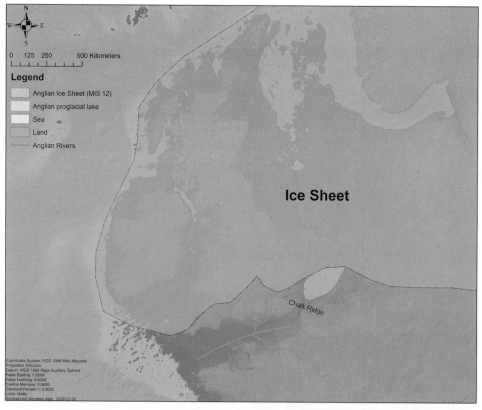

Figure 2.4. Hypothetical palaeogeographic reconstruction for MIS12 (Anglian glacial maxima). Based on Gibbard 1988, 1995; Toucanne et al. 2009; Huuse and Lykke-Anderson 2000; Stringer 2006; Westley and Bailey 2013. Basemap data from GEBCO 08 (www.gebco.net).

permit broad reconstructions at the temporal resolution of marine isotope stages (MIS). Over the course of the Pleistocene one of the most significant changes to occur in relation to physical connectivity between Britain and mainland Europe was the opening of the Straits of Dover, when the Weald-Artois chalk ridge (shown in Figure 2.4) was breached. The exact dating of when this occurred is still debated, with clear evidence existing for a breach in MIS 5e (Meijer and Preece 1996), but with the weight of evidence now suggesting that it probably occurred as early as MIS 12 (Gibbard 1995; Gupta *et al.* 2007, 344; Toucanne *et al.* 2009; Pettitt and White 2012, 102; Westley and Bailey 2013, 18).

Figure 2.4 provides a model of palaeogeography at the glacial-maxima of MIS12. Here due to lowered sea-levels an expanse of land exists where today we see the English Channel. A proglacial lake develops behind the Weald-Artois chalk ridge, fed by the Rhine, Meuse and Thames. Figure 2.5 shows a high stand (maximum sea-level reached) interstadial phase with the chalk ridge still in place. The relatively low number of finds from Britain for this period point to sporadic occupation between MIS 21 and MIS 13 (Ashton and Lewis 2002; Hosfield 2011; Pettitt and White 2012, 114). Thus although the presence of a physical connection

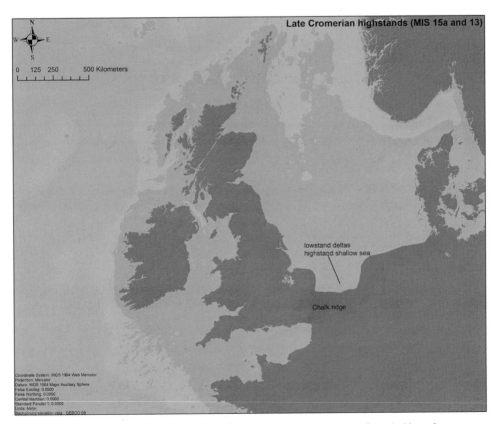

Figure 2.5. Map showing Late Cromerian highstand situations (no ice shown). Note the presence of the Weald-Artois ridge connecting Britain to the continent. Based on Bates et al. *2003; Stringer 2006; Peeters* et al. *2009; Westley and Bailey 2013. Basemap data from GEBCO 08 (www.gebco.net).*

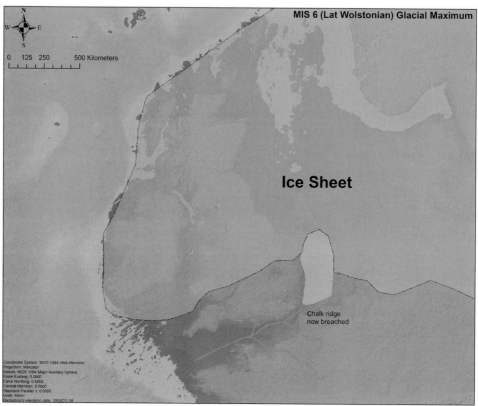

Figure 2.6. Map showing MIS 6 (Late Wolstonian glacial maxima). Note that the Weald-Artois ridge has been breached, with a river running from the proglacial lake. Based on Gibbard 1988; 1995; Toucanne et al. 2009; Huuse and Lykke-Anderson 2000; Coles 1998; Stringer 2006; Westley and Bailey 2013.

to the larger continental landmass may have made it easier for people to move back and forth, the resolution of the evidence makes it hard to understand to what degree this took place. As Gamble (1986), Roebroeks *et al.* (1992) and Brown *et al.* (2013) have argued, early human communities thrived on mosaic habitats, where large number of resources could be found in relatively short distances. It is entirely possible that the 'bridge' of the Weald-Artois ridge would have represented a particularly complex mosaic zone; with deltaic formations along its northern edges and shallow seas extending out and away into deeper water. As Stringer (2000) has suggested, such areas may have been highly desirable due to the variety of resources to be found within a small area. Thus, as Coles (1998) argued for later periods, this continental connection may have been more than a physical link, it could have been an extension of a favourable place to live, perhaps explaining the clustering of known evidence for this period.

Gupta *et al.* (2007, 344) conclude that the chalk ridge was removed when the amount of water trapped in the proglacial lake eventually led to the catastrophic breach of the Weald-Artois obstruction in a megaflood scenario. This has been inferred from the geomorphological

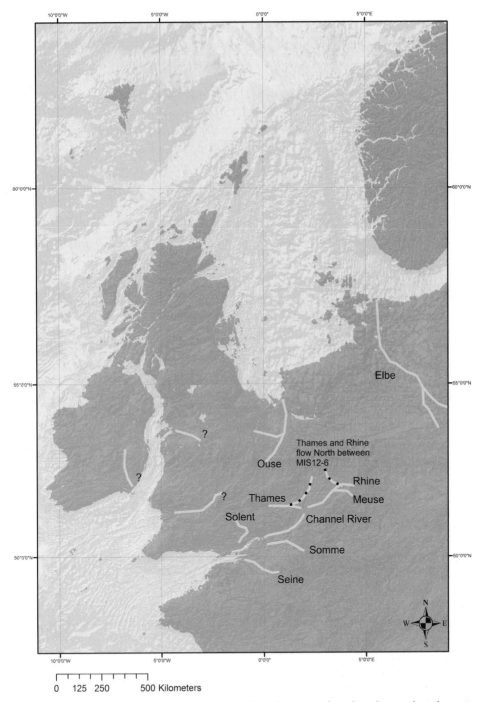

Figure 2.7. Map showing post-Anglian intermediate between glacial and interglacial maxima palaeogeography (from Westley et al. *2013, figure 1.7).*

features revealed via geophysical survey of the Channel floor. Toucanne *et al.* (2009) favour a more progressive development, with a major breach from MIS 12 and then development of the channel system over subsequent glaciations. Whichever model is followed, this event marks the first significant change in the nature of continental connections in north-west Europe. With the breaching of the Dover straits the continuous physical connection with the continent through high-stand phases was lost. However, it is significant for another reason. During low to mid-stand situations the presence of the new channel river system made for a formidable landscape feature, impacting on movement across the region. Even allowing for over-deepening due to continued erosion through time, the channel river sections revealed by Gupta *et al.* (2007) and discussed by Toucanne *et al.* (2009) indicate a substantial river, perhaps acting as more of a barrier than the presence of the English Channel in later periods.

This is significant, as it may have changed the axis of movement in post-Anglian periods. As Westley and Bailey (2013, 20) note, Figure 2.5 and 2.6 are the most common form of representation for palaeogeography of the Pleistocene. However, these represent maxima and minima scenarios, rather the more usual 'mean' situation. Figure 2.7 gives Westley *et al.*'s (2013, Figure 1.7) representation of post-Anglian intermediate (between glacial and interglacial maxima) palaeogeography and indicates how the presence of the Channel river may have changed movement patterns of animals and people in the Lower Palaeolithic. In many ways this best reflects the 'optimal' landscape of mosaic environments as the world moves from glacial to inter-glacial stages and back. Yet, as noted above, it is important not to underestimate the presence of the Channel river, as from 250,000 BP it "carried drainage from almost half of western Europe" and would have been a high energy anastomosing system, quite unlike any system we see today.

This in some ways highlights the problems with this form of palaeogeographic representation, where we rapidly absorb superficial landscape details (locations of rivers, lakes and shorelines) but struggle to understand the detail of what is represented. The changes in river formation, shoreline configuration, water depths and associated ecosystem re-configuration are just as significant, if not more so, than the moving land/sea boundary. As Brown *et al.* (2013) have argued, Lower and early-middle Palaeolithic communities seem to have sought out floodplain locations just beyond the tidal limit as their favoured places within the landscape. The process of inundation would have radically altered the location of this ecotone niche, indicating the need for more detailed understanding of the process of land/seascape reconfiguration discussed here.

Pettitt and White (2012, 112) have discussed the transition in environments over stadial and inter-stadial periods in relation to four phases. The first phase sees Britain as a cooling peninsula of mosaic environments, with sea-levels beginning to fall as temperatures drop. Phase two is the establishment of a glacial wasteland, Britain is connected to the continent due to the water trapped in glaciers, but it and the Dogger plain are inhospitable to people, animals and plant life. This eventually gives way to a warming transition, with re-establishment of mosaic communities. The physical connection to the continent remains for millennia (perhaps as many as 3,000 years), allowing a re-colonisation of the peninsula (Pettitt and White 2012, 14). Finally, Britain becomes an interglacial island, which 'traps' populations on the 'isolated' landmass. Here the nature of continental connectivity and associated environmental conditions is very much seen to dictate the nature of the archaeological record.

The next big shift with regard to palaeogeography and connectivity comes with the

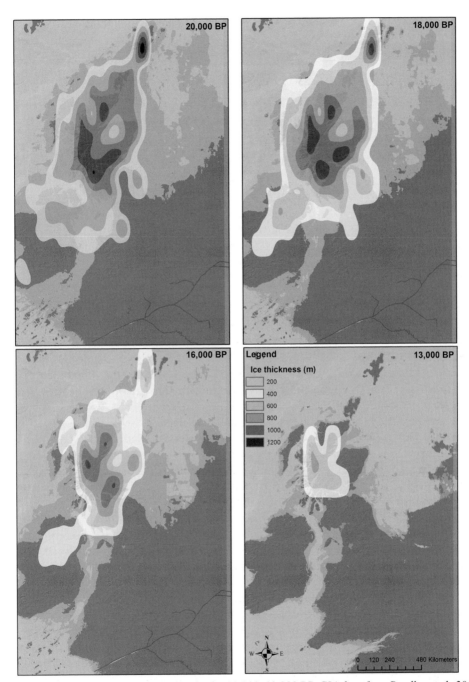

Figure 2.8. Map showing palaeogeography for 20,000–13,000 BP. GIA data from Bradley et al. 2011 and Brooks et al. 2011. Contributing topography and bathymetry from GEBCO 08 (www.gebco.net), Ordnance Survey, SeaZone and marine net. Note the difference between the GIA model (dark grey) and the simple reduction of sea-levels based on the Eustatic curve (as rendered below the solid shading).

LGM. Here two factors make it easier to understand the nature of both physical and social connectivity. First, the fact that this was the last period of major glaciation means that more substantial evidence survives for it and more precise modelling of its impacts can be carried out. As such, from this point on GIA models can be used to predict palaeogeographic change. Secondly, the resolution of the archaeological record increases. Figure 2.8 provides a GIA model output of palaeogeography *c.* 20,000 BP. A large ice sheet covers much of northern England, Scotland and Ireland, and Britain is once again a peninsula of Europe. However, as Pettit and White (2012) suggest, it would have been a largely cold and inhospitable place. In Figure 2.8 the impact of accounting for glacio-isostatic adjustment is clear. The central area of the figures gives the zone for which GIA data has been included, beyond those margins a simple drop in Eustatic sea-level has been used to reconstruct palaeogeography (with the same limits also visible more faintly in the central region). The degree of difference between GIA data and simplified reconstruction should act as a warning with regard to the accuracy of pre-LGM models. However, although the details of land extents may change, the key issues of connectivity and change would have been largely as discussed above.

With regard to the nature of social connectivity during the LGM it is important to note that Roebroeks *et al.* (2011) suggest that northern Germany and France were depopulated at this point in time. This reinforces the complexity of understanding inter-relationships between physical connectivity and human activity in the Palaeolithic. As populations responded to changing environmental conditions the loci of settlement shifted. Thus, the potential for occupation should not be taken as a direct predictor. In regard to the LGM, it would appear that between 31,000 BP and at least 22,000 BP (but more likely as late as 16,000 BP) there was no human occupation of Britain (Pettitt and White 2012, 424) and surrounding glacial margin areas. Figure 2.8 gives a GIA based model for palaeogeography at this time of human re-occupation of the British Isles as well as offering a final glimpse of the Pleistocene world prior to the transition to the Holocene at *c.* 11,600 BP.

This account of Pleistocene change has been necessarily brief but has highlighted the significant changes in the palaeogeography of north-west Europe and the uncertainties in our understanding of it. It is clear that these changes, and the environmental factors that drove them had a considerable impact on the nature of the archaeological record. Understanding the inter-relationship between people and environment, of Britain's connection to the continent or separation as island is fundamental to explaining the distribution of material. However, it is possible that we can do more than think about distribution alone, and consider more detailed questions of palaeoecology; of how these changing environments afforded by this shifting landscape and seascape may have been attractive or unattractive to groups living at the time. In addition it is clear that thinking in terms of national boundaries and current geographical extents certainly limits our understanding and more dynamic geographies of the past have to be engaged to create a fully convincing picture of past activity.

The Holocene

Figure 2.9 provides an overview of the changing palaeogeography of Europe between 11,000 and 2,000 BP in a simplified form. More complex representations of changing depths of water and areas inundated at 500 year intervals can be viewed in Sturt *et al.* (2013). Thanks to the work of Coles (1998) and Gaffney *et al.* (2007) the big picture story of the inundation of

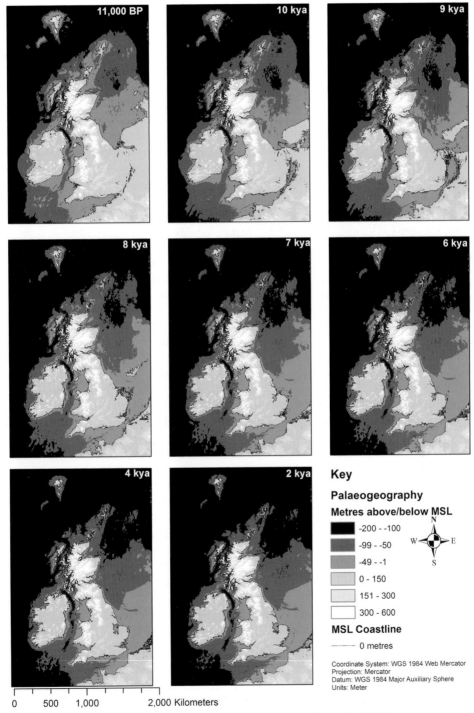

Figure 2.9. Changing palaeogeography from 11,000–2,000 BP.

Doggerland is now well known. This sees the large-scale relatively rapid transformation of north-west Europe from continental landmass to the more complex island landscape that we are familiar with today, over a three thousand year time period. As Figure 2.3 makes clear, the initial rates of sea-level change at the start of the Holocene were rapid, until *c.* 7,000 BP when a decline in vertical rise becomes apparent.

In addition to the general picture of eustatic sea-level rise, a series of meltwater pulses (caused by the collapse of melting ice-sheets and the release of large volumes of freshwater) saw very rapid vertical rise events. The most famous of these events is that which occurred *c.* 8,200 BP, with an almost instantaneous 1–3m rise (Hijma and Cohen 2010) in the North Sea region. The impact of meltwater pulses and the later Storegga slide tsunami (*c.* 8,000 BP) help to focus the mind on the fact that the images in Figure 2.9 smooth out the process of change. In addition, they draw the eye to land/sea boundary changes rather than the detail of the shifting environments, a theme that will be returned to later in this paper.

With regard to large-scale change Figure 2.9 illustrates that Ireland had become separated from Britain by at least 14,000 BP, and Britain becomes physically separated from the continent *c.* 9,000 BP – 8,000 BP. For the separation of Britain from the continent the GIA modelled date conforms well to physical evidence from coastal peat sequences along the south coast on England (Waller and Kirby 2002; Momber 2000; Gupta *et al.* 2004; Massey *et al.* 2008) and from the Seine Estuary, France (Frouin *et al.* 2007). In the case of Ireland surprisingly little work has been done in the Irish Sea with the result being a range of different models giving subtly different dates for separation (McCabe *et al.* 2008; Roberts *et al.* 2011; Edwards and Brooks 2006; Brooks *et al.* 2008; Shennan and Horton 2002), but all indicating a pre-Holocene split.

The next major event in terms of land loss is the submergence of Doggerland. Here the GIA model indicates inundation of this topographic high at *c.* 8,000 BP. As Gaffney *et al.* (2009) and Bell and Warren (2013, 35) suggest, this could mean that the final stage in the loss of Doggerland was in response to either the 8,200 BP meltwater pulse or the Storegga slide. However, it is quite possible that localised islets and inter-tidal sand islands remained beyond this 8,000 BP date to be more fully submerged over the following centuries. This focus on the detail of submergence helps to bring to the fore the fact that once covered over by tidal waters those topographic highs were not lost. Instead they became key features of seascapes; affecting the behaviour of currents, collecting drifting material and providing different sorts of fishing grounds to deeper waters. Thus we should not confuse inundation and the transformation from land to sea as a single stage process, but part of a shift to a different but potentially equally valuable) mosaic of resources.

In addition, as has been argued elsewhere (Sturt *et al.* 2013), focusing on the loss of large land areas such as Doggerland can negatively impact on our appreciation of the importance of more localised stories of change on patterns of connectivity and interaction. A good example of this can be seen in the different island groups along the southern margins of north-west Europe (the Channel Islands and Isles of Scilly). Guernsey separates from the continental mainland at *c.* 11,000 BP; and from its smaller island neighbour of Herm by 8,500 BP. However, Jersey gives a very different record of connectivity, with a finger of land slowly transforming into an inter-tidal causeway and cluster of small islands, with full separation not indicated until *c.* 6,000 BP. Furthermore, if we consider the implications of the bathymetry and topography of this region, it is clear that we need to do more than talk of causeways and connections. The process of inundation in this area would have led to large inter-tidal plains, punctuated with rocky outcrops. When exposed as land they would have been confusing fractal spaces to navigate, made more dangerous by the speed of the incoming tides over the low-lying ground. By boat they will have represented complex currents and tidal races, with rocky outcrops just below the water. However, these fast flowing waters with variable depths may also have acted as good fishing grounds.

Just as there is a more complicated story to tell for the Channel Islands when we look more closely, so too is there for the Isles of Scilly. Here the nature of the topography and bathymetry means that large scale transformation not only occurs in the earlier Holocene in response to rapid rates of vertical sea-level rise, but also in the later Holocene (Neolithic, Bronze and Iron Ages) as low lying landscapes are inundated and once larger islands are broken down into the configuration we see today at *c.* 3,000 BP. Thus in this landscape the texture of change takes on a different form and can help us consider the peculiarities of the records in both sets of island groups. However, this process of zooming in to appreciate variable histories pays dividends across the board. Just as the detail of landscape change is appreciatively different between Scilly and the Channel Islands, so too would it have been along different portions of the continental and British coastlines. In addition, as noted above, seaways will also have seen a corresponding change in behaviour. Once un-navigable routes due to low lying islets would have become more passable as sea-levels rose, but with new obstructions and deviating currents created as a part of this process. It is important to note here that the models presented in this paper do not account for changes in tidal range, and that every image reflects mean sea-level. As Uehara *et al.* (2006) and Neil *et al.* (2010) have shown, shifts in tidal range as the continental shelf becomes inundated can be profound, accelerating some of the changes visible in Figure 2.9.

Discussion and conclusion

Addressing one million years of palaeogeographic change is not a straightforward process. It becomes tempting to simplify things to a story of physical continuity and discontinuity – of land bridges. However, as Coles has argued (1998) this would be a mistake. Here I would like to emphasise that this is not only problematic in terms of how we understand terrestrial space, but also how we engage with marine space. Gaining an appreciation of how changes in water-depth will have created different biomes and different seafaring potential is just as significant as understanding the point of separation. This is especially important as we can infer from the 60km sea crossing undertaken as part of the colonisation of Australia and New Guinea *c.* 50,000 years ago (Balme 2013), and the presence of people on Flores *c.* 800,000 years ago, that the Channel itself was unlikely to pose an impenetrable barrier even in earlier periods if people ever chose to attempt to cross it. As Westley and Bailey argue (2013, 26), planned sea travel in skin boats must be entertained as a possibility from at least 40,000 years ago. Thus from this point onwards, we are not discussing barriers to connectivity, but a change in the medium over which that connection occurs.

It is at this juncture that work on changing palaeogeography begins to mesh with accounts of landscape and seascape. As Westerdahl (1992), Needham (2009) and Van de Noort (2011) have argued, understanding the changing characteristics of north-west Europe's seaways allows us to reconsider zones of interaction and societies' different understandings of maritime space. For Westerdhal (1992) and Needham (2009) we can split north-west Europe into a

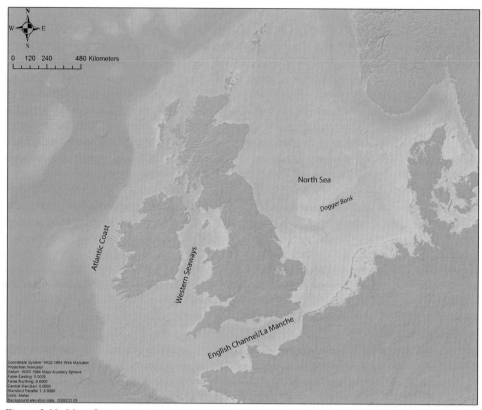

Figure 2.10. Map showing major marine interaction zones (after Sturt et al. *2013) – this also reflects Needham's (2009) 'maritory' zones.*

series of interaction zones or as Needham (*ibid.*) terms them 'maritories'. In some senses these maritime zones also reflect potential interaction spheres during lowstand phases when greater extents of land were exposed. This is due to the fact that they are largely driven by topographic features, which in turn influence hydroclimate and weather patterns. As Anderson-Whymark and Garrow (this volume) note, there is a long history of attempting to reconcile the nature of physical space with social changes indicated through material culture across bodies of water in graphical form; from the block diagrams of Childe (1929; Figure 5.1 in this volume), through to the more conceptual interaction spheres of Needham (2009) and triangles of Wilkin and Vander Linden (this volume).

Figure 2.10 illustrates these interaction spheres at their broadest level, with a North Sea zone (with a counter clockwise communication pattern envisaged, moving out from Europe, south down the east coast of Britain and then up the coast of France, driven by prevailing winds and currents), a channel zone (with strong east/west current driven movement), a western seaway (north/south directionality, again driven by currents) and an outer Atlantic zone. Each of these interaction spheres would have seen marked changes even once inundated as process of current reconfiguration took place. Figure 2.10 has been left deliberately free of arrows, circles and spheres, for as Needham (2009) has argued, these are not envisaged to be hard boundaries, more zones of heightened interaction due to ease of movement. As Westerdahl (1995) has shown, these zones can be further subdivided, based on predominant currents and wind patterns, but in the context of this paper and its deeper time view, such finessing may be misleading. The broad interaction zones are useful heuristic devices, helping to highlight how groups living along the western Atlantic margins would have had easier north/south movements by sea than perhaps east/west movement overland. This picks up on ideas mooted by Crawford (1936) when trying to explain the process via which the Neolithic may have reached Britain along the easier maritime route of his time, the western seaways.

However, in our accounts of interaction we need to be careful of presuming that ease and frequency go hand in hand with intensity of communication. As Van der Noort (this volume) notes, while the sea may have represented an at times dangerous environment to navigate, people's ideas of risk and their desire to take advantage of benign weather windows may have led to journeys of unexpected duration and direction. The motivation for this movement is highly likely to have been both contemporaneously variable, and to have changed through time; from curiosity and access to resources, to maintaining family ties or desire for profit. These journeys would have been matched to more localized quotidian activity along Europe's coast and out to deeper water fishing grounds. In essence, the key shift which needs to occur in our minds, is a movement away from visualizing blank palaeogeography, or distribution maps alone, to a consideration of how viewing both land and sea as inhabitable spaces changes our understanding of process and interaction.

Within this reconsideration the detail of palaeogeographic change is a lot more than just an improved backdrop to site location maps, it gives us the grain with, or against which, these changes occurred. In this way patterns of human activity attested through artefact types and distributions can be read as one analogue signal for social process, rather than as the single binary source (presence/absence) that we have tended towards in the past. Read together, rather than apart, these different lines of evidence help create new narratives of change. This is the epiphany that Clark (1936) came to with the discovery of the Leman and Ower harpoon. While for Clark it was the implications of a now submerged Mesolithic landscape beneath the North Sea, with Britain as a peninsula of Europe, for us it is the need to recognise the potential of both land and sea on equal footing.

In this paper I have tried to do more than just present palaeogeographic maps, hoping to encourage some discussion over the implications of the changing physical nature of connectivity. While not seeking to downplay the importance of appreciating the points in time at which Britain moves from peninsula to island, I have also hoped to highlight the significance of considering changes in sea behaviour, and more localised landscape reconfigurations. As Van de Noort (2006), Needham (2009) and Westerdahl (1992) have argued, understanding how to navigate the seascapes of Europe may have been a crucial and highly valued skill within prehistoric communities. However, more than this I have drawn on Evans' (2003) concept of 'texture', that understanding the environmental context within which archaeological activity occurred allows us to better understand the record it leaves behind. We know that continental connections have existed in physical and social forms since Britain was first occupied nearly one million years ago. The nature of these connections have changed through time, and in so doing have created different demands on those following them, and perhaps given them different social weights. Untangling the patterns they left behind, both on land and on water, is the challenge that now lies ahead.

Acknowledgements

I am very grateful for the input and insights gained from longstanding discussions of this topic with Justin Dix, Rachel Bynoe, Kieran Westley and Duncan Garrow. Duncan Garrow's comments and editorial insights were a great help in producing the final document.

References

Andersen, S. 1980. Tybrind Vig. Foreløbig meddelelse om en undersøisk stenalderboplads ved Lillebælt. *Antikvariske Stud.* 4, 7–22.

Andersen, S. 2013. *Tybrind Vig: Submerged Mesolithic Settlements in Denmark.* Aarhus: Aarhus University Press.

Ashton, N. and Lewis, S. 2002. Deserted Britain: declining populations in the British Late Middle Pleistocene. *Antiquity* 76, 791–798.

Ashton, N., Lewis, S. and Stringer, c. 2010. *The Ancient Human Occupation of Britain.* Amsterdam: Elsevier.

Balme, J. 2013. Of boats and string: the maritime colonisation of Australia. *Quaternary International* 285(8), 68–75.

Bell, M. and Warren, G. 2013. The Mesolithic. In J. Ransley, F., Sturt, J. Dix, J. Adams and L. Blue (eds) *People and the Sea: A Maritime Archaeological Research Agenda for England,* 30–49. York: Council for British Archaeology (Research Report 171).

Bates, M., Bates, C., Gibbard, P., Macphail, R., Owen, F. and Parfitt, S. 2000. Late Middle Pleistocene deposits at Norton Farm on the West Sussex coastal plain, southern England. *Journal of Quaternary Science* 15, 61–89.

Bradley, S., Milne, G., Shennan, I. and Edwards, R. 2011. An improved glacial isostatic adjustment model for the British Isles. *Journal of Quaternary Science* 26(5), 541–552.

Brooks, A., Bradley, S., Edwards, R., Milne, G., Horton, B. and Shennan, I. 2008. Postglacial relative sea-level observations from Ireland and their role in glacial rebound modelling. *Journal of Quaternary Science* 23, 175–192.

Brooks, A., Bradley, S., Edwards, R. and Goodwyn, N. 2011. The palaeogeography of Northwest Europe during the last 20,000 years. *Journal of Maps* 7(1), 573–587.

Brown A. G., Basell L. S., Robinson S. and Burdge G. C. 2013 Site Distribution at the Edge of the Palaeolithic World: A Nutritional Niche Approach. *PLoS ONE* 8(12), e81476. doi: 10.1371/journal.pone.0081476

Bintanja, R. &and van de Wal, R. 2008. North American ice-sheet dynamics and the onset of 100,000–year glacial cycles. *Nature* 454, 869–872.

Bridgland D., D'Olier B. Gibbard P. and Rowe, H. 1993. Correlation of Thames terrace deposits between the Lower Thames, eastern Essex and the submerged offshore continuation of the Thames-Medway valley. *Proceedings of the Geologists Association* 104, 51–57.

Bridgland, D., & D'Olier, B. 1995. The Pleistocene evolution of the Thames and Rhine drainage systems in the southern North Sea Basin. In R. Preece (ed.) *Island Britain: a Quaternary perspective,* 27-45. London: Geological Society (Special Publication 96).

Childe, V. G. 1929. *The Danube in Prehistory.* Oxford: Oxford University Press.

Clark, J. G. D. 1936. *The Mesolithic Settlement of Northern Europe.* Cambridge: Cambridge University Press.

Clark, J. G. D. and Godwin, H. 1956. A Maglemosian site at Brandesburton, Holderness, Yorkshire. *Proceedings of the Prehistoric Society* 22, 6-22.

Cohen, K., MacDonald, K., Joordens, J., Roebroeks, W. and Gibbard, P. 2012. Earliest occupation of north-western Europe: a coastal perspective. *Quaternary International* 271, 84–97.

Cohen, K., Gibbard, P. and Weerts, H. 2014. North Sea palaeogeographical reconstructions for the last 1 MA. *Netherlands Journal of Geosciences* 93, 7–29.

Coles, B. 1998. Doggerland: a speculative survey. *Proceedings of the Prehistoric Society* 64, 45–81.

Coles, B. 1999. Doggerland's loss and the Neolithic. In B. Coles, J. Coles, and M. Schon Jorgensen (eds) *Bog Bodies, Sacred Sites and Wetland Archaeology*, 51–67. Exeter: Wetland Archaeological Research Project.

Coles, B. 2000. Doggerland: the cultural dynamics of a shifting coastline. In K. Pye and S. Allen (eds), *Coastal and Estuarine Environments: Sedimnetology, Geomorphology and Geoarchaeology* Geological Society Special Publication No. 175, 393–401. London: Geological Society.

Crawford, O. G. S. 1936. Western Seaways. In L. Buxton (ed.), *Custom is King: Studies in Honour of R.R. Manett,* 181–200. London: Hutchinson's.

Evans, J. G. 2003. *Environmental Archaeology and the Social Order*. London: Routledge.

Edwards, R .J. and Brooks, A .J. 2008. The island of Ireland: Drowning the myth of an Irish land-bridge? In J. J. Davenport, D. P. Sleeman and P. C. Woodman (eds), *Mind the Gap: Postglacial Colonisation of Ireland*, 9–34. Special Supplement to *The Irish Naturalists' Journal*.

Edwards, R., Brooks, A., Shennan, I., Milne, G. and Bradley, S. 2008. Reply: Postglacial relative sea-level observations from Ireland and their role in glacial rebound modelling. *Journal of Quaternary Science* 23(8), 821–825.

Fagan, B. 2001. *Grahame Clark: an intellectual biography of an archaeologist*. Oxford: Westview Press.

Frouin, M., Sebag, D., Durand, A., Laignel, B., Saliege, J., Mahler, B. and Fauchard, C. 2007. Influence of paleotopography, based level and sedimentation rate on estuarine system response to the Holocene sea-level rise: the example of the Marais Vernier, Seine estuary, France. *Sedimentary Geology* 200, 15-29.

Gaffney, V., Thomson, K. and Fitch, S. 2007. *Mapping Doggerland: The Mesolithic Landscapes of the Southern North Sea*. Oxford: Archaeopress.

Gaffney, V., Fitch, S. and Smith, D. 2009. *Europe's Lost World: The Rediscovery of Doggerland*, Council for British Archaeology Research Report 160. York: Council for British Archaeology.

Gamble, C. S. 1986. *Palaeolithic Settlement of Europe*. Cambridge: Cambridge University Press.

Garrow, D. and Sturt, F. 2011. Grey waters bright with Neolithic Argonauts? Maritime connections and the Mesolithic–Neolithic transition within the "western seaways" of Britain, *c.* 5000–3500 BC. *Antiquity* 85 (327), 59–72.

Gupta, S., Collier, J., Parmer-Felgate, A., Dickinson, J., Bushe, K. and Humber, S., 2004. *Submerged Palaeo-Arun River: Reconstruction of prehistoric landscapes and evaluation of archaeological resource potential: final report*. London: Imperial College on behalf of English Heritage.

Gupta, S., Collier, J.S., Palmer-Felgate, A. and Potter, G. 2007. Catastrophic flooding origin of the shelf valley systems in the English Channel. *Nature* 448, 342–345.

Hijma, M. and Cohen, K. 2010. Timing and magnitude of the sea-level jump preluding the 8200 yr event. *Geology* 38(3), 275–278.

Hijma, M., Cohen, K., Roebroeks, W., Westerhoff, W. and Busschers, F. 2012. Pleistocene Rhine-Thames landscapes: geological background for hominin occupation of the southern North Sea region. *Journal of Quaternary Science* 27, 17–39.

Huuse, M. and Lykke-Andersen, H. 2000. Overdeepened Quaternary valleys in the eastern Danish North Sea: morphology and origin. *Quaternary Science Reviews* 19, 1233–1253.

Hosfield, R. 2011. The British lower Palaeolithic of the early middle Pleistocene. *Quaternary Science Reviews* 30, 1486–1510.

Jacobi, R. 1976. Britain inside and outside Mesolithic Europe. *Proceedings of the Prehistoric Society* 47, 67–84.

Jelgersma, S. 1979. Sea-level changes in the North Sea basin. In E. Oele, R. Schuttenhelm and A. Wiggers (eds), *The Quaternary History of the North Sea*, 233-48. Uppsala: Acta Universitatis Upsaliensis.

Lagarde, J. L., Amorese, D., Font, M., Laville, E. and Dugue, O. 2003. The structural evolution of the English Channel area. *Journal of Quaternary Science* 18(3–4), 201–13.

Louwe Kooijmans, L. 1971. Mesolithic bone and antler implements from the North Sea and from the Netherlands. *Berichten van de Rijksdienst Voor Het Oudheidkundz Bodemonderzoek* 20/21, 27–73.

Massey, A., Gehrels, W., Charman, D., Milne, G., Peltier, W., Lambeck, K. and Selby, K. 2008. Relative sea-level change and postglacial isostatic adjustment along the coast of south Devon, United Kingdom. *Journal of Quaternary Science* 23, 415–433.

McCabe, A. 2008. Comment: Postglacial relative sea-level observations from Ireland and their role in glacial rebound modelling. *Journal of Quaternary Science* 23, 817–820.

Meijer T. and Preece, R. 1996. Malacological evidence relating to the stratigraphical position of the Cromerian. In C. Turner (ed.) *The Early Middle Pleistocene in Europe*, 53–82. Balkema: Rotterdam.

Momber, G. 2000. Drowned and deserted: a submerged prehistoric landscape in the Solent. *International Journal of Nautical Archaeology* 29, 86–99.

Murphy, P. 2009. *The English Coast: A History and a Prospect.* London: Continuum.

Needham, S. 2009. Encompassing the sea: 'maritories' and Bronze Age maritime interactions. In P. Clark (ed.), *Bronze Age Connections: Cultural Contact in Prehistoric Europe*, 12–37. Oxford: Oxbow.

Neill, S. P., Scourse, J. D. and Uehara, K. 2010. Evolution of bed shear stress distribution over the northwest European shelf seas during the last 12,000 years. *Ocean Dynamics* 60. 1139–1156.

Peeters, H. and Murphy, P. 2009. *North Sea Prehistory Research and Management Framework.* Rijksdienst voor Cultureel Erfgoed/English Heritage.

Parfitt, S., Ashton, N., Lewis, S., Abel, R., Coope, G., Field, M., Gale, R., Hoare, P., Larkin, N., Lewis, M., Karloukovski, V., Maher, B., Peglar, S., Preece, R., Whittaker, J. and Stringer, C. 2010. Early Pleistocene human occupation at the edge of the boreal zone in northwest Europe. *Nature* 466, 229–33.

Pettitt, P. and White, M. 2012. *The British Palaeolithic: Hominin societies at the edge of the Pleistocene world.* London: Routledge.

Reid, C. 1913. *Submerged Forests.* Cambridge: Cambridge University Press.

Rainbird, P. 2007. *The Archaeology of Islands.* Cambridge: Cambridge University Press.

Roebroeks, W., De Loecker, D., Hennekens P. and Van Ieperen, M. 1992. "A veil of stones": on the interpretation of an early Middle Palaeolithic low density scatter at Maastricht-Belvédère (The Netherlands). *Analecta Praehistorica Leidensia* 25, 1–16.

Roebroeks, W., Hublin, J-J. and MacDonald, K. 2011. Continuities and discontinuities in Neanderthal presence: a closer look at Northwestern Europe. In N. Ashton, S. Lewis and C. Stringer (eds), *The Ancient Human Occupation of Britain,* 113–123. Amsterdam: Elsevier.

Roberts, M., Scourse, J., Bennel, J., Huws, D., Jago, C. and Long, B. 2011. Late Devensian and Holocene relative sea-level change in North Wales, UK. *Journal of Quaternary Science* 26(2), 141–155.

Rohling, E. Grant,K., Bolshaw, M., Roberts, A.P., Siddall, M., Hemleben, C. and Kucera, M. 2009. Antarctic temperature and global sea level closely coupled over the past five glacial cycles. *Nature Geoscience* 2, 500–504.

Shennan, I. and Horton, B. 2002. Holocene land-and sea-level change in Great Britain. *Journal of Quaternary Science* 17, 511–26.

Sturt, F., Garrow, D. and Bradley, S. 2013. New models of North West European Holocene palaeogeography and inundation. *Journal of Archaeological Science* 40, 3963–3976.

Toucanne, S., Zaragosi, S., Bourillet, J., Gibbard, P., Eynaud, F., Giraudeau, J., Turon, J., Cremer, M., Cortijo, E., Martinez, P. and Rossignol, L. 2009. A 1.2 Ma record of glaciation and fluvial discharge from the West European Atlantic margin. *Quaternary Science Reviews* 28, 2974–2981.

Uehara, K., Scourse, J., Horsburgh, K., Lambeck, K. and Purcell, A. 2006. Tidal evolution of the northwest European shelf seas from the Last Glacial Maximum to the present. *Journal of Geophysical Research: Oceans* 111(C9), C09025 1–15.

Van de Noort, R. 2006. Argonauts of the North Sea: a social maritime archaeology for the 2nd Millennium BC. *Proceedings of the Prehistoric Society* 76, 267–287.

Van de Noort, R. 2011. *North Sea Archaeologies: a maritime biography, 10,000 BC–AD 1500.* Oxford: Oxford University Press.

Warren, G. 2005. *Mesolithic Lives in Scotland.* Stroud: Tempus

Ward, I., Larcombe, P. and Lillie, M. 2006. The dating of Doggerland: post-glacial geochronology of the southern North Sea. Environmental Archaeology. *The Journal of Human Palaeoecology* 11(2), 207– 219.

Waller, M. and Kirby, J. 2002. Late Pleistocene/Early Holocene environmental change in the Romney Marsh region: new evidence from Tilling Green, Rye. In A. Long, S. Hipkin and H. Clarke (eds), *Romney Marsh: coastal and landscape change through the ages*, 22–39. Oxford: Oxbow.

Westley, K., Bailey, G., Davies, W., Firth, A., Flemming, N., Gaffney, V. and Gibbard, P. 2013. The Palaeolithic In J. Ransley, F. Sturt, J. Dix, J. Adams and L. Blue (eds), *People and the Sea: A Maritime Archaeological Research Agenda for England,* 10–29. York: Council for British Archaeology Research Report 171.

Westley, K., Flemming, N. and Gibbard, P. 2013. Palaeolithic Chapter – Technical Appendix: Sea-level Change, Palaeo-Environmental Change and Preservation Issues. The Palaeolithic, in J. Ransley, F. Sturt, J. Dix, J. Adams and L. Blue (eds), *People and the Sea: A Maritime Archaeological Research Agenda for England*. Council for British Archaeology: York. Available online at: http://archaeologydataservice.ac.uk/catalogue/adsdata/arch-1043 1/dissemination/pdf/publication_appendices/Appendix_2_Palaeolithic.pdf

Westerdahl, C. 1992. The Maritime Cultural Landscape. *International Journal of Nautical Archaeology* 21, 5–14.

Westerdahl, C. 1995. Traditional transport zones in relation to ship types. In O. Olsen, F. Rieck and J. Skamby Madsen (eds), *Shipshape. Essays for Ole Crumlin-Pedersen*, 213-230. Roskilde: Viking Ship Museum.

White, M. J. 2006. Things to do in Doggerland when you're dead: surviving OIS3 at the northwestern-most fringe of Middle Palaeolithic Europe. *World Archaeology* 38, 547–575.

White, M. J. and Schreve, D. C. 2000. Island Britain – peninsula Britain: Palaeogeography, Colonisation and the Lower Palaeolithic Settlement of the British Isles. *Proceedings of the Prehistoric Society* 66, 1–28.

Wymer, J. and Robins, P. 1994. A long blade flint industry beneath Boreal peat at Tichwell, Norfolk. *Norfolk Archaeology* 42, 13–37.

3

Attitudes and latitudes to seafaring in prehistoric Atlantic Europe

Robert Van de Noort

Introduction

This paper reconsiders a long-standing paradox or dichotomy in archaeological approaches to the sea, which is best encapsulated in the following question: is there a liminal boundary between the land and the sea, or were land and sea seamlessly interconnected?[1] Considering this question in the current context makes sense because the basic thinking behind this paradox continues to have a major influence on our understanding of ancient seafaring and on concepts such as the isolation or interconnectedness of prehistoric communities. Some archaeologists understand seafaring in prehistoric Atlantic Europe as something of an everyday occurrence (e.g. Butler 1963; O'Connor 1980; Muckelroy 1981; Cunliffe 2001); others understand sea-crossings as exceptional events, only undertaken in special circumstances and frequently surrounded by ritual and magic (e.g. Grinsell 1940; Helms 1988; Needham 2000; Kristiansen 2004; Westerdahl 2005). Such diverging opinions seem to vary, to a great extent, with the applications of different theoretical perspectives that have been adopted by archaeologists during the last century. These perspectives are closely aligned with the various ways in which cultural change in the prehistoric past was explained, through concepts such as migration, diffusion, trade and exchange, networks and interconnectedness, and I will commence this paper by providing an overview of these perspectives.

Within these debates, comparatively little attention has been paid to the material culture of the shipwrecks. Indeed, deciding whether prehistoric craft were seaworthy or not seems to have been determined, on many occasions, by the prevailing schools of thought of land-based archaeologists rather than by maritime-archaeological arguments. Nevertheless, the material culture of ancient seafaring provides us with a resource to reconsider the nature of prehistoric seafaring in Atlantic Europe, and experimental archaeology can assist in gaining further understanding of this. In the second part of this paper, I will set the scene on the possibilities and limitations of prehistoric seafaring by providing a summary overview of the prehistoric shipwrecks from Atlantic Europe. I will also reflect on the experimental archaeological construction of *Morgawr*, a Bronze Age-type sewn-plank boat based primarily on Ferriby-1, in the National Maritime Museum Cornwall (NMMC) in Falmouth. This project and *Morgawr*'s initial trials have offered a number of new insights into the seaworthiness and use of these craft, which were almost certainly the oldest in Atlantic Europe specifically constructed for cross-sea journeys. Through these reconsiderations, I will seek to shed some new light in the practice of seafaring in prehistoric Atlantic Europe.

Attitudes: The liminality *v* connectedness debate

There can be no doubt that boats existed in Late Glacial Atlantic Europe. Known logboats, such as these from Pesse in the Netherlands and from Noyen-sur-Seine and Nandy in northern France, date to the 8th millennium cal BC and this type of craft is represented in every subsequent millennium in Europe (Lanting 1997/8). Further but indirect evidence for boats being used on inland and coastal waters comes from the settlement patterns of the Ahrensburgian and Fosna/Hensbecka groups on the coast of Sweden and Norway, which can only be explained if these hunter-gatherers travelled by boat (e.g. Bjerck 2009), or from the late Mesolithic colonisation of the Orkney archipelago (Wickham-Jones 2006, 24).

There can also be no doubt that sea crossings took place in Atlantic Europe from at least around 4,000 BC, as evidenced by the introduction of domesticated animals and cereals from continental Europe to Britain and Ireland (Case 1969; Anderson-Whymark and Garrow, this volume). Furthermore, there can also be no doubt that during the Neolithic and throughout the Bronze Age and Iron Age, commodities and artefacts were traded or exchanged over great distances in Atlantic Europe, which would have included sea crossings. Materials such as beakers and other pottery types, jade axes, bronze and iron tools, weapons and shields, drinking cups, and jewellery of gold, silver, amber, jet and faience found on either side of the North Sea, Irish Sea and Channel have been subject of study for many decades (e.g. Butler 1963; O'Connor 1980; Raftery 1994; Sheridan 2007; Needham 2009; various chapters, this volume). Further early evidence for interaction across the sea comes in the form of similarity of monuments, in particular of the passage tombs, in France and Ireland (e.g. Sheridan 2003). Evidence of seafaring has also been found in human remains through stable isotope analysis, including the well-known case of the 'Amesbury Archer' (Fitzpatrick 2002), and from the Late Bronze Age and Iron Age burial site on the Isle of Thanet in Kent, where stable isotope analysis differentiated three distinct groups: one local, one from Scandinavia, and one from the Mediterranean (McKinley *et al.* 2013; Webley, this volume).

Deciding whether these prehistoric journeys across seas involved the crossing of liminal boundaries, or whether the land and sea were perceived in the past as being interconnected, has remained largely a matter of conjecture despite this wealth of material evidence. By placing this debate in the context of the main research traditions in archaeology in the twentieth century (cf. Trigger 1996, 211–483), certain trends become discernable. Inevitably, any summing-up of land-locked archaeologists' approaches to the sea, using the main archaeological schools of thought as a framework, risks over-simplifying the rich body of literature pertaining to this subject. Nevertheless, it is hoped that this summary provides an outline for understanding both the discussions from the past and those in the present.

For much of the 20th century, archaeologists accepted the reality of the movement of people in large numbers, or migrations, as a key mechanism for explaining cultural change in the past, and the extension of land-based migration to the sea was unquestioned. O. G. S. Crawford's (1936) appreciation of the importance of the Irish Sea as a maritime thoroughfare, and V. Gordon Childe's (1946) declaration of the Irish Sea as the 'grey waters bright with

Neolithic argonauts', are the best-know examples of this way of understanding the sea and seafaring, even though very little was known about the craft that would have enabled these journeys to take place. A large number of publications of later date continue to consider seafaring in this culture-historical vein: the distribution of certain materials such as beakers and bronzes in different parts of Atlantic Europe is attributed to movement of people made possible by frequent sea crossings (e.g. Harrison 1980). In other words, land and sea were seen as seamlessly connected from a culture-historical viewpoint, in the sense that the sea was not a barrier but a conduit for movement of large numbers of people in prehistoric Atlantic Europe, and 'cultures' could sometimes by found on opposite sides of seas. During the first half of the 20th century, only logboats had been recognised as prehistoric craft in Atlantic Europe. In the absence of a specialist field of maritime archaeology, the expertise to ascertain the seaworthiness of these craft was lacking. This is, for example, shown in the mistaken identification of log-coffins as being reused logboats (one even believed to have a keel and stem), as in the examples of mound burials at Loose Howe and Gristhorpe in Yorkshire, Shap in Cumbria, and Disgwylfa Fawr in Ceredigion, Wales (Grinsell 1940, 375; McGrail 2001, 193).

With the development of an anthropologically-focussed and science-conscience archaeology in the 1960s and '70s, we notice a shift in understanding and explaining cultural change in the prehistoric past. Archaeologists adopted concepts such as trade, exchange and various variants of networks to explain changes in the material culture, and rejected the notion of migrations. Belatedly inspired by anthropologist Branislaw Malinowski's (1922) *Argonauts of the Western Pacific*, this shift is exemplified by the adoption of the concept of prestige-goods exchange in the 1980s by archaeologists studying the prehistory of western Europe. Prestige goods were understood to have played a role in the reproduction or legitimisation of inequality following the emergence of elite groups in Atlantic Europe in the late Neolithic and Early Bronze Age (e.g. Rowlands 1980; Shennan 1982; 1986; Bradley 1984; Barrett 1994), and the journeys that were undertaken to obtain these prestige or exotic goods were therefore exceptional. Sea crossings in the pre-Roman Iron Age were similarly viewed as supporting trade and exchange involving elite groups in Britain and Ireland, and therefore relatively rare events. Not till the late Iron Age did overseas trade result in the developments of ports and port settlements. Hengistbury Head and other so-called 'gateway communities' received goods from overseas, but few of these goods found their way further inland (Cunliffe 1991, 194; Hill and Willis 2013, 79–80). In essence, processual archaeology understood sea crossings as events serving the needs and desires of selected individuals who were part of elite networks, but for the majority of the population the sea was a real or perceived boundary that was rarely crossed.

Maritime archaeology emerged as a distinct sub-field during the period when processual archaeology was the dominant school of thought, and the publications by the early pioneers such as Keith Muckelroy (1978) and Sean McGrail (1987) reflect this, with a focus on methodology and technology, and a modern science-based approach to the seafaring capabilities of boats. The latter frequently meant that craft were considered to be unable to cross major water bodies in adverse weather conditions, which only served to reinforce the disconnection of archaeological studies of long-distance connections from the practice of prehistoric seafaring (e.g. Cunliffe 2001, 69; see also below).

New ideas have emerged in the last three decades. These include a renewed emphasis on the importance of symbols and ritual, the role of individuals and different groups within societies who exercise their agency, and landscape as the stage for social action and performance. However, few post-processual archaeologists have embraced the study of the sea. The sea, with its limited visible traces from the past, does not lend itself easily to post-processual archaeology, especially phenomenological approaches. Nevertheless, the renewed emphases on symbols and rituals have sparked new ideas on prehistoric sea crossings and seafaring as being ritually-imbued. In turn, this has altered the significance attributed to exotic objects that were transported across seas and the symbolic connotations of the seafaring craft (e.g. Beck & Shennan 1991; Broodbank 1993; Crumlin-Pedersen and Thye 1995; Needham 2000; 2009; Kristiansen 2004; Kristiansen and Larsen 2005; Van de Noort 2006). Much of this body of work is inspired by Mary Helms' publications (1988; 1993; 1998), which continue to provide a coherent theoretical framework for linking exotic material culture with the practice of travelling great distances, including seafaring.

Current maritime archaeological thinking is, probably, best encapsulated by Christer Westerdahl's recent work: within the maritime cultural landscape, he recognises a binary divide between the realms of the land and the sea which each has its own sets of rules of engagement, technologies, taboos, language and culture, but this divide can be crossed by using liminal agents. In the Baltic Sea in prehistory, such liminal agents included the seal, elk and horse (e.g. Westerdahl 2002; 2005; 2009; 2011). Such a hybrid approach has validity for much of Atlantic Europe during prehistory. On the one hand, going to sea was always a high-risk venture with loss of the craft, cargo and crew a genuine possibility, and whilst the value attributed to commodities and artefacts from overseas was very high, these were intended for elite networks or selected coastal communities. People lower down the social order or living some distance away from the coast were simply not engaged with the sea and overseas goods and ideas. On the other hand, the transformational sea crossings added significant value to the exotic objects and foreign knowledge that could be obtained from distant lands, and these were treated as exclusive to specific individuals in society and surrounded by rituals and taboos, and this may have involved liminal agents. The stories and myths that were told about these journeys, and the experience of the seafarers, made the sea a more knowable place. Nevertheless, the sea was never fully socialized and, when compared to the land, remained a largely unknown and unknowable place (Van de Noort 2011, 42–3). The recent publication of *People and the Sea; a Maritime Archaeological Research Agenda for England* (Ransley and Sturt 2013), echoes this way of thinking by considering, in a diachronic framework, the range of coastal activities and seafaring before turning to matters of maritime identities and perceptions of maritime space.

Latitudes: prehistoric shipwrecks

Despite the recognition that shipwrecks hold important information on prehistoric seafaring and on many aspects of society in which they operated (e.g. Gibbins and Adams 2001), shipwrecks have as yet barely featured in this paper. This is quite deliberate and reflects most discussions on long-distance exchange in prehistory: in these discussions, overseas goods and ideas continue to 'appear in the archaeological record', a phrase that denotes the praxis of simply by-passing the process and practice of overcoming geographical distance.

Maritime archaeologists have, maybe paradoxically, contributed to this situation, because the use of many types of vessels at sea has been rejected by them. The latter point is, in my view, closely linked to the processual origins of maritime archaeology in Atlantic Europe. The seaworthiness of prehistoric craft is assessed by maritime archaeologists from a predominantly etic perspective, or one that is based on modern (and western) concepts of maritime design. However, seaworthiness in the prehistoric past would have been defined in very different terms. For example, it seems most likely that sea crossing would simply not have been attempted in adverse weather conditions, and strong winds and storms could have been interpreted as bad omens. Thus, what constituted seaworthiness in a prehistoric context is not the same as seaworthiness today.

    Three broadly-defined categories of craft are likely to have played a role in seafaring: hide- or skin-covered boats, logboats and plank boats. Each category will be considered below in turn. This section will also reflect on the early lessons from the experimental archaeological construction of a full-size sewn-plank boat, *Morgawr*. The maritime iconographic evidence of Danish bronze etchings and Norwegian and Swedish rock carvings is not discussed here further, as the type of boats illustrated continue to be matters of extensive debate which is unlikely to be resolved any time soon (cf. Van de Noort 2011, 187–91, for a summary of this debate). However, recent analysis of the landscape context of the rock carvings leaves no doubt that these boats were used along the island-rich coasts of Sweden and Norway (Ling 2013).

Hide and skin boats
In the absence of archaeological evidence of prehistoric hide- and skin-covered boats from Atlantic Europe, discussions on the role of this type of craft in seafaring remains largely hypothetical. On one side of the debate are those who, referring to historical and ethnographic studies of coastal and sea-going hide- and skin-covered boats used in the recent past, such as the umiaks of the Inuit in Greenland (Petersen 1986), the curraghs of Ireland (e.g. McGrail 1987; 2001) or the sewn craft of the Saami (Westerdahl 1985a; 1985b), believe that this type of craft was used for seafaring in prehistoric Atlantic Europe. Key arguments are that these light craft had considerable freeboard that provided relative safety from swell and waves and that, therefore, these would have been the choice of craft for sea crossings in the Mesolithic and Neolithic. The technologies required for the construction of such craft, such as the binding of timbers for the frame and the sewing together of the hides, are all archaeologically attested from as early as the Upper Palaeolithic (McGrail 2001). On the other side of the debate are those who consider the placing of large seafaring skin boats back into prehistory an anachronistic practice. After all, skin boats are only known from the last few centuries. The long-distance seafaring capabilities of some of these craft are also placed in doubt: for example, the maximum period of time these craft could be on open sea before the hides became waterlogged has been stated at 24 to 36 hours, even if the skin had been well-oiled before departure (Fair 2005). Using seal skins as pokes for blubber would have offered the possibility for maintaining the skins water-resistant whilst on the move, but landfalls would have been required every couple of days (Schmitt 2013).

    Without finds of prehistoric skin boats, it appears improbable that this debate is resolvable. Nevertheless, is has been argued that the indirect evidence for the existence of large and probable sea-going skin boats before 2,000 cal BC exists in the form of the Bronze Age sewn-plank boats (see below; Van de Noort *et al.* 1999; Coates 2005). These craft may have adopted two techniques from earlier skin boats: the sewing or stitching of the elements that made up the hull, and the elaborate system of cleats and transverse timbers that ensured the stability of the bottom of the boat. In the absence of nails and treenails, the former technique could not have been dispensed with when the transition from skin boat to plank boat was made, but the latter technique seems 'over-engineered', and could be a skeuomorphic adaption.

Logboats
Whilst logboats are known from Atlantic Europe from the 8th millennium cal BC (see above), their seafaring capabilities remain very much in doubt. Logboats are well-suited for travelling inland rivers, deltas and estuaries. The ability of logboats to deal with waves, swell, currents and winds would have been greatly increased with additional side-strakes to increase the freeboard, with outriggers or as paired logboats, but archaeological evidence for any of these innovations in prehistoric Atlantic Europe is absent (e.g. McGrail 1977; Mowat 1996). Nevertheless, it seems not improbable that some of the larger logboats, such as those from Hasholme (Millett and McGrail 1987), would have managed coastal navigation in very good weather conditions reasonably well. The location of the late Iron Age Poole logboat, in Poole Harbour, makes the use of logboats in coastal environments a more than probable hypothesis (McGrail 1978: 9). Some archaeologists have argued that logboats were customarily used in sea crossings in the Neolithic (Peacock *et al.* 2009).

The biggest database of dated logboats in Europe contains 551 boats dated through radiocarbon assay and an additional 58 craft dated through dendrochronology (Lanting 1997/8; Figure 3.1). Surprisingly little use has been made by this meta-dataset by maritime archaeologists. The reason for this appears to be that the explanatory concept used by the author to explain the distribution of logboats, diffusion, is not supported by the ways in which these logboats were constructed (e.g. Maarleveld 2008). Nevertheless, the database is an important source of information on the existence of logboats in the different regions of Europe. The earliest logboats in the Netherlands (Pesse 8,250–7,750 cal BC) and northern France (Noyen-sur-Seine and Nandy 7,180–6,550 cal BC), and the continued presence of logboats thereafter in a region that extends northwards into southern Denmark, implies a 'core' zone where logboats have been used for most of the Mesolithic, the Bronze and Iron Ages (Figure 3.2). For most of the rivers in central Europe away from the coast, logboats date to the very end of the Mesolithic, with those in the Rhine-Saône-Rhône corridor radiocarbon dated from 4,350 cal BC. Ireland and Britain are relatively latecomers, with the earliest reliably known logboats dating from the Neolithic for Ireland and the Bronze Age for Britain. Scandinavian logboats are of much later date still: the oldest logboat, from Skäggered, Göteburg, is dated to 810–390 cal BC.

Looking afresh at Lanting's database, one can draw a few conclusions on the use of logboats in prehistoric Atlantic Europe. First, that logboats were used on inland rivers and in deltas and estuaries in the core region from the early Mesolithic onwards, and from the late Mesolithic for the rest of continental Europe. There is ample evidence for fishing and utilisation of marine and coastal resources from this core region from the Mesolithic onwards, and the presence of early logboats here is unsurprising. Second, the younger dates of logboats in Ireland and Britain imply either the use of hide- and skin-covered boats during the Mesolithic and much of the Neolithic (and part of the Early Bronze Age in Britain as

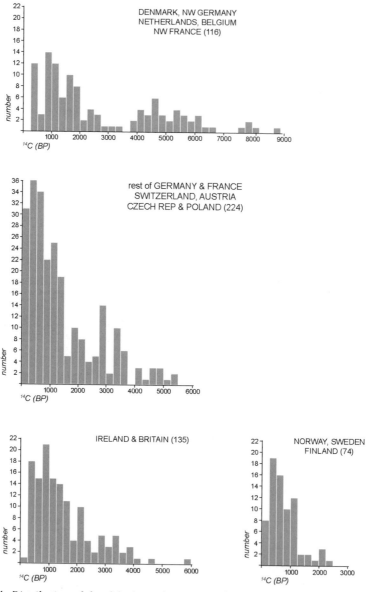

Figure 3.1. Distribution of dated logboats by groups of countries in 200-year periods. Based on Lanting 1997/8.

well), or that the concept of building logboats comes with the earliest Neolithic contacts, soon after 4,000 cal BC. Third, the absence of logboats in Scandinavia should be explained in reference to the significant glacio-isostatic adjustment experienced by this landmass, which has lifted early Mesolithic coasts by as much as 55m. This would have rendered the old coastlines unsuited for the preservation of prehistoric logboats.

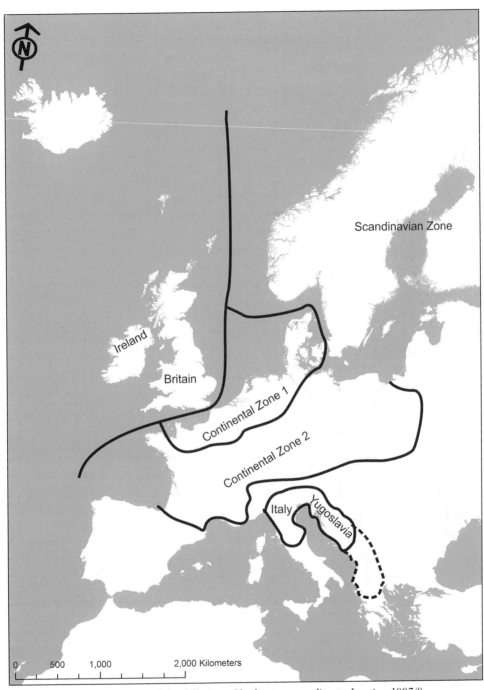

Figure 3.2. Map of the diffusion of logboats, according to Lanting 1997/8.

Plank boats

Around 2,000 BC, the construction of planks boats represent an important – possibly the most important – step-change in the seafaring capabilities in prehistoric Atlantic Europe. The remains of ten sewn-plank boats of Bronze Age date are known to us, but some of these are of a very fragmentary nature (see Van de Noort 2006 for a detailed discussion of these). The earliest of these craft is Ferriby-3, dated to 2,030–1,780 cal BC (Wright *et al.* 2001) and the latest the Brigg 'raft', dated to 825–760 cal BC (Switsur in McGrail 1981; recalibrated in Wright *et al.* 2001). All plank boats have in common that the planks are sewn or stitched together using withies of tree branches and the use of integral cleats and transverse timbers to give rigidity to the (bottom of the) hull. In the absence of any mast steps or oar locks or holes, it is generally accepted that these craft were paddled, with crews of up to 20.

Where substantive parts of sewn-plank boats have been recovered, it is evident that each boat was designed as a unique object which is, in part, undoubtedly the result of having to work with trees of different size and shape. An important observed change is the shift from single stitches in the sewn-plank boats before *c.* 1,250 cal BC to the continuous stitch in the sewn-plank boats after that date. Over time, the sewn-plank boats seem to have evolved from canoe-like shapes with a length:width ratio of 6.3:1 (for Ferriby-1; but see below) to wider and shorter craft with a length:width ratio around 4.5:1 (for the Brigg 'raft'). This evolution could represent the need to transport larger cargoes. In the wider context of trade and exchange in the Bronze Age, this would make sense. Bronze tools and weapons and exotic imports were in the Early Bronze Age were relatively scarce resources and the latter were reserved for elite groups. Over time, bronze become more readily available and was frequently recycled, as shown by the cargoes of the Middle Bronze Age wrecked boats at Langdon Bay (Muckelroy 1981; Northover 1982; Needham and Dean 1987) and Salcombe (Needham *et al.* 2013). Exotic objects had lost their exclusiveness by this time as well.

There has been much discussion on the seafaring capabilities of the sewn-plank boats (e.g. Wright 1990; Roberts 1992; Clark 2004; Coates 2005; Crumlin-Pedersen 2006; Crumlin-Pedersen and McGrail 2006; Sanders 2007). In essence, maritime archaeologists have discussed the technical aspects of these boats that make them more or less seaworthy: hull-shape, rocker and freeboard are the most important of these. From a landscape contextual perspective, it has been noted that all sewn-plank boats have been found on coasts, estuaries and rives with tidal reach, implying that these craft were used for seafaring rather than inland navigation, even if this was mainly coastal in nature (Van de Noort 2006). Maybe these discussions miss the key point. Surely, the reason for constructing the sewn-plank boat, a craft that was longer and sturdier than anything known around 2,000 BC, is difficult to explain if it were not for the sea-change in the importance attributed to long-distance exchange involving sea crossings, brought about by the introduction of bronze tools and weapons in Atlantic Europe.

Morgawr

The experimental construction of a Bronze Age-type sewn-plank boat was the centrepiece of the exhibition '2012 BC: Cornwall and the Sea in the Bronze Age' at the National Maritime Museum Cornwall (NMMC) in Falmouth. The exhibition ran from April 2012 till the end of January 2013 and the boat, which we named *Morgawr*, was built under the supervision of shipwright Brian Cumby by a group of some 100 volunteers (Figure 3.3). The organisation

Figure 3.3. The construction of Morgawr in the National Maritime Museum Cornwall, Falmouth.

of the project may have reflected boat-building practices in the Bronze Age, when peripatetic shipwrights (with their entourage) could have offered their expertise and skills, but with most of the work undertaken by local communities (Van de Noort 2011).

Morgawr was based on the 'hypothetical reconstruction of a complete boat', which in turn was based principally on Ferriby-1 but with elements from Ferriby-2 and -3, and the wash strake from the Iron Age-period Ferriby-4 incorporated, and published by Ted Wright and John Coates (in Wright 1990, chapter 5). The fundamental principles of the project to build *Morgawr* were: only Bronze Age methods and technology were to be used for the finished craft; only yew withies were to be used for the stitching of the planks; and moss would be used for caulking, all in accordance with the archaeological evidence. However, the aim of the reconstruction was to construct a usable and possible seaworthy craft, and the shipwright was given the task to achieve this, but any diversions from the published 'complete boat' had to be recorded and explained. Such diversions included the reduction in the amount of rocker, leaving it capable of taking a 1m swell but retaining enough height for paddlers for and aft in the boat to contribute to the propulsion; the narrowing of the maximum beam to 2m as to ensure that the paddlers' effort was optimised; and the addition of a seventh frame over the weakest part of the boat (Van de Noort *et al.* 2014).

Morgawr was launched on the 6 March 2013, and the initial trials in Falmouth Harbour have shown that the boat is remarkably stable, can take easily a crew of 20 paddlers plus a significant cargo, behaves well in windy conditions and waves up to 0.5m high, but is difficult to steer in high winds (Figure 3.4). Of course, in the absence of harbours or jetties

Robert Van de Noort

Figure 3.4. Morgawr on the day of the launch.

in the Bronze Age, precise steering would not have been a big issue. The top speed with a not-so-well-trained crew was estimated at 2.5 knots, over short distances. In the opinion of the crew, drawn from local gig clubs, the boat would be suitable for seafaring in calm conditions. Trials are planned for 2014 and 2015, and these are likely to include full trails at sea.

Discussion and conclusion

This paper commenced with the question: is there a liminal boundary between the land and the sea, or were land and sea interconnected? The matter was considered relevant to this conference because it has played an important role in determining the nature of prehistoric seafaring.

Over the last 100 years or so, seafaring in prehistoric Atlantic Europe has been perceived in different ways that closely reflect the way in which cultural change has been explained by the dominant research traditions in archaeology: culture-historical archaeology viewed sea crossings as an extension of the concept of migrations; in processual archaeology these sea crossings enabled trade and exchange within elite networks; and post-processual archaeology has added ritual and symbolic meanings to the sea crossings, the exotic objects and the seagoing craft.

The contribution from maritime archaeologists to this debate has been limited, mainly because of their critical assessment of the seaworthiness of known prehistoric shipwrecks. However, hide- and skin-covered boats and large logboats could have been used for sea crossings if the conditions were optimal. The construction of the sewn-plank boats has been described here as the first attempt to build craft designed for sea crossings, with these boats being considerably longer and sturdier than other types. The recent experience with *Morgawr* reinforces the view that these craft were capable of coastal and cross-sea journeys, albeit favourable conditions were still required.

In conclusion, the sea in prehistoric Atlantic Europe was a place of real danger, but also signified opportunities for some individuals and groups to gain wealth and power. Seafaring was almost certainly an activity that was exclusive to specific individuals and groups, and these groups could only go to sea under the guidance of an experienced traveller/shipwright. The material culture for much of prehistoric Atlantic Europe seems to support Christer Westerdahl's notion of a binary divide between land and sea. The use of liminal agents to cross the boundary between land and sea is most clearly demonstrated for the Baltic, but it seems likely that similar liminal agents were used elsewhere as well.

Note
1   I use the term 'liminal' in the broader sense of its meaning (as has become customary in archaeology), that is as a real or perceived boundary or threshold the crossing of which creates ritual, social and/or political ambiguity and change.

References

Barrett, J. 1994. *Fragments from Antiquity. An Archaeology of Social Life in Britain, 2900–1200 BC*. Oxford: Blackwell.

Beck, C. and Shennan, S. 1991. *Amber in prehistoric Britain*. Oxford: Oxbow Books.

Bjerck, H. 2009. Colonizing seascapes: comparative perspectives on the development of maritime relations in Scandinavia and Patagonia. *Arctic Anthropology* 46, 118–131.

Bradley, R. 1984. *The social foundations of prehistoric Britain*. London: Routledge.

Broodbank, C. 1993. Ulysses without sails: trade, distance, knowledge and power in the early Cyclades. *World Archaeology* 24, 315–331.

Butler, J. 1963. *Bronze Age connections across the North Sea*. Groningen: Biologisch-Archeologisch Instituut, Rijksuniversiteit Groningen (Palaeohistoria 9).

Case, H. 1969. Neolithic explanations. *Antiquity* 43, 176–186.

Childe, V. G. 1946. *Scotland before the Scots*. London: Methuen.

Clark, P. (ed.). 2004. *The Dover Bronze Age Boat*. London: English Heritage.

Coates, J. 2005. The Bronze Age Ferriby Boats: seagoing ships or estuary ferry boats? *International Journal of Nautical Archaeology* 35 (1), 38–42.

Crawford, O. G. S. 1936. Western seaways. In L. Buxton (ed.), *Custom is King. Essays presented to R. R. Marett on his seventieth birthday*. London: Hutchinson.

Crumlin-Pedersen, O. 2006. The Dover Boat: a reconstruction case-study. *International Journal of Nautical Archaeology* 35 (1), 58–71.

Crumlin-Pedersen, O. and Thye, B. (eds). 1995. *The Ship as Symbol in Prehistoric and Medieval Scandinavia*. Copenhagen: National Museum of Denmark.

Crumlin-Pedersen, O. and McGrail, S. 2006. Some principles for the reconstruction of ancient boat structures. *International Journal of Nautical Archaeology* 35 (1), 53–57.

Cunliffe, B. 1991. *Iron Age Communities in Britain*. London: Routledge.

Cunliffe, B. 2001. *Facing the Ocean: the Atlantic and its people*. Oxford: Oxford University Press.

Fair, S. 2005. The northern umiak: shelter, boundary, identity. In K. Breish and A. Hoagland (eds), *Building Environments*. Knoxville, *Perspectives in Vernacular Architecture* 10, 233–248.

Fitzpatrick, A. 2002. 'The Amesbury Archer': a well-furnished Early Bronze Age burial in southern England. *Antiquity* 76, 629–30.

Gibbins, A. and Adams, J. 2001. Shipwrecks and maritime achaeology. *World Archaeology* 32, 279–291.

Grinsell, L. 1940. The boat of the dead in the Bronze Age. *Antiquity* 14, 360–369.

Harrison, R. 1980. *The Beaker Folk. Copper Age Archaeology in Western Europe*. London: Thames and Hudson.

Helms, M. 1988. *Ulysses' Sail. An Ethnographic Odyssey of Power, Knowledge, and Geographical Distance*. Princeton: Princeton University Press.

Helms, M. 1993. *Craft and the Kingly Idea. Art, Trade, and Power.* Austin: University of Texas.

Helms, M. 1998. *Access to Origins. Affines, Ancestors, and Aristocrats.* Austin: University of Texas.

Hill, J. D. and Willis, S. 2013. Middle Bronze Age to the end of the pre-Roman Iron Age, c. 1500 BC to AD 50. In J. Ransley and F. Sturt (eds), *People and the Sea: a Maritime Archaeological Research Agenda for England*, 75–92. York: Council for British Archaeology.

Kristiansen, K. 2004. Sea faring voyages and rock art ships. In P. Clark (ed.), *The Dover Bronze Age Boat in Context. Society and Water Transport in Prehistoric Europe*, 111–121. Oxford: Oxbow Books.

Kristiansen, K. and Larsson, T. 2005. *The Rise of Bronze Age Society: travels, transmissions and transformations*. Cambridge: Cambridge University Press.

Lanting, J. 1997/8. Dates for origin and diffusion of the European logboat. *Palaeohistoria* 39/40, 627–650.

Ling, J. 2013. *Rock Art and Seascapes in Uppland*. Oxford: Oxbow Books.

Maarleveld, T. 2008. Boten zonder geschiedenis, of wie is er bang voor een boomstamboot? In R. Oosting and J. Van den Akker (eds), *Boomstamkano's, overnaadse schepen en tuigage. Inleidingen gehouden tijdens het tiende Glavimans Symposion, Lelystad, 20 april 2006*, 5–25. Amersfoort: Stichting Glavimans Symposion.

Malinowski, B. 1922. *Argonauts of the Western Pacific*. London: Routledge.

McKinley, J., Schuster, J. and Millard, A. 2013. Dead-sea connections. A Bronze Age and Iron Age ritual site on the Isle of Thanet. In J. Koch and B. Cunliffe (eds), *Celtic from the West 2; Rethinking the Bronze Age and the arrival of Indo-Europeans in Atlantic Europe*, 157–183. Oxford: Oxbow Books.

McGrail, S. 1978. *Logboats of England and Wales*. British Archaeological Report 51. Oxford: British Archaeological Reports.

McGrail, S. 1981. *The Brigg 'raft' and her prehistoric environment*. Oxford: British Archaeological Report 89 and Greenwich: National Maritime Museum Archaeological Series 6.

McGrail, S. 1987. *Ancient Boats in North West Europe*. London: Longman.

McGrail, S. 2001. *Boats of the World*. Oxford: Oxford University Press.

Millett, M. and McGrail, S. 1987. The archaeology of the Hasholme logboat. *Archaeological Journal* 144, 69–155.

Mowat, R. 1996. *The Logboats of Scotland*. Oxford: Oxbow Books.

Muckelroy, K. 1978. *Maritime Archaeology*. Cambridge: Cambridge University Press.

Muckelroy, K. 1981. Middle Bronze Age trade between Britain and Europe. *Proceedings of the Prehistoric Society* 47, 275–297.

Needham, S. 2000. Power pulses across a cultural divide: Armorica and Wessex. *Proceedings of the Prehistoric Society* 66, 151–194.

Needham, S. 2009. Encompassing the sea: 'maritories' and Bronze Age maritime interactions. In P. Clark (ed.), *The Dover Bronze Age Boat in context: society and water transport in prehistoric Europe*, 12–37. Oxford: Oxbow Books.

Needham, S. and Dean, M. 1987. La garcaison de Langdon Bay à Douvre; la signification pour les échanges à travers la manche. In C. Mordant and A. Richard (eds), *Les relations entre la continent et les Iles Britanniques à l'Age du Bronze*, 119–124. Amiens: Revue Archeologique de Picardie, supplément.

Needham, S., Parham, D. and Frieman, C. 2013. *Claimed by the Sea. Salcombe, Landon Bay, and other marine finds of the Bronze Age*. York: Council for British Archaeology.

Northover, P. 1982. The exploration of the long-distance movement of bronze in Bronze and Early Iron Age Europe. *Bulletin of the University of London Institute of Archaeology* 19, 45–72.

O'Connor, B. 1980. *Cross-Channel relations in the later Bronze Age: relations between Britain, North-Eastern France and the Low Countries during the later Bronze Age and the Early Iron Age, with particular reference to the metalwork* British Archaeological Report 91. Oxford: British Archaeological Reports.

Peacock. D., Cutler, L. and Woodward P. 2009. A Neolithic voyage. *International Journal of Nautical Archaeology* 39, 116–124.

Petersen, H. 1986. *Skinboats of Greenland*. Roskilde: Viking Ship Museum.

Raftery, B. 1994. *Pagan Celtic Ireland; the enigma of the Irish Iron Age*. London: Thames and Hudson.

Ransley, J. and Sturt, F. (eds) 2013. *People and the Sea: a Maritime Archaeological Research Agenda for England* Council for British Archaeology Research Report 171. York: Council for British Archaeology.

Roberts, O. 1992. The Brigg 'raft' reassessed as a round bilge Bronze Age boat. *International Journal of Nautical Archaeology* 21 (3), 245–258.

Rowlands, M. 1980. Kinship, alliance and exchange in the European Bronze Age. In J. Barrett and R. Bradley (eds) *Settlement and Society in the British Later Bronze Age,* British Archaeological Report 83, 15–55. Oxford: British Archaeological Reports.

Sanders, D. 2007. The Dover Boat: some responses to Ole Crumlin-Pedersen and Seán McGrail concerning its propulsion, hull-form, and assembly, and some observations on the reappraisal process. *International Journal of Nautical Archaeology* 36 (1), 184–192.

Schmitt, L. 2013. A note concerning flake axes and umiaks. *Oxford Journal of Archaeology* 32, 119–122.

Shennan, S. 1982. Ideology, change and the European Early Bronze Age. In I. Hodder (eds), *Symbolic and Structural Archaeology*, 155–161. Cambridge: Cambridge University Press.

Shennan, S. 1986. Interaction and change in the third millennium BC western and central Europe. In C. Renfrew and J. Cherry (eds), *Peer Polity Interaction and Socio-Political Change*, 137–148. Cambridge: Cambridge University Press.

Sheridan, A. 2003. Ireland's earliest passage tombs: a French Connection? In G. Burenhult and S. Westergaard (eds), *Stones and Bones. Formal Disposal of the Dead in Atlantic Europe during the Mesolithic-Neolithic interface 6000–3000 BC,* 9–25 British Archaeological Report S1201. Oxford: Archaeopress.

Sheridan, A. 2007. From Picardie to Pickering and Pencraig Hill? New information on the 'Carinated Bowl Neolithic' in northern Britain In A. Whittle and V. Cummings (eds), *Going over: the Mesolithic-Neolithic Transition in North-West Europe*, 441–492. Oxford: Oxford Books.

Trigger, B. 1996. *A History of Archaeological Thought*. Cambridge: Cambridge University Press.

Van de Noort, R. 2006. Argonauts of the North Sea: a social maritime archaeology for the 2nd Millennium BC. *Proceedings of the Prehistoric Society* 72, 267–288.

Van de Noort, R. 2011. *North Sea Archaeologies: a Maritime Biography, 10,000 BC–AD 1500*. Oxford: Oxford University Press.

Van de Noort, R., Middleton, R., Foxon, A., and Bayliss, A. 1999. The 'Kilnsea-boat', and some implications from the discovery of England's oldest plank boat. *Antiquity* 73, 131–135.

Van de Noort, R., Cumby, B., Blue, L., Harding, A., Hurcombe, L., Monrad Hansen, T., Wetherelt, A., Wittamore, J. and Wyke, A. 2014. *Morgawr*: the reconstruction of a Bronze Age-type sewn-plank boat based on the Ferriby boats. *International Journal of Nautical Archaeology* 43, 292–313.

Westerdahl, C. 1985a. Sewn boats of the North: a preliminary catalogue with introductory comments. Part 1. *International Journal of Nautical Archaeology* 14, 33–62.

Westerdahl, C. 1985b. Sewn boats of the North: a preliminary catalogue with introductory comments. Part 2. *International Journal of Nautical Archaeology* 14, 119–142.

Westerdahl, C. 2000. From land to sea, from sea to land. On transport zones, borders and human space. In J. Litwin (ed.), *Down the River to the Sea; proceedings of the 8th ISBSA Conference Gdansk 1997*, 11–20. Gdansk: Polish Maritime Museum.

Westerdahl, C. 2002. The ritual landscape at sea. In K. Krüger and C.-O. Cederlund (eds), *Maritime Archäologie heute. Maritime Archaeology Today. 3rd International Marine Archaeological Conference of the Baltic Sea Area, 2001*, 51–72. Rostock.

Westerdahl, C. 2005. Seal on land, elk at sea. Notes on and applications of the ritual landscape at the seaboard. *International Journal of Nautical Archaeology* 34, 2–23.

Westerdahl, C. 2009. The horse as liminal agent. *Archaeologica Baltica* 11, 314–327.

Westerdahl, C. 2011. The binary relationship of sea and land. In B. Ford (ed.), *The Archaeology of Maritime Landscapes*, 291–310. New York: Springer.

Wickham-Jones, C. 2006. *Between the Wind and the Water: World Heritage Orkney.* Bollington: Windgather Press.

Wright, E. 1990. *The Ferriby Boats. Seacraft of the Bronze Age.* London: Routledge.

Wright, E. Hedges, R., Bayliss, A. and Van de Noort, R. 2001. New AMS dates for the Ferriby boats; a contribution to the origin of seafaring. *Antiquity* 75, 726–734.

4

Britain and Ireland inside Mesolithic Europe

Graeme Warren

Introduction

The Mesolithic period is pivotal to understanding connections between the British-Irish Isles[1] and the continent, as it was during this period that the physical connection between Britain and continental Europe was inundated (the fact that Ireland was an island from the Late Glacial is often neglected in discussion). This physical separation looms large in archaeological accounts, which stress the isolation of Britain and Ireland from continental Europe. This paper triangulates between Ireland, Britain and the rest of Europe and highlights the complex ways in which Britain and Ireland were linked to broader historical processes of social change in the European Mesolithic. Some of these, but not all, may have been connected to environmental change. This discussion also requires consideration of how archaeologists approach the identification of 'contact and connections', in particular the problems of relying on material culture to identify these. I begin by reviewing existing models of contact and connections and summarising information on sea-level and seafaring.

Early, Later, Latest

My title is drawn from the late Roger Jacobi's seminal 1976 paper 'Britain inside and outside Mesolithic Europe' (Jacobi 1976) which argued that over time Britain was isolated from developments in the continental European Mesolithic. Jacobi highlighted the difficulties caused by multiple regional terminologies and proposed a simplified division into a European Early, Later and Latest Mesolithic. The Early and Later Mesolithic in Britain (and Ireland, which was discussed as part of Britain) was paralleled across Northern Europe. The Latest Mesolithic in Europe was defined by the appearance of 'trapeze' industries, which Jacobi argued spread from the south of Europe, reaching the north-west by *c.* 6,500 BC.[2] This took place after the final physical separation of Britain and the continent, which Jacobi dated to *c.* 7,400 BC. As trapezes were absent from Britain, 'there is no artefactual evidence for social connections by ... *(c. 6500 BC)*...' (Jacobi 1976, 78). Jacobi (*ibid.*, 80) also argues that the absence from Britain of *feuilles de gui*, a distinctive retouched point characteristic of the north European plain, and the distinctive Wommerson quartzite associated with this technocomplex meant that Britain had 'ceased to be even socially connected with the Continent by ... *(c. 7,300–7,050 BC)'*. The distinction in artefact types was considered to indicate an absolute absence of contact across the newly formed water bodies that separated Britain and the rest of the Continent: '...the detectable 'Foreign Relations' of Britain, the newly created island, did indeed end until the 'Neolithic Period'.' (*ibid.*, 80). Britain was 'inside' the European Mesolithic, and then it was 'outside'.

Distinctions in artefact types and raw materials are still key evidence of the presence or absence of 'Continental Connections'. For example, the Later Mesolithic lithic industry of Ireland is distinct from that of Britain, both are distinct from continental Europe, and there is little evidence of raw material movement linking these regions. Alison Sheridan therefore argues that the hunter-gatherer communities of these islands were insular, and that the impetus for the appearance of new Neolithic material culture and practices in the Irish Sea region is social change in France (Sheridan 2007; 2010). On the other hand, Julian Thomas argues on the basis of ethnoarchaeological data that you cannot use material culture as an index for contact; that we must *assume* these connections did exist; and that Neolithisation arose through the movement of materials and ideas in these networks (Thomas 2004; 2008). Precisely the same data is being used in these discussions to back up diametrically opposed interpretation. Whilst this is a nice example of equifinality in archaeological interpretation, it is also somewhat of an analytical impasse. In this regard, it is interesting to note that genetic variation in modern snail populations has recently been used to argue that "trading links were established between Iberia and Ireland in the Mesolithic, providing ample opportunities for land snails to be transported in the cargo" (Grindon and Davison 2013, 5). Sometimes different data sets tell us very different stories.

Sea level

The relationship between the sea and the land in northern Europe changed, substantially, during the Mesolithic period (see Bell and Warren 2013, 33–40 for a summary with detailed references; Sturt, this volume). Relative sea level resulted from the complex interplay of water being released from bodies of ice and the rebound of the land as it was released from the weight of these bodies of ice. Significant 'meltwater pulses' are recognised, such as a jump of *c.* 1–3m at *c.* 6,200 BC, also known as Melt Water Pulse 3 (MWP3). In terms of considering the connections between different parts of Northern Europe three events are especially significant (for review see Bell and Warren 2013).

- Ireland and Britain were separated by the Irish Sea by *c.* 12,000 BC. Britain at this time was still connected to continental Europe
- The English Channel was flooded, mainly from the West, with the Straights of Dover flooded at *c.* 7,000 BC.
- The North Sea plain, or Doggerland, was finally submerged by *c.* 6,000 BC as part of long term sea level rise, with the final submergence possibly being driven by MWP3 or the Storegga slide tsunami (see below).

Isostatic rebound was more significant in northern Britain and Ireland and in these areas uplift has broadly surpassed sea level rises, leading to the preservation of Mesolithic shorelines. Sea level rise could be dramatic and a number of arguments have linked social and environmental change at this time (see below). In general the impact of sea level rise during the period was to reduce the land area available for settlement and this has frequently been commented upon in the literature. Sea level rise also served to increase the length of sea crossings between different parts of the British-Irish Isles.

Boats

The nature of maritime technologies is reviewed in Bell and Warren (2013, 45–6). Little material evidence for Mesolithic seafaring exists: dugout boats are well known from Continental Europe but no certain examples exist in Britain or Ireland and there is no direct evidence of skin/hide boats. The occupation of islands that required long or difficult sea journeys (the Isles of Scilly, the Outer Hebrides, possibly Shetland, the crossing of Swnt Enlli) provides indirect evidence of sea faring capacity. Fish species in archaeological contexts are argued to show little evidence of off-shore fishing, possibly because of the unpredictable and sometimes difficult sea conditions (Pickard and Bonsall 2004). That seafaring was highly seasonal seems likely. For the purpose of this paper I assume that seafaring capabilities were sufficient to enable contact across the bodies of water that surrounded the islands of Britain and Ireland if such contact was desired: this, of course, glosses over many complexities surrounding the timing, character and ease of those journeys.

An(other) island perspective

The problems of using material culture as evidence of contact are highlighted by the Mesolithic of the Isle of Man, where a microlithic 'early' Mesolithic gives way to a 'heavy-bladed' 'later' Mesolithic which developed by at least 5,000 BC and probably before (McCartan 2003, 2004; Woodman 1978). McCartan suggests that Manx industries originated in Ireland, but that isolation led to insular developments (2004, 279). The relationship between Man, Ireland and Britain is therefore a microcosm of the relationships between Ireland, Britain and Europe.

The Isle of Man is a comparatively small island (*c.* 572km^2) and generalisations about possible Mesolithic population levels can be obtained by comparing ethnographically-observed and predicted population densities for hunter-gatherers in similar environments (see Table 4.1). Whilst these numbers should be treated as crude estimates only, it is important to note that most of these population levels fall below the level of *c.* 200–500 often considered to be a minimum viable long term human population. Only the average population densities recorded for north-west American and Californian hunter-gatherers, the most densely aggregated hunter-gatherers known from the recent historical past and living in more productive environments than Man, would have sustained a viable population.

There are several possibilities to consider here:

- Firstly, *Mesolithic communities in Britain and Ireland may have lived at much higher population densities than those recorded in comparable environments world-wide.* There are over 300 Mesolithic sites on Man, and it is possible that settlement was intensive, but there is little evidence for settlement on this scale in the Mesolithic of Britain and Ireland and the balance of probability is against this.

Graeme Warren

Table 4.1. Possible population densities for Mesolithic Isle of Man. Data from Gamble et al. 1999, Binford 2001, Kelly 1995. Bold indicates population density likely to be viable in the long term. Populations for Britain and Ireland at same densities shown for comparative purposes.

		density per 100km²	Population of **Isle of Man**	Population of **Ireland**	Population of **Britain**
Models for Britain and Ireland					
Gamble et al 1999 (sparse)		2	11.4	1,688	4,597
Gamble et al 1999 (low)		5	28.6	4,221	11,492
Gamble et al 1999 (high)		9	51.5	7,598	20,686
Binford 2001 (low)		8	45.8	6,754	18,388
Binford 2001 (high)		16	91.5	13,507	36,776
Ethnographic averages (Kelly 1995)					
North American Northwest Coast (low)	Bella Coola	10	57.2	8,442	22,985
North American Northwest Coast (average)		68.4	**391.2**	57,743	157,216
North American Northwest Coast (high)	Puyallup	195	**1115.4**	164,619	448,204
Californian (low)	Kawaiisu	11.9	68.1	10,046	27,352
Californian (average)		157	**898.0**	132,539	360,861
Californian (high)	Chumash	843	**4822.0**	711,661	1,937,619
temperate forests (low)	Shoshone Bannock	1.31	7.5	1,106	3,011
temperate forests (average)		13	74.4	10,975	29,880
temperate forests (high)	Sanpoil	38	**217.4**	32,080	87,342

- Secondly, *the Manx evidence indicates a small population surviving at the margins of what is demographically viable in long term.* This is possible, but this degree of isolation seems inherently unlikely given other evidence for sea-faring in the period.
- Thirdly, and most likely, *the population of Mesolithic Man was too small to be viable in the long term and was maintained by contacts with other areas.* Both McCartan (2003; 2004) and Woodman (1981) have previously proposed that mating networks were maintained over the Irish Sea during the Mesolithic.

The Manx example therefore highlights that using differences in stone tool technologies and raw materials is not necessarily an index of the presence/absence of contact. Significant challenges remain in understanding the character and nature of the social interaction that comprised this contact – including its frequency and intensity – but the contacts must have been there.

On scale

As many have noted, the dominance of the regional and local scale approaches to the European Mesolithic has led to a proliferation of regional terminology which makes broad scale synthesis difficult. It is, for example, remarkable that the terminology for the British and Irish Mesolithic periods does not match: with the Early/Earlier Mesolithic in Ireland equating to the Later Mesolithic of Britain. (In passing, it is worth noting that this distinction is not always appreciated in the archaeological community). The proliferation of national terminologies has recently been argued to 'reflect(s) an idea of a static, isolated prehistoric lifestyle during the early Holocene' (Sørensen *et al.* 2013, 2), and this reminds us that considering the broad scale is central to understanding the multi-scalar histories and dynamics of specific hunter-gatherer societies (Sassaman and Holly 2011) who may not respect the national boundaries that articulate so much of our research. It is important to note that genetic research is less cautious about the large scale, and maps with arrows indicating specific population movements for the Mesolithic and Neolithic are common, if problematic (Oppenheimer 2006).

In an attempt to provide some synthesis, my discussion is based on a broad chronological

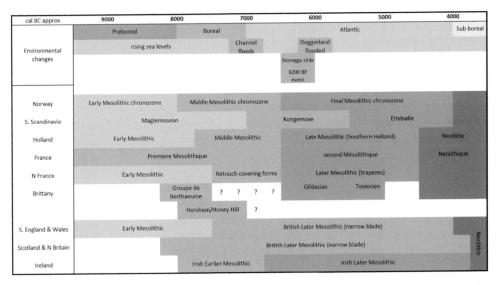

Figure 4.1. Approximate chronological relationships for areas discussed in text. See main text for references. Please note that these are rounded to approximately 250 years and show broad associations only.

review using secondary sources of the Mesolithic from France to Norway: see Figure 4.1 (Costa and Marchand 2006; Ducrocq 2009; 2010; Ducrocq *et al.* 2008; Bjerck 2008; Blankholm 2008; Valdeyron 2008; Verhart 2008; Ghesquière and Marchand 2011; Marchand *et al.* 2009; Perrin *et al.* 2009). This chronology is itself based on synthesis, and there is a compelling need for a European level review of high quality radiocarbon dates (Schulting *et al.* 2009). Change over time in the Mesolithic of Britain and Ireland is very badly understood. The chronologies presented here are imprecise: they are rounded to *c.* 250 year intervals – compressing 10 to 12 human generations. They hopefully serve to demonstrate the broad synchronicity of some processes and raise some possibilities for consideration.

My discussion is broadly chronological and considers the following themes:

- Ireland outside of Mesolithic Europe?
- Long distance links and regionalisation in the Early Mesolithic
- Houses and moving your world
- The second Mesolithic?

Ireland outside of Mesolithic Europe? (*c.* 12,700–9,500 BC)

The initial (re)colonisation of the British-Irish Isles following the Late Glacial Maximum (LGM) was part of the final expansion of Palaeolithic settlement into northern Europe. The retreat of the ice provided opportunities for hunter-gatherers to explore and (re)colonise new areas. Environmental changes led to major social changes as communities adapted to new landscapes. We often consider this movement North in expansionist terms, as an exploration of new lands or even an expression of the so-called human universals to explore and travel. But it is worth remembering that some, at least, of these communities may have been facing serious challenges as their world changed: as McCannon describes it "... their skills and folkways (were) rendered obsolete by changes to their habitat. Many were refugees, fleeing environmental shocks and stresses" (McCannon 2012, 40).

Similarities in material culture, art and settlement types suggest that the post-LGM settlement of Britain (but not Ireland) following *c.* 12,700 BC was part of a European tradition of hunter-gatherer settlement, behaviour and belief (Jacobi and Higham 2011; Pettitt and White 2012), perhaps with particular links to Belgium and northern Europe. These communities changed over time and receive different archaeological names, but Britain is clearly part of these broader European histories. At the start of the Holocene, across north-west Europe, 'Early Mesolithic' industries develop from Ahrensburgian and other traditions and again, these changes are apparent in Britain (Warren 2013, and refs within). Britain (but not Ireland) at this time was physically connected to Europe, and appears to have been very much part of this social world. These communities presumably lived at low population densities, and kinship links must have been vital in maintaining them through routines of dispersal and aggregation, meeting and leaving. Their settlement of Britain may have been small scale, and ebbed and flowed with significant environmental change.

There is no evidence for Late Glacial settlement in Ireland, and classic European 'Early Mesolithic' (Maglemosean) evidence is not found in Ireland, which appears to first be settled in the years following 8,000 BC (Woodman 2012). Ireland was an island from *c.* 12,000 BC but the crossing was comparatively short and probably did not provide an insuperable technological challenge. Woodman has drawn attention to a number of important methodological and research history problems which may have led to a low archaeological visibility for early settlement in Ireland (e.g. Woodman 1986a; 1986b; Woodman and Wickham-Jones 1998), but for the purpose of this paper it is assumed that the absence is real. This distinction requires explanation: Ireland, it appears, was completely outside of Early Mesolithic Europe. Why?

Woodman has suggested that the delayed colonisation of islands is relatively common globally (e.g. 2003, 58). This is possible, but given the general diversity of settlement in Early Mesolithic Europe (see below) it would be preferable to seek more particular explanations. The most important argument for the absence of early human settlement in Ireland is the impoverished fauna of the island (Woodman *et al.* 1997). Key Late Glacial absences include the wild horse, elk and auroch. In the early Holocene red deer were absent from the native fauna (Woodman 1986a, 11; Woodman *et al.* 1997) and are a Neolithic introduction to the island of Ireland (Carden *et al.* 2011; 2012). Wild boar, and other animals, may also have been absent in the early Holocene (see below).

The absence of horse is especially significant in determining the presence of Late Glacial settlement, as this was a key resource for the first (Magdalenian) settlers of Britain (see Woodman 1986b; Jacobi and Higham 2011, 243). The Magdalenian colonisation of Britain, therefore may have stopped short of Ireland because of the absence of a key resource: wild horse. But what of later settlement? Federmesser, Ahrensburgian and other archaeological complexes have different landscape distributions than Magdalenian material, and these include sites in Western Scotland (Ballin *et al.* 2010). Early Holocene strategies are also diverse. In Germany, for example, from late in the pre-boreal we see the development of economies with a very significant emphasis on hazelnuts (Holst 2010). In Scandinavia the development of an arctic marine adaptation allows the very rapid colonisation of the north. By *c.* 9,500 BC a marine adaptation led people into Northern Scandinavia within a short distance of the ice cap (Bjerck 1995; 2009). Yet Ireland was still not settled. The evidence of human ingenuity and diversity at this time is at odds with a failure to colonise an island simply because it was an island. What, in particular, made this landscape unattractive?

Fuglesveldt (2011; 2012) argues that the recolonisation of Northern Europe was the final extension northwards of Upper Palaeolithic ways of life, and that one of the key aspects of this way of life was the spiritual relationship that linked hunters and large game, especially reindeer. When people followed their world north they therefore did not just follow resources but a world view, as "... the reindeer played a central role not only in terms of subsistence, but also in the Late Upper Palaeolithic and Early Mesolithic pantheon of spirits" (*ibid.*, 39). There is compelling evidence from Early Holocene Britain of similar relationships with large game. The well known red deer antler head dresses at Star Carr which demonstrate a process of 'becoming deer' (Conneller 2004) are also paralleled in Europe with the special treatment of the heads of the large animals that were the 'co-inhabitants' of Mesolithic hunters (Fuglesveldt 2011, 42). These suggest that a spiritual relationship linked early Holocene hunters and large game animals. Given the importance of this relationships, the absence of large game from Ireland may have made the island *conceptually* impossible to settle: this was a land outside the world-view that made the early Mesolithic of Europe possible.

Long distance links and regionalisation in the Early Mesolithic (*c.* 9,500–8,000 BC)

As noted above regionalisation is notable across Europe in the early Mesolithic and the earliest part of the Holocene can be seen as a time of diversification and the breaking apart of the Late Glacial life way. This period also sees startling long distance movements and connections and remarkable historical events. Sørensen *et al.* (2013) demonstrate how at this time the 'conical core pressure blade concept' spreads through northern Scandinavia from north-west Russia as part of a movement of Boreal forest adapted peoples and as a diffusion of ideas. Groups migrating from the east, with a terrestrial focus on beaver and elk and the maritime based hunter gatherers of western Scandinavia who had colonised from the south met in Northern Scandinavia (Sørensen *et al.* 2013; see also Blankholm 2009). These meetings of different groups and individuals, carrying different traditions and, possibly, differentiated by their genetic backgrounds have not often appeared in our accounts of the early Holocene.

The spread of the pressure blade concept demonstrates remarkable long distance connections. Sørensen *et al.* argue that the presence of skilled blade production in flint at Sujala, Finland demonstrates a movement of people of >1000km in one generation from east to west, as the skills of blade production required access to high quality flint, which was absent in the 'quartz world' of the northern Fennoscandinavia shield which Sujala lies on the western edge of. The scale of these movements and connections should alert us to the unusual and the new and clearly demonstrates the problems of an overly regional approach. Naomi Woodward's doctoral research, for example, argues that a 'northern tradition' of tanged points in Orkney and the north of Scotland has strong links with early Holocene lithic assemblages in Northern Scandinavia (including the Hensbacka-Fosna technocomplex). Our maps of Mesolithic continental connections do not often extend in this direction.

Regionalisation continues around the North Sea region (Deeben 2003, 143; Bjerck 2008, 78; Verhart 2005; 2009) and includes the development of the 'Horsham' group (*c.* 8,500–7,800 BC: Ghesquière and Marchand 2011, 93), originally defined in the 1930s and then rediscovered in France in the 1970s. These lithic industries include very regular blades, picks and tranchet axes, and basally retouched points. The Horsham and Honey Hill groups are geographically distinct in England and Wales: the Horsham to the south and west, the Honey Hill to the east. They are also found on both sides of the Channel; the Horsham, in the earlier phases, mainly restricted to the east of the Channel, but expanding to Brittany later. Ghesquière and Marchand (2011, 136) argue that:

> "Ces liens stylistique entretenus sur les deux rives de la manche suggèrent des relations de chaque côte d'un bras d'eau de 50 à 100 kilomètres de largeur. L'existence d'une population commune et de contacts réguliers sous-entend une maîtrise confirmée de la navigation dans un secteur ou les courants marins sont loin d'être négligeables [The maintenance of these stylistic links from both shores of the Channel suggests relationships on each side of a stretch of water from 50 to 100 kilometers wide. The existence of a common population and of regular contacts implies an experienced command of navigation in an area where ocean currents are far from negligible]".

The sea here is not a barrier to the maintenance of a common cultural tradition although the final formation of the Channel is still widely seen to be significant in ending these close links (Ghesquière and Marchand 2011, 136; Ducroq 2009). (In passing, it is very surprising that Barton and Roberts' (2004) review of the Horsham material makes no reference to its appearance across the Channel).

England and Wales can therefore be argued to involved in the regionalisation characteristic of France, Holland and Belgium. These industries are not present in Scotland, which, on the basis of current evidence develops the 'later Mesolithic' at this time (see below). Possibly, northern Britain is part of a northern world not a lowland European one. Continental connections may link different parts of Britain and Ireland to different places.

Houses and moving your world (*c.* 8,000–7,000 BC)

The centuries following 8,000 BC see more regionalisation and diversification of economy across northern Europe. In Northern Britain this period sees the start of the 'later' Mesolithic, which is also present in Ireland where it is called the 'earlier' Mesolithic. In both areas a new and distinctive tradition of round-house architecture appears and is associated with new stone tool industries, sometimes described as 'narrow-blade' or 'geometric'. These timber buildings are also contemporary with the first settlement of Ireland. Waddington *et al.* (2007, 207) have argued that the appearance of these buildings and narrow blade microliths around Northern Britain and Ireland is a consequence of the inundation of the North Sea plain which is ongoing throughout this period with the houses acting as 'territorial markers' in the context of increasing competition and pressure for resources. The loss of land, and readjustment of people's routines is likely to be a key factor in changing settlement patterns at this time, but it is also important to note that this period sees technological change across large areas of north-western Europe (see also Woodman 2012, 11–13), including those not immediately adjacent to the North Sea. In France, for example, in the centuries surrounding 8,000 BC isosceles triangles become rare and points with retouched base become common (e.g. Ducrocq 2009; Blanchet *et al.* 2006). Without neglecting the importance of sea level change in understanding social change at this time, we must consider other possibilities. It is also important to note that whilst sea level rise might require people to move their settlements, it does not explain why particular new types of stone tools and houses develop.

Instead, it may be useful to complement the focus on sea level change by asking how these buildings enabled communities to cope with change; how these buildings made the colonisation of Ireland possible (this may take part as a movement of people 'pushed' by sea level change – but whatever their motivation, it leads to the settlement of an island that was previously beyond the limits of Mesolithic Europe). These 6m diameter timber framed buildings are substantial constructions that make considerable demands in terms of materials and labour: they almost certainly required the labour of more than an immediate nuclear family. The houses are therefore *products* of successful social relations; of bringing people together.

Their repeated architectural form across a large area suggests some common understandings of the right ways of organising domestic space. Whilst this may indicate the importance of tradition and/or world view in determining how space is used it is important to note that such commonalities of practice provide a context for hospitality. People from other areas can be welcomed to a house which will in many senses be familiar. There is some evidence of long-distance contacts and connections in terms of practices at this time, for example, cremation burials in northern France and the Netherlands include placing small amounts of cremated bone in pits (e.g. at 7,400 BC Oirschot, Netherlands; Verhart 2008), providing a close parallel to the contemporary token cremations placed in pits and marked with posts at Hermitage, Ireland (Collins 2009). It is not at all clear whether this reflects a shared tradition, maintained over time in the absence of contact, or a common form of practice, maintained through interaction. It is therefore possible that alongside increased regionalisation evidence in other aspects of the archaeological record (manifest for example in more use of local raw materials and a reduction in the size of tools) these houses demonstrate the importance of hospitality and contact and connection.

The importance of houses may suggest that the spiritual relations with large game outlined above were no longer so important. The Upper Palaeolithic way of life had changed, adapted to new circumstances, and created new potentials for social relations: indeed, the first colonisation of Ireland appears to have involved the deliberate importation of wild boar (Warren *et al.* 2014). As well as the houses structuring space in a predictable way, Mesolithic communities would alter landscapes by importing animals. This may indicate a profoundly different world view: rather than following your world as it moves north, contacts and connections to different places were made by bringing your world with you.

The second Mesolithic? (*c.* 7,000–5/4,000 BC)

The 7th millennium sees major change. Gronenborn argues that the centuries following 7,000 cal BC are a time of 'crisis' for Mesolithic groups in Central Europe (Gronenborn 1999, 137), and in France, this period sees the divide between a 'premiere' and 'seconde' Mesolithic. In Britain no technological change is identified at this time, but Ireland changes from the 'earlier' to 'later' Mesolithic (Woodman 2012). At a broad scale two phenomena are especially significant for understanding Continental connections – the appearance of 'trapezes' and the final loss of Doggerland.

The impacts of the final inundation of Doggerland and the possibly catastrophic tsunami associated with the Storegga submarine slide (Weninger 2008; Sturt this volume) in the second half of the seventh millennium BC are difficult to assess in absence of good chronological information. Sea level rise and disastrous events would have had significant impact on Mesolithic communities, especially in the generally low-lying North Sea plain, but given the broader evidence of social change in this period (see below), it would certainly be limiting, perhaps even facile, to identify single processes as driving change. Even if one does consider environmental processes to be the most likely cause of change in hunter-gatherer communities (and this would be a very problematic assumption, see Sassaman and Holly 2011), we would then need to pick apart the influence of sea level rise and the 8,200 cal BP event, a major cooling episode with implications for the archaeology of the Mesolithic period across Europe (e.g. Berger and Guilaine 2010). There is certainly no reason to suppose that the rise of the sea necessarily posed any insuperable technical challenge to contact between different regions. Contact may have been lost across these bodies of water (see below), but this was a choice, not a necessity.

The appearance of 'trapezes' in European stone tool industries has been somewhat neglected recently, especially in the English language literature. Despite this neglect, their appearance has recently been argued to be a "major historical phenomenon affecting the European continent" (Perrin *et al.* 2009, 178), and once again, the significance of the phenomena becomes apparent when it is examined across national boundaries. Although often discussed in isolation, the 'trapezes' form part of a suite of changes to the nature of stone tool assemblages (Perrin *et al.* 2009):

- A shift to the removal of large and regular flint blades by pressure/indirect percussion.
- Trapezoid arrowheads. These may differ from the triangular projectile points they replace in emphasising cutting, not piercing (this is only true of symmetrical trapezes).
- Laterally notched bladelets. Their function is unknown, but would seem to imply a new task of some kind.

Therefore the appearance of trapezes is not just a change of stone tools, but "an entire technical system ... including new actions, styles, techniques and knowledge" (Perrin *et al.* 2009, 174). The origin of trapezes is uncertain, possibly lying in North Africa or the Ukraine, but they spread into Western Europe from Sicily after *c.* 7,000 BC, reaching the English Channel by *c.* 6,500 BC. By this stage the Channel has formed, and Britain and Ireland are not part of the 'second' Mesolithic in terms of lithic technology (but see below). It is critically important to note that the spread of trapezes had previously involved crossing water bodies (from/to Sicily, for example).

Perrin *et al.* suggest that because three independent aspects of stone tool industries change at the same time this indicates "l'existence de phénomènes sociaux cohérents, impliquant tout ou partie du corps social [the existence of coherent social phenomena, involving all or part of the social body]"[3] (*ibid.*, 170). They do not see any link between the spread of trapezes and domesticates, but suggest substantial change in settlement patterns associated with the appearance of the new technologies. The 7th millennium BC therefore sees significant change in Mesolithic communities across Europe, even if the detail of what this meant for specific groups is not clear. Clearly, not all aspects of this need change be associated with the loss of Doggerland. Perrin *et al.* suggest that population movement across Europe is a possible explanation for the scale and nature of the change, but is not sustained by current evidence.

In Britain there are few meaningful chronological data to assess change at this time, but Ireland sees a transition from an 'earlier' Mesolithic characterised by microliths to a 'later' non-microlithic Mesolithic *c.* 6,800/6,700 BC (Woodman 2012). This seemingly insular and distinctive approach has been the cause for much speculation about the contacts and connections between Britain and Ireland and the continent. However, the differences in some aspects of stone tool typology can sometimes mask commonalities. In Brittany at this time, for example, trapezes become significant at (broadly) the same time as the Irish later Mesolithic appears (Costa and Marchand 2006). But despite the differences in the nature of stone tools many aspects of technical change in the two areas at the time are shared: including greater use of local raw materials which they argue to indicate a reduction in the size of territories (Costa and Marchand 2006). Costa and Marchand argue that the strength of these connections:

> "ne peut que renforcer l'importance du phénomène, nous obligeant par là-même à nous demander s'il ne s'agit pas d'un mécanisme inherent à l'évolution structurelle des sociétés de la fin du Mésolithique, au moins dans cette zone atlantique [can only reinforce the importance of the phenomenon, obliging us thereby to consider if it is a process inherent to the structural evolution of societies at the end of the Mesolithic, at least in the Atlantic zone]". (*ibid.*, 284–5)

This suggests that despite the differences in raw materials and typology, Ireland should be considered to be undergoing the same processes and dynamics as other neighbouring parts of Mesolithic Europe. Whilst parallel evolution of isolated Mesolithic communities in different places is certainly possible, it is more plausible to consider these commonalities as reflecting contact between these areas. Within Ireland, there is some evidence for long distance movement of small numbers of raw materials during the Later Mesolithic (e.g. Kador 2007), but this does not appear to extend beyond the shores of Ireland. Rather than meaning that there was no contact beyond the confines of the island, it may be that the nature of this contact was such that it was not marked by the movement of lithic materials. Indeed, the appearance of a domesticated cow at Ferriter's Cove, Co. Kerry (Woodman *et al.* 1999; Tresset 2003; Anderson-Whymark and Garrow, this volume) may indicate that connections between Ireland and France were marked in different ways at different times.

Discussion

The Mesolithic of Britain and Ireland must be considered as part of the Mesolithic of Europe rather than being inside or outside it. For much of the period clear evidence demonstrates contacts and connections between what now form the British-Irish Isles and other parts of continental Europe. Stone tools and raw materials are not always reliable guides to the presence or absence of these contacts. Commonalities in stone tool typologies and raw materials simply demonstrate that people were choosing to show their connections to other communities through these media. In passing, it is important to note that during the Neolithic the significance of demonstrating connections over distance appears to have risen (Cooney *et al.* 2012) – this does not mean that the contacts were not present before, it implies that they were not a matter of material celebration.

For much of the Mesolithic the historical processes apparent in Europe are present in Britain and Ireland – a general trend to regionality, diversity and smaller territories over time. Whilst it is conceivable that these indicate a parallel evolution from a common starting point it seems much more likely that these commonalities result from a shared history. Some events, such as the spread of trapezes, do initially appear to have stopped short of Britain and Ireland. But it is important to note that when the broader historical phenomenon of the appearance of 'trapezes' is considered considerable parallels in terms of social process can be adduced between Ireland and France at this time. Data are not available to assess how Britain may have participated in these changes. Furthermore, although it cannot be demonstrated, it is highly likely that Mesolithic communities in Britain and Ireland encountered trapezes and *chose* not to adopt them or to partake in the broader historical process that trapezes represent. This is not to say that they were 'outside' of Europe, simply to recognise that the individuals and communities who inhabited Britain at this time developed their own social strategies and responses to the changing worlds in which they lived.

As well as the sea level and environmental changes that have often featured in our explanations of change, broad historical processes characterised Mesolithic Europe, and these are often very poorly understood. In several instances these are broadly synchronous, as for example in the mid seventh millennium: when the inundation of Doggerland and the appearance of trapezes in northern Europe take place. Neither historical event should be neglected in our accounts, which should try and understand how they relate to each other. A key challenge for the Mesolithic of the British-Irish Isles is discriminating between these different processes and understanding what may be causing change at any given time and why it relates to the particularity of the changes we encounter as archaeologists. This is why simply identifying broadly synchronous events as causally related is problematic.

Britain and Ireland were *inside* Mesolithic Europe. The nature and intensity of the continental connections changed over time, but it is difficult to sustain any argument that suggests they were isolated from the broader processes and dynamics that characterised the continent. Rather than arguing that specific communities are inside or outside, connected nor not, it would be more helpful if we started to think seriously about why these varied communities chose to do some things and not others.

Acknowledgements

My thanks to Duncan, Fraser and Hugo for the invitation to contribute to this volume – and my apologies if this is not quite the paper they (or I) expected. Thanks to Gregor Marchand for advice on Mesolithic France and Rowan Lacey for assistance with matters linguistic. Many thanks to Duncan and to Thomas Kador for useful comments on an early draft of this paper. All errors, inaccuracies and failures of judgement are the sole responsibility of the author.

Notes
1   The use of the term 'British Isles' to describe the islands that comprise Britain and Ireland is problematic, but no widely accepted alternative exists: the region is here described as the British-Irish Isles.
2   Jacobi presented his argument in uncalibrated radiocarbon years BC, I provide approximate calibrations for convenience, but these dates should be treated as very general. Unless otherwise specified, all dates in this paper are in cal BC.
3   All translations in this paper are the author's own.

References

Ballin, T., Saville, A., Tipping, R. and Ward, T. 2010. An Upper Palaeolithic flint and chert assemblage from Howburn Farm, South Lanarkshire, Scotland: first results. *Oxford Journal of Archaeology* 29, 323–360.

Barton, N. and Roberts, A. 2004. The Mesolithic period in England: current perspectives and new research. In A. Saville (ed.), *Mesolithic Scotland and its Neighbours: the early Holocene prehistory of Scotland, its British and Irish Context and some Northern European perspectives,* 339–358. Edinburgh: Society of Antiquaries of Scotland.

Bell, M. and Warren, G. 2013. The Mesolithic. In J. Ransley and F. Sturt (eds), *People and the Sea: A Maritime Archaeological Research Agenda for England,* Council for British Archaeology Research Report 171, 30–49. York: Council for British Archaeology.

Berger, J.-F. and Guilaine, J. 2010. The 8200 cal BP abrupt environmental change and the Neolithic transition: A Mediterranean perspective. *Quaternary International* 200, 31–49.

Binford, L. 2001. *Constructing Frames of Reference: an analytical method for archaeological theory building using ethnographic data sets.* Berkley: University of California Press.

Bjerck, H. 1995. The North Sea Continent and the Pioneer Settlement of Norway. In A. Fischer (ed.), *Man and Sea in the Mesolithic: Coastal Settlement Above and Below Present Sea Level*, 131–144. Oxford: Oxbow.

Bjerck, H. 2008. Norwegian Mesolithic trends: a review. In G. Bailey and P. Spikins (eds), *Mesolithic Europe*, 60–106. Cambridge: Cambridge University Press.

Bjerck, H. 2009. Colonizing seascapes: comparative perspectives on the development of maritime relations in Scandinavia and Patagonia. *Arctic Anthropology* 46, 118–131.

Blanchet, S., Kayser, O., Marchand, G. and Yven, E. 2006. Le Mésolithique moyen en Finistère: de nouvelles datations pour le groupe de Bertheaume. *Bulletin de la Société Préhistorique Française* 103, 507–518.

Blankholm, H. 2008. Southern Scandinavia. In G. Bailey and P. Spikins (eds), *Mesolithic Europe*, 107–131. Cambridge: Cambridge University Press.

Blankholm, H. 2009. *Målsnes 1: an Early Post-Glacial Coastal Site in Northern Norway*. Oxford: Oxbow.

Carden, R., Carlin, C., Marnell, F., McElholm, D., Hetherington, J. & Gammell, M. 2011. Distribution and range expansion of deer in Ireland. *Mammal Review* 41, 313–325.

Carden, R., McDevitt, A., Zachos, F., Woodman, P., O'Toole, P., Rose, H., Monaghan, N., Campana, M., Bradley, D. and Edwards, C. 2012. Phylogeographic, ancient DNA, fossil and morphometric analyses reveal ancient and modern introductions of a large mammal: the complex case of red deer (*Cervus elaphus*) in Ireland. *Quaternary Science Reviews* 42, 74–84.

Collins T. 2009. Hermitage, Ireland: life and death on the western edge of Europe. In S. McCartan, P. Woodman, R. Schulting and G. Warren (eds), *Mesolithic Horizons: Papers presented at the Seventh International Conference on the Mesolithic in Europe, Belfast 2005*, vol 2, 876–879. Oxford: Oxbow.

Conneller, C. 2004. Becoming deer. *Archaeological Dialogues* 11, 37–56.

Cooney, G., Mandal, S., O'Keeffe, E. and Warren, G. 2012. Rathlin in early prehistory. In W. Forsythe and R. McConkey (eds), *Rathlin Island: an archaeological survey of a maritime landscape*, 46–84. Belfast: TSO Belfast, Northern Ireland Archaeological Monograph 8.

Costa, L. and Marchand, G. 2006. Transformations des productions lithiques du premier au second Mésolithique en Bretagne et en Irlande. *Bulletin de la Société Préhistorique Française* 103, 275–290.

Deeben, J. and Arts, N. 2005. From tundra hunting to forest hunting: Late Upper Palaeolithic and Early Mesolithic. In L. Louwe Kooijmans, P. van den Broeke, H. Fokkens and A. van Gijn (eds), *The Prehistory of the Netherlands*, vol 1, 139–156. Amsterdam: Amsterdam University Press.

Ducrocq, T. 2009. Élements de chronologie absolue du Mésolithique dans le Nord de la France. In P. Crombé, M. Van Strydonck, J. Sergant, M. Boudin and M. Bats (eds), *Chronology and Evolution within the Mesolithic of North-West Europe: Proceedings of an International Meeting, Brussels, May 30th–June 1st 2007*, 345–361. Newcastle: Cambridge Scholars Publishing.

Ducrocq, T. 2010. Des traces discrètes d'occupations paléolithiques et mésolithiques dans le marais de Warluis (Oise): les sites VI et IX. *RAP* 1/2, 1–36.

Ducrocq, T., Bridault, A. and Coutard, S. 2008. Le gisement mésolithique de Warluis (Oise): approche préliminaire. In J.-P. Fagnart, A. Thevenin, T. Ducrocq, B. Souffi, and P. Coudret (eds), *Le début du Mésolithique en Europe du Nord-Ouest: Actes de la table ronde d'Amiens, 9 et 10 octobre 2004*, 85–106. Mémoire XLV de la Société préhistorique française.

Fuglestvedt, I. 2011. Humans, material culture and landscape: outline to an understanding of developments in worldviews on the Scandinavia Peninsula, ca. 10,000–4500 BP. In A. Cannon (ed.), *Structured Worlds: The Archaeology of Hunter-Gatherer Thought and Action*, 32–53. Sheffield: Equinox Publishing.

Fuglestvedt, I. 2012. The pioneer condition on the Scandinavian peninsula: the last frontier of a 'Palaeolithic Way' in Europe. *Norwegian Archaeological Review* 45, 1–29.

Ghesquière, E. and Marchand, G. 2011. *La Mésolithique en France: Archéologie des deniers chasseurs-cueilleurs. Archéologies de al France*. Paris: La Découverte.

Grindon, A. and Davison, A. 2013. Irish *Cepaea nemoralis* land snails have a cryptic Franco-Iberian origin that is most easily explained by the movements of mesolithic humans. *PLoS ONE* 8(6), e65792

Holst, D. 2010. Hazelnut economy of early Holocene hunter-gatherers: a case study from Mesolithic Duvensee, northern Germany. *Journal of Archaeological Science* 37, 2871–2880

Jacobi, R. 1976. Britain inside and outside Mesolithic Europe. *Proceedings of the Prehistoric Society* 42, 67–84

Jacobi, R. and Higham, T. 2011. The Later Upper Palaeolithic recolonisation of Britain: new results from AMS radiocarbon dating. In N. Ashton, S. G. Lewis and C. Stringer (eds), *Developments in Quaternary Sciences* 14, 223–247.

Kador, T. 2007. Stone age motion pictures: an objects' perspective from early prehistoric Ireland. In V. Cummings and R. Johnston (eds), *Prehistoric Journeys*, 33–44. Oxford: Oxbow Books.

Kelly, R. 1995. *The Foraging Spectrum: diversity in hunter-gatherer lifeways*. London: Smithsonian Institute Press.

Marchand, G. 2007. Mesolithic fragrances: Mesolithic-Neolithic interactions in Western France. In A. Whittle and V. Cummings (eds), *Going Over: the Mesolithic-Neolithic Transition in North-West Europe*, 225–242. London: British Academy.

Marchand, G., Dupont, Oberlin, C. and Delque-Kloic, E. 2009. Entre «effet réservoir» et «effet de plateau: la difficile datation du Mésolithique de Bretagne». In P. Crombé, M. Van Strydonck, J. Sergant, M. Boudin and M. Bats (eds), *Chronology and Evolution within the Mesolithic of North-West Europe: Proceedings of an International Meeting, Brussels, May 30th–June 1st 2007*, 29–3247. Newcastle: Cambridge Scholars Publishing.

McCartan, S. 2003. Mesolithic hunter-gatherers in the Isle of Man: adaptations to an island environment? In L. Larsson, H. Kindgren, K. Knutsson, D. Loeffler and A. Åkerlund (eds), *Mesolithic on the Move*, 331–339. Oxford: Oxbow Books.

McCartan, S. 2004. The Mesolithic in the Isle of Man: an Island Perspective. In A. Saville (ed.), *Mesolithic Scotland and its Neighbours: The Early Holocene Prehistory of Scotland, its British and Irish Context and some Northern European Perspectives*, 271–284. Edinburgh: Society of Antiquaries of Scotland.

Perrin, T., Marchand, G., Allard, P., Binder, D., Collina, C., Garcia-Puchol, O. and Valdeyron, N. 2009. Le second Mésolithique d'Europe occidentale: origine et gradient chronologique (the late Mesolithic of Western Europe: origins and chronological stages). *Annales de la Fondation Fyssen* 24, 160–177.

Pettitt, P. and White, M. 2012. *The British Palaeolithic: human societies at the edge of the Pleistocene world*. London: Routledge.

Pickard, C. and Bonsall, C. 2004. Deep-sea fishing in the European Mesolithic: fact or fantasy? *European Journal of Archaeology* 7, 273–290.

Sassaman, K. E. and Holly, D. H. (eds). 2011. *Hunter-Gatherer Archaeology as Historical Process*. Tucson: The University of Arizona Press.

Schulting, R. and Richards, M. 2001. Dating women and becoming farmers: new palaeodietary and AMS dating evidence from the Breton Mesolithic cemeteries of Téviec and Hoëdic. *Journal of Anthropological Archaeology* 20, 314–344.

Sheridan, A. 2007. From Picardie to Pickering and Pencraig Hill? New information on the 'Carinated Bowl Neolithic' in northern Britain. In A. Whittle and V. Cummings (eds), *Going Over: the Mesolithic-Neolithic Transition in North-West Europe*, 441–492. London, British Academy.

Sheridan, A. 2010. The Neolithization of Britain and Ireland: the 'Big Picture'. In B. Finlayson and G. Warren (eds), *Landscapes in Transition*, 89–105. Oxford: Oxbow Books/Council for British Research in the Levant.

Sørensen, M., Rankama, T., Kankaanpää, J., Knutsson, K., Knutsson, H., Melvold, S., Eriksen, B.V. and Glørstad, H. 2013. The first eastern migrations of people and knowledge into Scandinavia: evidence from studies of Mesolithic technology, 9th–8th millennium BC. *Norwegian Archaeological Review* 46, 1–38.

Thomas, J. 2004. Current debates on the Mesolithic-Neolithic transition in Britain and Ireland. *Documenta Praehistorica* 31, 113–130.

Thomas, J. 2008. The Mesolithic-Neolithic transition in Britain. In J. Pollard (ed.), *Prehistoric Britain*, 58–89. Oxford: Blackwell.

Tresset, A. 2003. French Connections II: of cows and men. In I. Armit, E. Murphy, E. Nelis, and D. Simpson (eds), *Neolithic Settlement in Ireland and Western Britain*, 18–30. Oxford: Oxbow.

Valdeyron, N. 2008. The Mesolithic in France. In G. Bailey & P. Spikins (eds.) *Mesolithic Europe*, 182–202. Cambridge: Cambridge University Press.

Verhart, L. and Groenendijk, H. 2005. Living in abundance: Middle and Late Mesolithic. In L. Louwe Kooijmans, P. van den Broeke, H. Fokkens and A. van Gijn (eds), *The Prehistory of the Netherlands*, vol 1, 161–178. Amsterdam: Amsterdam University Press.

Verhart, L. 2008. New developments in the study of the Mesolithic of the Low Countries. In G. Bailey and P. Spikins (eds), *Mesolithic Europe*, 158–181. Cambridge: Cambridge University Press.

Waddington, C., Bailey, G., Bayliss, A. and Milner, N. 2007. Howick in its North Sea context. In C. Waddington (ed.), *Mesolithic Settlement in the North Sea Basin: a case study from Howick, North-East England*, 203–224. Oxford: Oxbow Books.

Warren, G. 2013. Transformations? The Mesolithic of north-west Europe. In V. Cummings, P. Jordan and M. Zvelebil (eds), *The Oxford Handbook of the Archaeology and Anthropology of Hunter-gatherers*, 537–555. Oxford: Oxford University Press.

Warren, G., Davis, S., McClatchie, M. and Sands, R. 2014. The potential role of humans in structuring the wooded landscapes of Mesolithic Ireland: a review of data and discussion of approaches. *Journal of Vegetation History and Archaeobotany* 22(5), 629–646.

Weninger, B., Schulting, R., Bradtmöller, M., Clare, L., Collard, M., Edinborough, K., Hilpert, J., Jöris, O., Niekus, M., Rohling, E. and Wagner, B. 2008. The catastrophic final flooding of Doggerland by the Storegga Slide tsunami. *Documenta Praehistorica* 35, 1–24.

Wickham-Jones, C. and Woodman, P. 1998. Studies on the early settlement of Scotland and Ireland. *Quaternary International* 49/50, 13–20.

Woodman, P. 1978. *The Mesolithic in Ireland*. Oxford: British Archaeological Report British Series 58. Oxford; British Archaeological Reports.

Woodman, P. 1986. Problems in the colonisation of Ireland. *Ulster Journal of Archaeology* 49, 7–18.

Woodman, P. 1986. Why not an Irish Upper Palaeolithic? In D. A. Roe (ed.), *Studies in the Upper Palaeolithic of Britain and Northwest Europe*, 43–54. Oxford: British Archaeological Report S296.

Woodman, P. 2012. Making Yourself at Home on an Island: The First 1000 Years (+?) of the Irish Mesolithic. *Proceedings of the Prehistoric Society* 78, 1–34.

Woodman, P., Anderson, E. and Finlay, N. 1999. *Excavations at Ferriter's Cove, 1983–95: last foragers, first farmers in the Dingle Peninsula*. Bray: Wordwell.

Woodman, P., McCarthy, M. and Monaghan, N. 1997. The Irish quaternary fauna project. *Quaternary Science Reviews* 16, 129–159.

Seaways and shared ways: imagining and imaging the movement of people, objects and ideas over the course of the Mesolithic–Neolithic transition, *c.* 5,000–3,500 BC

Hugo Anderson-Whymark and Duncan Garrow

Introduction

'The Neolithic' still fits well into a culture historical framework, even half a century after that mode of understanding was broadly superseded. At a macro European scale, the practices of farming crops and animals, the new technology of pottery-making, and (in some cases) the act of settling more permanently, clearly did spread out geographically from the 'fertile crescent' over time (Scarre 2013, chapter 5); although inevitably, at the micro scale, the picture becomes somewhat more complicated. The processes by which the spread of 'the Neolithic' occurred have long been a key topic of discussion within later prehistoric archaeology. The central question has been whether those changes happened as a consequence of people, or just ideas, moving. Back in 1934, for example, Childe suggested that "the ideas embodied in the first [Neolithic] revolution must ... have been diffused, spread by colonising movements or by prolonged, enduring and repeated intercourse [interaction]" (Childe 1934, 297).

Intriguingly, and in some ways disappointingly, this same question is one which has dominated recent discussions of the Mesolithic–Neolithic transition specifically in Britain and Ireland as well. Especially since Thomas (1991) first constructed a substantial case that indigenous adoption may have been the primary causal factor in the uptake of Neolithic practices in Britain and Ireland, many pages have been given over to discussions as to how the British and Irish transition occurred (Sheridan 2003; 2010; Thomas 2008; 2013; etc.). This debate has often been very polarised, and sometimes the same evidence has been used to support diametrically opposed arguments. Over the past few years, however, there has been a clear move towards accounts which incorporate substantial elements of both indigenous adoption and colonisation (e.g. Whittle *et al.* 2011, 858; Cummings and Harris 2011), and it has been suggested that we should perhaps not try to understand the process in such binary terms (Garrow and Sturt 2011). However, even in these more mixed and/or conciliatory accounts of the process, the age-old indigenous adoption/colonisation opposition is still maintained to a substantial extent, even if both are allowed for.

In the first part of this paper, we look briefly back at some of the classic culture-historical discourse surrounding Neolithic 'culture change'. Our aims in doing so are to understand better the origins of this debate, and also to see whether theorisations of process which occurred then, during the heyday of culture-history, have the potential to inform current discussions of what are essentially the same issues. Ultimately, we argue that the tendency within this early work (a) to try to identify source areas of innovation or distinctive material culture, (b) to equate objects with people, and (c) to establish single directions of flow for cultural change, remain present in most recent discussions too. We suggest that these should no longer feature so prominently, and argue instead for a somewhat messier process of transformation without clear directionality, which must be understood as having been played out in the very long-term (over a millennium or more), not just the couple of centuries either side of 4,000 cal BC.

Another issue we will be considering within our paper is the way in which 'culture change' has been depicted graphically – imagined/imaged – in past discussions of the transition. Traditionally, within many early twentieth century culture historical accounts, the relationships between different culture groups were shown as tessellating blocks, depicting difference in two dimensions across space and through time (Figure 5.1). These images arguably led to a more static visual depiction of change than was actually present within the textual passages they accompanied (see below). There have, since then, broadly speaking been two other main methods of depicting change from Mesolithic to Neolithic. The second is the contour map – perhaps the most classic instance of its use being in Ammerman and Cavalli-Sforza's (1971) 'wave of advance' paper (Figure 5.2); in this case, the primary visualisation is of differential brackets of time. The third method is the use of arrows (a recent example being Whittle *et al.* 2011, Figure 15.8 – see Figure 5.3); in this case, the element being visualised is the movement of people and/or material culture and/or ideas across space. As will become clear below, our feeling is that all three of these visualisation techniques – and especially the latter two (which have most commonly been used in recent years) – represent the process(es) of transition in too straightforward a way. Of course, simplicity, and particularly visual simplicity, is absolutely necessary in certain contexts. However, in this case, it is possible to suggest that our imaging of the transition has served to mask the complex character of the process those images are trying to represent. We explore other possible ways of visualising the change towards the end of the paper.

Culture-historical debates

Given his prolific output, strong theoretical reputation and pioneering role in the establishment of culture-historical modes of thinking, it is hardly surprising that the work of Gordon Childe is in many ways the richest source of information about early culture-historical theorisations of culture change and diffusion. Two sections of his work stand out particularly as being explicit theorisations of the process – a chapter in *New Light on the Most Ancient East* entitled 'the mechanism of diffusion' (Childe 1934, chapter 10) and a short section of his book *Social Evolution* (Childe 1951, 170–177). In the former, Childe used the example of the seal to illustrate how diffusion, even of one thing, could happen in multiple ways (1934,

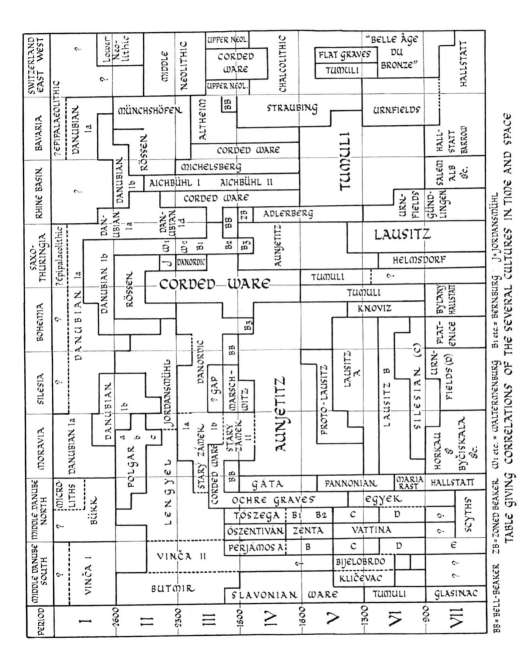

Figure 5.1. Blocks. Childe's depiction of the relationships between different culture groups (Childe 1929).

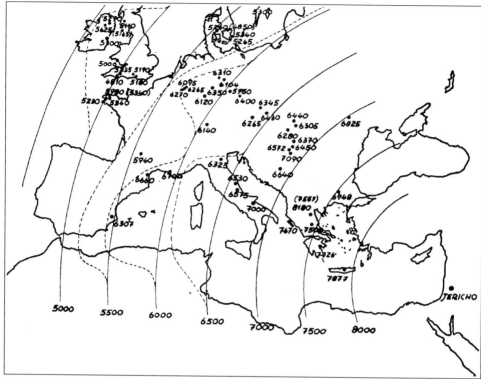

Figure 5.2. Contours. Ammerman & Cavalli-Sforza's depiction of the spread of the Neolithic across Europe (Ammerman & Cavalli-Sforza 1971, Figure 6).

294). Interestingly, he then immediately went on to discuss the spread of the Neolithic in particular, suggesting (as seen in the quote within our opening paragraph) that the movement of both people and ideas would have been key, and that is was actually difficult to define the role played by either (1934, 297). Some years later, Childe was to expand on this difficulty: "for as material objects can be transmitted from one community to another, so can ideas" (1951, 170). He then went on to make a complicating point, that "diffusion is not an automatic process ... One society can borrow an idea ... only when it fits into the general pattern of the society's culture" (*ibid.*, 172).

In relation to the arrival of the Neolithic in Britain and Ireland specifically, intriguingly, in his first book *The Dawn of European Civilisation*, Childe attributed a very significant role in the process to the indigenous population: "no actual colonization on any large scale is presupposed in the phenomena of our new stone age. The neolithic arts and the idea of megalithic architecture may simply have been taken over by the natives from traders touching on the shores" (1925, 291). However, fifteen years later (notably perhaps *after* the outbreak of the Second World War), his understanding of the process had changed considerably: "immigrants from across the Channel brought, fully formed, the oldest neolithic culture recognisable in the archaeological record" (Childe 1940, 34). Seventeen years after this statement, Childe's view of the process in Britain and Ireland outlined in the sixth edition of

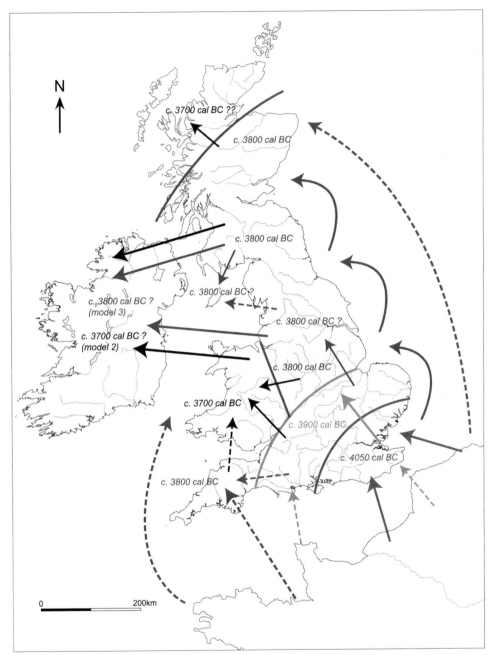

Figure 5.3. Arrows. Whittle et al.*'s schematic depiction of the spread of the Neolithic across Britain and Ireland (Whittle* et al. *2011, Figure 15.8).*

The Dawn was completely different to that described above in the first: "Great Britain and Ireland were relatively well populated with mesolithic hunters and fishers. But a neolithic culture of distinctive western type was first introduced by peasants who crossed over to southern England from northern France or Belgium and did not mingle with the pre-existing food-gatherers ... The neolithic farmers owed hardly an item in their equipment to their mesolithic forerunners and competitors" (1957, 322). Interestingly, with more material culture excavated and analysed than there had been three decades before, and a different interpretive scheme within which to explain those objects, Childe felt obliged to comment on the fact that there were nonetheless clear differences in Neolithic material culture either side of the Channel: "would-be colonists embarking in frail craft must discard unessential equipment and relax the rigid bonds of tribal custom. Any culture brought to Britain must be insularized by the very conditions of transportation" (*ibid.*).

Childe's argument in 1957 was presumably influenced to some extent by the publication of Piggott's *The Neolithic Cultures of the British Isles* three years earlier (1954). Piggott too had argued for very little interaction between the indigenous population and colonising farmers, at least at first: "it is difficult to detect signs of contact between the two groups – aboriginal hunter-fishers and immigrant agriculturalists – in the British Isles during what must have been the first phases of colonisation" (1954, 15). However, intriguingly, Piggott introduced the notion of a 'secondary neolithic' where "elements derived from Mesolithic sources can be detected, often contributing very strikingly to the make-up and producing distinctive insular variants of Neolithic culture unknown on the Continent" (*ibid.*). Later in the book, Piggott, like Childe, felt obliged to deal with the discrepancies observed between the colonisers' primary Neolithic (Windmill Hill) material culture group and the presumed source culture groups. He noted, for example, the absence of leaf-shaped arrowheads in assemblages from Brittany, as well as the absence of certain Michelsberg pottery forms from Britain (*ibid.*, 98–99). Clearly struggling to explain these discrepancies, he explicitly stated that "in short, we have certain similarities, but nothing to warrant derivation of one from the other" (*ibid.*, 99). Confusingly, in direct contradiction to the argument he had made at the beginning of the book, he then went on to discuss how "intrusive Neolithic and established Mesolithic ideas" about material culture had been "blended together" to make up the distinctively different Windmill Hill culture (*ibid.*, 100–101).

In summary then, this brief overview of debates occurring in the middle decades of the 20th century has demonstrated that people were certainly wrestling with many of the same issues that confront (and confuse) us now. The extent of migration was described variously as very minimal to large scale. Discussions about the directionality and origins of change also varied considerably, with the former sometimes being recognised as potentially bi-directional (involving British/Irish mariners as well as continental Europeans) and the latter as having been potentially multiple. The material culture of this period, then as now, also caused difficulties. Whilst there was a clear arrival of 'Neolithic' things, their transfer from mainland Europe was nonetheless difficult to understand fully – bits of the supposed source assemblages were missing, or had changed.

As a result of these difficulties, the overall culture-history story is in some ways confusing: Childe's account of the causes of change switched completely from 1925 to 1940, Piggott essentially contradicted his own argument within a hundred pages of one book. In recent years, contradictory perspectives about the transition have certainly prevailed as well.

Equally, the evidence remains often confusing and certainly open to different interpretations. However, it is not our intention just to look negatively upon these long term difficulties. Rather, as discussed above, we argue that it is perhaps possible to learn something from these original culture historical debates. In their openness to admitting that 'diffusion' was a highly complex process and a very difficult one to pin down, both Childe and Piggott both perhaps had a lesson for us today. Equally, in their (admittedly variable) willingness to view the process of transition as something best understood as a culmination of long-term processes, and their focus on the role of indigenous populations in transforming 'the Neolithic' into multiple Neolithics, again we would argue that we have something to learn. We explore these ideas further towards the end of this chapter.

Mesolithic connections

Although this paper is primarily concerned with contact between already 'Neolithic' communities on the continent and 'Mesolithic'/'Earliest Neolithic' communities in Britain and Ireland, it is pertinent to step back in time and consider earlier relationships between Mesolithic groups in what was a dynamic post-glacial landscape (see also Warren, this volume). Ireland became an island early in the post glacial period and as a result the range of fauna differs significantly from that in Britain, with large ungulates, such as red deer and aurochs, representing the most notable absence. In contrast, the landmass that was to become Britain was connected to mainland Europe (at low tide) until *c.* 6,500 BC, according to the most recent palaeogeographical modelling (Sturt *et al.* 2013; Sturt this volume), when the land-bridge between the Channel River and North Sea was fully inundated.

Prior to the formation of the Channel, the material culture of southern Britain shared many affinities with northern France and the Low Countries. Ghesquière (2012, 107) has demonstrated clear parallels between Middle Mesolithic 'Horsham-type' assemblages of south-east England and the Picardie region of France, and 'Honey Hill-type' assemblages that occur across southern England and the Nord-Cotentin region in France. In the Middle Mesolithic (*c.* 8,000–6,500 BC) these regions were, however, separated by the wide estuary of the Channel River, with the land bridge lying further east, indicating that contact between them was probably maintained by boat, with journeys across many kilometres of open water.

In the Late Mesolithic, following the formation of the Channel, distinctly different microlith industries developed on each side of the Channel (trapeze-dominated assemblages in France and micro-blade rod/scalene triangle assemblages in southern Britain). This potentially indicates that cross-Channel contact diminished or ended entirely. However, these differences between microlith assemblages should perhaps be viewed simply as evidence of cultural difference; any contact would not necessarily have resulted either in an exchange of material culture between these communities or in any material convergence (Hodder 1982, 21; McCartan 2004; Garrow and Sturt 2011, 66; Thomas 2013, 210). A strong tidal race in the newly formed Channel may, therefore, have presented navigational challenges, potentially hindering contact, but for seafaring communities these problems would not have been insurmountable.

Turning to Ireland, it has long been observed that later Mesolithic material culture, based on broad flakes, differs significantly from that of Britain (see also Warren, this volume). This has been used to suggest an insular Mesolithic; however, parallels between lithic assemblages on the Isle of Man and Ireland demonstrate potentially significant degrees of maritime contact in and across the Irish Sea. The maritime mobility of Mesolithic populations has therefore been underplayed in many accounts of contact (Garrow and Sturt 2011; Thomas 2013, 263).

Early interactions *c.* 5,300–4,050 BC

In eastern France, Neolithic communities first appear in the archaeological record *c.* 5,300 cal BC, while in the far west of France and the Channel Islands the earliest Neolithic dates perhaps to *c.* 5,000 cal BC (Marcigny *et al.* 2010; Garrow and Sturt forthcoming). Whittle *et al.*'s (2011, 839) recent programme of Bayesian modelling indicates that the earliest Neolithic sites in Britain occur in south-east England between *c.* 4,075–3,975 cal BC (95% probability). This suggests that it took more than a millennium for Neolithic practices and things to cross the Channel into Britain – a distance of only 33km – and considerably longer for the Neolithic to become established in the north and west. The question of contact in the intervening period (*c.* 5,000–4,000 BC) is a hotly debated subject as hard evidence is sparse and that which is available is open to interpretation. Moreover, the same evidence has been presented and reworked on so many occasions that there is a risk of 'transition fatigue'. It is not our desire to go over old ground in detail again, as more detailed arguments and counter-arguments can be found in the referenced texts. It is, however, necessary that we run briefly through some key lines of evidence.

Ferriter's Cove cattle bones
The earliest evidence during this period for contact between continental 'Neolithic' communities and 'Mesolithic' hunter gatherers in Britain and Ireland comprises six eroded mid-shaft fragments of a cattle radius and tibia and a charred fragment of cattle metatarsus that were recovered from a Mesolithic midden at Ferriter's Cove, Co. Kerry, Ireland (see Thomas 2013, 266–267 for a useful summary of other similar (if less convincing) sites in Ireland). A fragment of one of the long bones from Ferriter's Cove yielded an early date of 4,495–4,195 cal BC at 95% probability (Woodman and McCarthy 2003, 33); a second earlier date has been discounted as unreliable as the measurement was made on charred bone (see Sheridan 2010, 92). In the absence of large ungulates in Ireland and domesticates in Britain at this time, it has been argued that these remains belong to an animal originating from western France (Woodman and McCarthy 2003; Tresset 2003; Tresset and Vigne 2007; Sheridan 2010). The context of recovery offers no light on how these bones came to be in Ireland, but as they were fragmented and one was charred it is probable that the meat on the bones was consumed before deposition in the midden. Sheridan (2003; 2010) considers these bones to result from a failed attempt at colonisation, proposing a possible explanatory scenario featuring:

> "a very small scale immigration of pioneering farmers from France; the hunting of their stock by the indigenous inhabitants of Ferriter's Cove; and the consequent failure of a Neolithic way of life to take root at that point, owing to the absence of a critical mass of people and of domesticates" (Sheridan 2010, 92).

However, archaeological evidence for these Neolithic pioneers in Ireland, such as ceramics or settlement, remains elusive. The presence of these bones also fails to provide incontrovertible evidence for the presence of cows in Ireland: it is possible that the bones were transported as a joint of beef rather than a live cow or calf (Whittle 2003; Thomas 2013, 267). The direction of contact is also open to question and, as Thomas has stated (2008, 64), it is equally possible that contact with Neolithic farmers in France resulted from a journey initiated by a Mesolithic community in Ireland. In light of the plethora of alternative theories and absence of firm evidence, we consider these bones simply as enigmatic evidence of early contact between very distant communities. We will return to the issue of the direction of movement in the discussion below.

Jadeitite axe-heads
The recent research of Pétrequin and the *Projet JADE* team has revolutionised our understanding of the origins and movement of jadeitite axe-heads – originally quarried in the Alps – across Europe in the Neolithic (Pétrequin *et al.* 2008). Moreover, detailed biographies have been written for many of the axe-heads found in Britain revealing patterns of reworking that betray long and complex patterns of movement across Europe. It has been suggested that many of these axe-heads entered Britain around 4,000 BC through northern France, when Neolithic practices and things first arrived in the south-east. However, Sheridan (2011) has argued that a number of examples from south-west Britain that show evidence of re-shaping in the Morbihan area of southern Brittany may have reached Britain via a western route across the Channel (Sheridan's *Trans-Manche Ouest*).

The omphacitic jadeitite axe-head deposited in shallow water beside the Sweet Track, Somerset, shortly after the track was constructed in 3,807/6 BC represents a prime example (Coles and Orme 1984; Coles *et al.* 1974). This axe-head was already several centuries old when it was deposited: it originated in the north Italian Alps (probably the Mont Viso massif) and was probably re-shaped in the Morbihan area of southern Brittany at some point between 4,300 and 3,900 BC, before circulating around north-west/northern France and being brought to south-west England (Sheridan 2011, 31). Other examples include the Breamore axe-head from Hampshire that had also probably been re-shaped in the Morbihan, and a fragmentary Tumiac-type axe from High Peak, Sidmouth, Devon that exhibits an aborted attempt to perforate the butt (a Morbihan characteristic; see Sheridan 2011, 31 and Sheridan *et al.* 2010 for a complete list of jadeitite axe-heads from south-west and south-central England, respectively).

The date at which these axe-heads entered Britain is still very much open to debate (see Thomas 2013, 273–283 for a useful summary). Sheridan (2010, 99) speculates that the *Trans-Manche Ouest* route was most active *c.* 4,000–3,750 BC, but there is no reason that these axe-heads could not have entered Britain at an earlier date. As with the Ferriter's Cove bones, there is no definitive evidence as to the direction of movement or nature of contact that brought these axe-heads into Britain. Sheridan (2011, 31) argues that the Sweet Track axe-head may have been brought to Britain "as a treasured possession of a group of early immigrant farmers, complete with legends about its ancient distant origin and its history" and further suggests that its ritualised deposition in water is consistent with practices for Alpine axe-heads in north and north-western France, with no indigenous Mesolithic precedent for such depositions. It is, however, impossible to know for how long and between whom this axe circulated before deposition: it may have been in Britain for centuries. Moreover, contrary to Sheridan's assertion, there are indications that British Mesolithic populations deliberately deposited artefacts in watery contexts, such as rivers, establishing practices that became more prominent in the Neolithic (Bradley 1998, xvii–xviii; Chatterton 2006; Lamdin-Whymark 2008, 43).

It is an interesting possibility that these axes may have been exchanged between French 'Neolithic' and British 'Mesolithic' communities in the late 5th millennium BC (with no indication in which direction contact was initiated). Axes were objects that 'Mesolithic' and 'Neolithic' people were both familiar with, and there is little question regarding the intrinsic allure of jadeitite. It is also worth noting that other diagnostically 'Neolithic' stone objects (such as schist rings) were being exchanged between 'Neolithic' and 'Mesolithic' groups in Normandy, Brittany and the Channel Islands around this time as well (Garrow and Sturt forthcoming).

Achnacreebeag 'simple' passage grave and its pottery
Another line of evidence for early contact, presented by Sheridan (e.g. 2000; 2003; 2010) as part of her Atlantic 'Breton' strand of neolithisation, is the presence of one near-complete pot and fragments from two others (which are argued by some to be French late Castellic-style vessels) within a funerary monument at Achnacreebeag, Argyle and Bute. This monument has two phases of construction: the first being a closed chamber surrounded by a low stone cairn, and the second phase comprising the insertion of simple passage grave on the south-east side of the cairn. The pottery vessels at stake were recovered from deposits sealed in the passage of the second phase monument (Sheridan 2000; 2003). Sheridan has convincingly argued on stylistic grounds that the Achnacreebeag ceramics are paralleled in Armorican Middle Neolithic II assemblages and a near identical vessel recovered from a simple passage grave at Vierville, Normandy is particularly notable (Verron 1986; 2008; Sheridan 2003). Human bone from the Vierville tomb has recently been radiocarbon dated and results form a consistent series at 4,350–4,050 cal BC (Schulting *et al.* 2010, 164). If these vessels are accepted to be derived from France itself, then Sheridan's statement that "Occam's Razor decrees that some movement of people from Brittany is the least unlikely interpretation" (2000, 13) might be viewed as reasonable.

However, some caution must be expressed over accepting these vessels as evidence akin to a 'smoking gun' for evidence of colonisation. Fabric analysis has failed to reveal conclusively if these vessels were manufactured in France (Sheridan 2010a, 192) and despite an estimated date of *c.* 4,000 BC based on French monument and ceramic chronologies (Sheridan 2003), no radiocarbon dates are available for either phase of the Achnacreebeag monument. The latter is particularly concerning as the dating of monuments in Scotland on the basis of parallels and perceived developmental sequences is notoriously problematic; for example dating recently revealed the two small henge monuments thought to be Neolithic actually date from the middle and late Bronze Age (Bradley 2011). Moreover, Bayesian modelling of radiocarbon dates associated with Castellic pottery indicate that it did not go out of use until 4,120–3,610 cal BC at 95% probability (Whittle *et al.* 2011, 850). This potentially indicates that Sheridan's Breton strand of contact extends later than her proposed date range of 4,300/4,200–4,000 BC (2010) and may overlap with Whittle *et al.*'s (2011, 850) Bayesian modelled start date for the arrival of 'Neolithic things and practices' in southern Scotland of 3,875–3,760 cal BC at 95% probability. Therefore, whilst the simple passage grave and pottery at Achnacreebeag may provide further evidence of long distance contact, it is not at present possible to say when this happened, or indeed if that contact was particularly early.

The wider question of the date and distribution of simple passage graves, such as Broadsands, and other monument types, such as rotunda, that form part of Sheridan's (2010, 99) '*Trans-Manche Ouest*', indicated as dating from *c.* 4,000–3,750 BC, will be considered below.

Opposing views?
The limited and vague nature of evidence for contact prior to the establishment of the Neolithic in Kent at some point after 4,050 BC allows little to be stated confidently about the degree and nature of contact between Britain, Ireland and the continent in the 5th millennium BC. Potentially key monuments, such as Achnacreebeag, and plausibly early Neolithic monuments including simple passage graves, remain undated. The evidence provided from British and Irish Mesolithic sites is also infuriatingly limited, in part due to the fact that most Mesolithic deposition practices involve surface contexts that fail to preserve bone – flint scatters are often all that commonly survive. If cattle bone from cross-Channel contact was present on many of the late Mesolithic sites in southern Britain, quite simply we would never know.

The direction of movement is also ambiguous and while it has been tempting (for some people at least) to see Neolithic communities as the ones pushing the boundaries, Mesolithic populations were certainly highly mobile and competent seafarers.

4,050 cal BC or so... The arrival of the Neolithic in south-east Britain
Whittle *et al.*'s (2011) radiocarbon dating programme, which primarily sought to refine the date of causewayed enclosures using Bayesian modelling, has provided invaluable new evidence for the arrival and spread of Neolithic practices and things in Britain. In this model 'the Neolithic' appears in south-east England between 4,075–3,975 cal BC at 95% probability and gradually spreads across East Anglia and much of south-east England by *c.* 3,900 cal BC; a subsequent 'surge' beginning late in the 39th century cal BC spreads Neolithic practices to the rest of Britain and Ireland (Whittle *et al.* 2011, 839). The appearance and slow spread of 'the Neolithic' across south-east England over *c.* 100–150 years – perhaps 4–6 generations – has significant implications for both traditional models of colonisation and models of acculturation (e.g. Thomas 1999) in terms of the speed and scale of change.

Breaking with mid-20th century models of large-scale population movements, Whittle *et al.* propose a colonisation scenario for initial change involving "small scale, piecemeal and perhaps episodic fissioning from continental communities" (Whittle *et al.* 2011, 858). Central to the formulation of this hypothesis is the absence of a single clear source area for the Neolithic practices and things that appear in Britain in this early period. In essence, the Neolithic in Britain was not imported as a complete 'package'; selected elements of material culture and practices were adopted and others were not, a process of 'selection and recombination' previously described by Thomas as *bricolage* (2003; 2008, 77).

Early Neolithic lithic and ceramic assemblages demonstrate this point very effectively. Parallels for the British Early Neolithic Carinated Bowl ceramic assemblages have long been sought on the continent, and it has proved possible to identify close parallels within the Michelsberg complex (Piggott 1954; Whittle 1977; etc) and more recently with Chasséen vessels in the Nord-Pas de Calais and northern Picardie regions of France (Sheridan 2007). However, as Piggott and Childe both discussed, the very assemblages that yield convincing parallels also contain vessels forms unlike any found in Britain. For example, the Michelsberg enclosure at Spiere de Hel, Flanders, which is located only 100km from the Kent coast and dates from *c.* 4,000 cal BC, contains carinated bowls that are readily paralleled in British assemblages, along with closed jars ('bottle' and 'bottle-shaped' vessels) that are not (Vanmontfort 2001; 2002; Whittle *et al.* 2011, 859). Further west in France, the carinated bowls of the MN II are accompanied by 'vase supports', which likewise do not appear in British assemblages.

Lithic assemblages provide another case in point as the arrival of the Neolithic was accompanied by a variety of new tool types, including polished flint and stone axe-heads and leaf-shaped arrowheads. As we have already seen with the jadeite examples, polished axe-heads can readily be paralleled in continental Neolithic assemblages and it should be noted that geological differences across both Britain and France result in the predominance of stone axes in the west, and flint axes in the east, of each country. The production of polished flint axe-heads in Britain is also associated with the appearance of deep mining, for example on the South Downs, which is again paralleled on the continent. The British leaf arrowhead can be broadly paralleled with the leaf-shaped points found in Michelsberg assemblages. However, Michelsberg assemblages also contain triangular arrowheads and chisel arrowheads, the former being most characteristic of Chasséen assemblages, that do not appear in British early Neolithic assemblages. Moreover, leaf-shaped arrowheads in Michelsberg assemblages frequently only exhibit semi-invasive retouch, whereas in Britain it is usual for the retouch to be fully invasive (see for example Manolakakis and Garmond 2011).

3,800 onwards: adoption of the Neolithic across Britain and Ireland
In the late 39th century the pace at which the Neolithic was spreading across Britain significantly increased and by *c.* 3,700 BC Neolithic practices and things are present across Britain, except for the north of Scotland and its archipelagos, and Ireland (Whittle *et al.* 2011). Whittle *et al.* (2011) describe this episode as the 'surge', a term that initially conjures images of extensive and rapid population movement. The manner in which the Neolithic 'expanded' is, however, open to considerable debate, an issue explored in depth in Whittle *et al.*'s discussion (2011, 861–871). Did the expansion result from the movement of the established Neolithic populations in southern Britain? Does it reflect a new wave of immigration from the continent? Or, does it relate to adoption of Neolithic life-ways by Mesolithic communities?

In all probability we are dealing with complex processes involving elements of internal expansion, continued continental colonisation/immigration and acculturation. However, as this paper is primarily focussed on cross-Channel connections we wish to dwell on this issue in particular. In south-east Britain specific direct evidence for continued continental contact (whether immigration or two-way contact) is difficult to identify, not least as aspects of British Neolithic material culture have their origins in this region. The presence of several 'Scandinavian' style axe-heads in the River Thames and a fine example beneath the mound of Julliberrie's Grave earthen long barrow in Kent, provide some evidence of continued continental contact (if much further north than previously seen) although these implements are comparatively rare (Jessup 1939; Lamdin-Whymark 2008).

In western Britain and Ireland several lines of evidence attest to continental contact with regions of western France. It is however debatable if the beginning of the Neolithic in these regions is solely the product of contact with western France (leaving aside the question of colonisation or acculturation), or rather a fusion of contact between western France influences from Neolithic communities already well established in south-east Britain at this time. We will first consider evidence from south-west Britain, before expanding the discussion to encompass a wider region.

Bayesian modelling indicates that 'the Neolithic' in south-west Britain began between 3,940–3,735 cal BC at 95% probability (Whittle *et al.* 2011, 516). The simple passage grave at Broadsands, Devon, which was constructed 3,840–3,710 cal BC at 95% probability, is therefore early within the regional sequence (Whittle *et al.* 2011, 520; see also Sheridan *et al.* 2008 and Scarre, this volume). This monument type, although unique in Devon, can be paralleled with numerous simple passage graves widely distributed in western Britain and Ireland, but they are not a feature of the Neolithic in eastern Britain. Their 'origins' arguably lie in the Morbihan of south-west Brittany *c.* 4,300 and by 3,700 cal BC this monument type was widely spread along the Atlantic facade (Sheridan *et al.* 2008, 18). Close parallels can be found in Normandy (Vierville: Verron 1986; 2008), Brittany (Carn: Giot *et al.* 1996) and Jersey (La Sargenté: Patton 1993; see Sheridan *et al.* 2008 for further discussion).

The date and morphology of the Broadsands simple passage grave alone arguably provides sufficient evidence to assert that there was contact with western France at the very beginning of the Neolithic in this region (Sheridan *et al.* 2008; Sheridan 2010; 2011), although this is certainly open to question (Scarre, this volume). However, when considering aspects of material culture that belong to Sheridan's (2010) *Trans-Manche Ouest* strand of neolithisation, we are presented with many of the same issues of selectivity seen between the earliest Neolithic in south-east Britain and the Michelsburg culture. Sheridan *et al.* (2008) suggest that two sherds of bowl pottery from Broadsands, which were manufactured locally, may replicate French MNII vessels rather than the British Carinated Bowl tradition; however this assertion has been refuted by other authors who consider the vessels to sit well within British Carinated Bowl assemblages (Whittle *et al.* 2011, 516). The trumpet lugs on Hembury Ware/south-western-style pottery can, however, only be paralleled in contemporary ceramics from north-west France, although the form of the vessels can be traced to the earlier Carinated Bowl tradition (Sheridan 2011, 32). An assemblage from Bestwall Quarry, Poole, that includes deep baggy vessels with solid knob-lugs (one of which had a charred organic residue that has been dated to 3,900–3,650 cal BC at 95% probability) has no parallels with contemporary Carinated Bowl assemblages (*ibid.*, 25; Woodward 2009). However, arguably the most distinctive elements of contemporary French MNII ceramic assemblages, such as 'Vase Supports' and decorated forms, are particularly notable by their absence.

Lithic assemblages present a similar picture. The manufacture of axes of igneous rock in south-west Britain is readily paralleled in Brittany and Jersey, although one may view this as a reflection of the local geology as much as a specific practice. The struck flint assemblages are, however, quite different. The specialised blades, tranchet tools and tranchet arrowheads of the French MNII are not paralleled in south-west Britain. Indeed it is notable that leaf-shaped arrowheads are associated with Hembury Ware, not the chisel forms of the MNII. The Neolithic in western Britain and Ireland is therefore perhaps best viewed as a fusion of Neolithic practices arriving from western France and the spread of the British Carinated Bowl Neolithic from south-east Britain. Moreover the degree to which we can seen the French influence as straightforward colonisation is questionable as influences persist over much of the early Neolithic as is demonstrated by parallels with Cotswold rotunda (which are poorly dated but pre-date long barrows) and portal dolmens (see Whittle *et al.* 2011, 520 for dates from Zennor and Sperris Quoits).

At a somewhat less specific level, the arrival of causewayed enclosures in Britain and Ireland represents further evidence for ongoing contact with the European mainland. As Whittle *et al.* (2011) have discussed in detail, the phenomenon of Neolithic enclosures is one which extends back as far as the 6th millennium BC. The broad 'theme' of enclosure is taken up in different ways by various Neolithic communities from that point onwards. In several parts of continental Europe close to Britain and Ireland, there appears to have been a significant increase in the numbers of enclosures constructed during the early centuries of the fourth millennium (Whittle *et al.* 2011, 881). This pattern fits extremely well with the developments seen in southern England especially, where the heyday of causewayed enclosure construction was *c.* 3,650–3,450 cal BC (Whittle *et al.* 2011, Ch. 14). Thus while, in certain places, direct material culture connections are perhaps harder to identify, it is clear that Britain and Ireland witnessed very similar trajectories of change to parts of continental Europe at a broader level.

Discussion

In order to assess the nature of cross-Channel connections over the period in which we are interested within this paper, we broke down the evidence into three main periods. The Neolithic arrives in western France probably around 5,000 BC. From that point onwards, occasional 'Neolithic' items – including the Ferriter's Cove cow (possibly in beef joint form) and perhaps also some jadeitite axes – do seem to have made it across the Channel into 'Mesolithic' Britain and Ireland. Exactly where these items came *from* and *who* was responsible for their movement is difficult to establish. As we move into and through the first two centuries of the 4th millennium BC, Neolithic practices appear to take hold fully enough for us to begin to feel comfortable describing much of Britain as 'being' Neolithic. Whittle *et al.*'s recent modelling of the available radiocarbon dates suggests an earliest take-up of 'the Neolithic' in south-east England, with an at first gradual and then subsequently 'surging' movement north and west. Intriguingly, while the first Neolithic assemblages in southern England share *elements* of their material culture repertoires with north-western and northern France and Belgium, they remain just elements. A full artefactual repertoire from any one of these regions is not discernible in the British Early Neolithic record. In the century or so following 3,800 BC, indicators of the Neolithic are observed spreading right across Britain and Ireland. The processes by which this spread occurred are, however, not easy to pin down. Arguments can be made in favour of indigenous adoption (by the existing population) of Neolithic practices, of continued (small scale?) migration into Britain by people travelling from the European mainland, and of migration by 'Neolithic' people previously living in Britain to the south and east. As in the previous phase, certain characteristic elements of Neolithic material culture elsewhere do seem to be taken on in Britain, but in complex ways, often being incorporated and merged into pre-existing and already-changed (from the 'original' source continental styles) Neolithic repertoires.

The picture of transition therefore appears to be a highly complex one. As discussed at the beginning of the chapter, the ways in which we depict any culture change graphically are revealing about the ways in which we theorise that process intellectually as well. Given the complex picture just outlined, traditional graphic representations relating to the Mesolithic–Neolithic transition in Britain and Ireland appear overly simple. Our understanding of the process has perhaps been too readily influenced by the macro European-scale picture, which is one of relatively straightforward south-east to north-west movement (although in many areas this simple story would also become more complex and multi-directional once investigated at a larger scale). In contrast to the block, contour and arrow images of transition described at the beginning of the chapter, the process of transition in Britain and Ireland was a 'messy' one, with material culture and ideas being taken up at different points from different locations, and with people (and things?) moving in different directions. Even where clear links between places can be established materially (e.g. an Alpine jadeitite axe found in southern England), the paths of those objects to those places may well still have been complex (e.g. several of those axes appear to have been re-shaped in Brittany) and it is also difficult to know who was doing the moving and why. The age old diffusionist problem of interpreting the process(es) behind the appearance of 'different' objects in any given place remains.

We have seen that the archaeology of the earliest Neolithic in Britain and Ireland has long been resisting simple interpretation, causing Childe, Piggott and the rest to be confused, and to change their minds between, and even within, books. It has continued to confuse and confound in recent years as well. As Garrow and Sturt (2011) and others have argued, it is important not to see the transition in black and white terms – as colonisation or indigenous adoption, as a switch from clearly 'Mesolithic' to clearly 'Neolithic'. Equally, at the end of this chapter, we can perhaps conclude that it is also important to embrace the messiness and complexity of the process(es), at least to some degree.

To return to one of this chapter's main themes, how then can and should we image that messy process, without dissolving entirely the simplified story that a diagram should represent? The problem here is that a diagram necessarily represents a simplified, mostly synchronic 'snapshot' of what is actually a complicated set of diachronic processes. It would be possible to construct a diagram with arrows going all over the place, perhaps also changing direction and strength over time in a series of 'time slice' images. Yet it seems doubtful whether such a series of diagrams would actually clarify much at all, even if it did represent a more 'accurate' picture of process in some ways. Another possibility would be a representation along the lines of Needham's visualisation of the 'maritory' concept, in which he shows *spheres* of interaction across and around the Channel region during the Bronze Age (Figure 5.4). There, the different interaction zones are depicted by circles, with no directionality implied.

In Figure 5.5, we have depicted some of the connections described in the main section of the paper, drawing on Needham's 'maritory' conceptualisation for inspiration. Certain elements of this visualisation of the transition are appealing: the lack of clear directionality, the overlap (in space and by implication also time) between the different sized circles and other shapes, the relatively complex nature of the image. However, the image nonetheless still simplifies the process, artificially imposing boundaries where there probably were none. Nor does it adequately capture any of the diachronic changes seen between 5,000 and 3,500 BC. The movement of people, objects and ideas over the course of the Mesolithic–Neolithic transition is, as we have seen, a complex affair. At the end of this consideration of the process, are we to conclude that it is perhaps simply too complicated to depict in diagrammatic form?

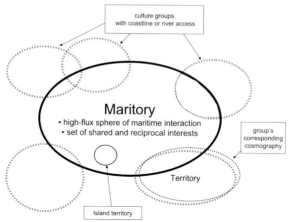

Figure 5.4. Needham's schematic representation of a 'maritory' (Needham 2009, Figure 2.3).

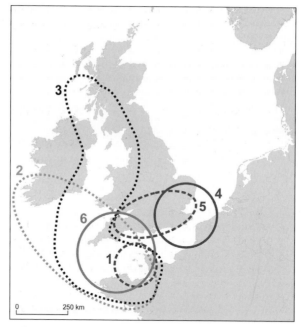

Figure 5.5. Continental connections c. 5,000–3,500 BC, re-imaged. Key to numbered shapes: (1) Interactions between mainland France and the Channel Islands, leading to the arrival of the Neolithic in the latter c. 5,200–4,800 BC; (2) Interaction(s) across the Channel leading to the presence of the Ferriter's Cove cow bones in south-west Ireland c. 4,500–4,200 BC; (3) Interactions around the western seaways possibly leading to similar pottery forms or actually exchanged pots between north-west France and Scotland, c. 4,300–3,600 BC; (4) Interaction around the Straits of Dover Channel region, leading to the very earliest Neolithic dates in England being seen in the south-east; (5) Interaction between people in south-east England and those in south/south-west England, leading to the spread of Neolithic practices westwards c. 3,900 BC; (6) Interaction overland and across the sea leading to the spread of Neolithic practices further westwards, and some similarities in tomb forms on both sides of the Channel c. 3,800 BC.

Otherwise, perhaps, are we simply asking the wrong questions? Trying to trace a process which did not exist? In defining 'a Mesolithic' and 'a Neolithic' in the first place, we are of course simplifying a complex multiplicity of states, identities and processes. In trying to capture the change from one of those 'states' to another, it is therefore unsurprising that we struggle. The complexity, which we have already simplified with our labels 'Mesolithic' and 'Neolithic', simply re-emerges. As we have discussed throughout the chapter, the complexity of the archaeological record has been challenging simple explanations for decades. Perhaps, if we are able to embrace that complexity, at least to a reasonable extent, we might be able to *imagine* the changes that occurred between 5,000 and 3,500 BC in a less confusing way, even if it still proves difficult to *image* the complexity of the long-term process in a satisfactory way.

Acknowledgements

We are very grateful to the Journal of the Royal Anthropological Institute/John Wiley & Sons, Stuart Needham, Alasdair Whittle and Oxbow Books for granting us permission to reproduce Figures 5.2, 5.3 and 5.4. We would also like to thank Anwen Cooper and Fraser Sturt for their helpful comments on an earlier draft of this paper.

References

Ammerman, A. J. and Cavalli-Sforza, L. L. 1971. Measuring the rate of spread of early farming in Europe. *Man* (n.s.) 6, 674–688.

Bradley, R. 1998. *The Passage of Arms: an archaeological analysis of prehistoric hoards and votive deposits*. 2nd Edition. Oxford: Oxbow Books.

Bradley, R. 2011. *Stages and Screens: an investigation of four henge monuments in northern and north-eastern Scotland*. Edinburgh: Society of Antiquaries of Scotland.

Chatterton, R. 2006. Ritual. In C. Conneller and G. Warren (eds), *Mesolithic Britain and Ireland: new approaches*, 101–120. Stroud: Tempus.

Childe, V. G. 1925. *The Dawn of European Civilisation*. London: Keegan Paul.

Childe, V. G. 1929. *The Danube in Prehistory*. Oxford: Oxford University Press.

Childe, V. G. 1934. *New Light on the Most Ancient East*. London: Keegan Paul.

Childe, V. G. 1940. *Prehistoric Communities of the British Isles*. London: W. R. Chambers.

Childe, V. G. 1951. *Social Evolution*. London: Watts and Co.

Childe, V. G. 1957. *The Dawn of European Civilisation* (6th edn). London: Routledge and Keegan Paul.

Coles, J. M., Orme, B., Bishop, A. C. and Woolley, A. R. 1974. A jade axe from the Somerset Levels, *Antiquity* 48, 216–220.

Coles J. M. and Orme, B. J. 1984. *Ten Excavations along the Sweet Track (3200 bc)*. *Somerset Levels Papers* 10. Cambridge: Somerset Levels Project.

Cummings, V. and Harris, O. 2011. Animals, people and places: the continuity of hunting and gathering practices across the Mesolithic-Neolithic transition in Britain. *European Journal of Archaeology* 14(3), 361–82.

Garrow, D. and Sturt, F. 2011. Grey waters bright with Neolithic argonauts? Maritime connections and the Mesolithic–Neolithic transition within the 'western seaways' of Britain, *c.* 5000–3500 BC. *Antiquity* 85, 59–72.

Garrow, D. and Sturt, F. forthcoming. The Mesolithic-Neolithic transition in the Channel Islands: maritime and terrrestrial perspectives. In T. Darvill and A. Sheridan (eds,) *Hands Across the Water: the archaeology of the cross-channel Neolithic*. London: British Academy.

Ghesquière, E. 2012. *Le Mésolithique de Basse-Normandie*. Toulouse: Université de Toulouse. Ph.D.

Giot, P.-R., L'Helgouach, J. and Monnier, J. 1996. *Prehistoire de la Bretagne* (3rd ed.). Rennes: Ouest-France Universite.

Hodder, I. 1982. *Symbols in Action: Ethnoarchaeological studies of material culture*. Cambridge: Cambridge University Press.

Jessup, R. F. 1939. Further excavation at Julliberrie's Grave, Chilham. *Antiquaries Journal* 19, 260–281.

Lamdin-Whymark, H. 2008. *The residue of ritualised action: Neolithic deposition practices in the Middle Thames Valley*. British Archaeological Report 466. Oxford: Archaeopress.

Manolakakis, L. and Garmond, S. 2011. Différencier les armatures de flèches du Chasséen et du Michelsberg en Bassin parisien. *Revue archéologique de Picardie* Numéro spécial 28, 349–363.

Marcigny C., Ghesquière, E., Juel, L. and Charraud, F. 2010. Entre Néolithique ancien et Néolithique moyen en Normandie et dans les Iles anglo-normandes: parcours chronologique. In C. Billard and M. Legris (eds), *Premiers néolithiques de l'Ouest, 28e Colloque interrégional sur le Néolithique, Archéologie et culture*, 117–162. Rennes: Presses Universitaires de Rennes.

McCartan, S. 2004. The Mesolithic of the Isle of Man: an island perspective. In A. Saville (ed.), *Mesolithic Scotland and its neighbours, the Early Holocene prehistory of Scotland, its British and Irish context, and some Northern European perspectives*. Society of Antiquaries of Scotland Monograph Series 28, 271–83. Edinburgh: Society of Antiquaries of Scotland.

Needham, S. 2009. Encompassing the sea: 'maritories' and Bronze Age maritime interactions. In P. Clarke (ed.), *Bronze Age Connections: cultural contact in prehistoric Europe*, 12–37. Oxford: Oxbow Books.

Patton, M. 1993. *Statements in Stone: monuments and society in Neolithic Britta*ny. London: Routledge.

Pétrequin P., Sheridan, A., Cassen, S., Errera, M., Gauthier, E., Klassen, L., Le Maux, N. and Pailler Y. 2008. Neolithic Alpine axe-heads from the continent to Great Britain, the Isle of Man and Ireland. In H. Fokkens, B. J. Coles, A. L. Van Gijn, J. P. Keleijne, H. H. Ponjee and C. G. Slapp Endel (eds), *Between Foraging and Farming: An extended broad spectrum of papers presented to Leendert Lowe Kooijmans. Analecta Praehistorica Leidensia* 40, 261–279. Leiden: Leiden University.

Piggott, S. 1954. *The Neolithic Cultures of the British Isles*. Cambridge: Cambridge University Press.

Scarre, C. 2013. *The Human Past*. London: Thames and Hudson.

Schulting, R., Sebire, H. and Robb, J. E. 2010. On the road to Paradis: new insights from AMS dates and stable isotopes at Le Déhus, Guernsey, and the Channel Island Neolithic. *Oxford Journal of Archaeology* 29(2), 149–173.

Sheridan, A. 2000. Achnacreebeag and its French connections: vive the 'auld' alliance. In J. Henderson (ed.), *The Prehistory and Early History of Atlantic Europe*. British Archaeological Report S861, 1–16. Oxford: Archaeopress.

Sheridan, A. 2003. French connections I: spreading the marmites thinly. In I. Armit, E. Murphy, E. Nelis and D. Simpson (eds), *Neolithic Settlement in Ireland and Western Britain*, 3–17. Oxford: Oxbow Books.

Sheridan, A. 2004. Neolithic connections along and across the Irish Sea. In V. Cummings and C. Fowler (eds), *The Neolithic of the Irish Sea*, 9–21. Oxford: Oxbow Books.

Sheridan, A. 2007. From Picardie to Pickering and Pencraig Hill? New information on the 'Carinated Bowl Neolithic'. In A. Whittle and V. Cummings (eds), *Going over: the Mesolithic–Neolithic Transition in north-west Europe*. Proceedings of the British Academy 144, 441–92. Oxford: Oxford University Press.

Sheridan, A. 2010. The Neolithization of Britain and Ireland: The 'Big Picture'. In B. Finlayson and G. Warren (eds), *Landscapes in Transition*, 89–105. Oxford: Oxbow Books.

Sheridan, A. 2010. The earliest pottery in Britain and Ireland and its continental background. In B. Vanmontfort (ed.), *Pots, Farmers and Foragers: Pottery traditions and social interaction in the earliest Neolithic of the Lower Rhine area*, 189–207. Amsterdam: Amsterdam University Press.

Sheridan, A. 2011. The earlier Neolithic of south west England: New insights and new questions. In S. Pearce (ed.) *Recent archaeological work in south-western Britain: Papers in honour of Henrietta Quinnell*. British Archaeological Reports British Series 548, 21–39. Oxford: Archaeopress.

Sheridan, A., Schulting, R., Quinnell, H. and Taylor, R. 2008. Revisiting a small passage tomb at Broadsands, Devon. *Proceedings of the Devon Archaeological Society* 66, 1–26.

Sheridan, A., Field, D., Pailler, Y., Petrequin, P., Errera, M. and Cassen, S. 2010. The Breamore jadeitite axehead and other Neolithic axeheads of Alpine rock from central southern England. *Wiltshire Archaeological and Natural History Magazine* 103, 16–34.

Sturt, F., Garrow, D. and Bradley, S. 2013. New models of North West European Holocene palaeogeography and inundation. *Journal of Archaeological Science* 40, 3963–3976.

Thomas, J. 1991. *Rethinking the Neolithic*. Cambridge: Cambridge University Press.

Thomas, J. 2003. Thoughts on the 'repacked' Neolithic revolution. *Antiquity* 77, 67–74.

Thomas, J. 2008. The Mesolithic-Neolithic transition in Britain. In J. Pollard (ed.), *Prehistoric Britain*: 58–89. Oxford: Blackwell.

Thomas, J. 2013. *The Birth of Neolithic Britain*. Oxford: Oxford University Press.

Tresset, A. 2003. French connections II: Of cows and men. In I. Armit, E. Murphy, E. Nelis and D. Simpson (eds), *Neolithic Settlement in Ireland and Western Britain*, 18–30. Oxford: Oxbow Books.

Tresset, A. and Vigne, J. D. 2007. Substitution of species, techniques and symbols at the Mesolithic-Neolithic transition in Western Europe. In A. Whittle and V. Cummings (eds), *Going over: the Mesolithic–Neolithic transition in north-west Europe*. Proceedings of the British Academy 144, 189–210. Oxford: Oxford University Press.

Vanmontfort, B. 2007. Bridging the gap. The Mesolithic-Neolithic transition in a frontier zone. *Documenta Praehistorica* 34, 105–118.

Vanmontfort, B., Geerts, A.-I., Casseyas, C., Bakels, C., Buydens, C., Damblon, F. Langohr, R., Van Neer, W., Vermeersch, P. M. 2001/2002. Del Hel in de tweede helft van het 5de millenium v.Chr. Een midden-Neolithische enclosure te Spiere (prov. West-Vlaanderen). *Archaeologie in Vlaanderen* VII (2004), 9–77.

Verron, G. 1986. Les civilisations Néolithiques de la Normandie, développements récents. In J. P. Demoule, and J. Guilaine, (eds), *Le Néolithique de la France*, 193–206. Paris: Picard.

Verron, G. 2008. Un monument funéraire complexe du Néolithique moyen à Vierville. In C. Marcigny, E. Ghesquière, and J. Desloges (eds), *La Hache et la Meule. Les Premiers Paysans du Néolithique en Normandie*, 139–42. Le Havre: Muséum d'Histoire Naturelle du Havre.

Whittle, A. W. R. 1977. *The Earlier Neolithic of Southern England and its Continental background*. British Archaeological Report S35. Oxford: British Archaeological Reports.

Whittle, A. 2003. *The Archaeology of People*. London: Routledge.

Whittle, A., Bayliss, A. and Healy, F. 2011. *Gathering Time: Dating the early Neolithic enclosures of southern Britain and Ireland*. Oxford: Oxbow Books.

Woodman, P. C. and McCarthy, M. 2003. Contemplating some awful(ly interesting) vistas: Importing cattle and red deer into prehistoric Ireland. In I. Armit, E. Murphy, E. Nelis, and D. Simpson (eds), *Neolithic Settlement in Ireland and Western Britain*, 31–39. Oxford: Oxbow Books.

Woodward, A. 2009. The pottery. In L. Ladle and A. Woodward, *Excavations at Bestwall Quarry, Wareham 1992–2005. Volume* 1: *the Prehistoric Landscape,* 200–271. Dorchester: Dorset County Museum.

Parallel lives? Neolithic funerary monuments and the Channel divide

Chris Scarre

Introduction

Funerary monuments of timber, earth and stone are one of those classic features of the west European Neolithic that were somehow carried from the Continent, where they had been present for several centuries, to Britain. The multiplication of radiocarbon dates seen in recent years has demonstrated that monuments of significant scale (such as the classic long barrows) did not, on the whole, characterise the very earliest Neolithic of Britain and Ireland, but in most regions followed after a gap of several generations (Whittle 2007; Whittle *et al.* 2011, 750, 871). If we envisage the Neolithic as having been brought to Britain by voyagers from northern France, as several recent models propose (e.g. Sheridan 2003; Sheridan *et al.* 2008; Pailler and Sheridan 2009; Collard *et al.* 2010; Whittle *et al.* 2011, 853), we must accept either that these first British Neolithic communities carried the germ of the monumental tradition in their memories, seeking to revive and realise it as soon as suitable circumstances arrived; or that cross-Channel contacts persisted for a period of centuries and brought a stream of Continental ideas to these shores including, in due course, the practice of monument construction (see also Anderson-Whymark and Garrow, this volume).

At the broader scale, of course, this particular story is part of a much wider narrative of the monument traditions that became current throughout western and northern Europe during the 5th and 4th millennia BC. Earlier generations interpreted this pattern in terms of a travelling 'megalithic people', a construct that goes back at least to the 18th century (Caylus 1766, 386–387), and was widely accepted during the 19th century (e.g. Westendorp 1822; Bertrand 1864; Bonstetten 1865; Fergusson 1872). Diffusionist notions of megalithic origins persisted well into the 20th century, crystallised for example in Childe's vision of "missionaries or prospectors" whose arrival, from southern France to northern Scotland, was marked by the construction of megalithic collective tombs that "can only have been built or inspired by voyagers arriving by sea" (Childe 1950, 88–89). It is interesting and perhaps instructive to note how human mobility patterns have in recent years returned to take centre stage in many narratives of regional Neolithic origins.

Were specific monument forms of recognisably Continental origin introduced directly to southern Britain? Monuments do not equate with peoples, of course, nor are they to be considered in isolation from other aspects of material culture, subsistence or ritual. Yet they are part of the transformation of social practice that was associated with the earlier Neolithic, and it is pertinent, therefore, to scrutinise the evidence they provide, alongside the ceramic forms or the newly introduced domestic fauna (Sheridan 2007; Tresset 2003; Thomas 2013). At the same time, however, it is important to look beyond the issue of origins, fascinating as they are, and to review the broader pattern of monument sequences on the two sides of the Channel during the 4th and 3rd millennia BC. Such a review highlights a crucial contrast between the initial period of relative convergence in the early 4th millennium BC, and the following thousand years during which the British and French monument sequences parted to go their different ways. Thus an early period of contact was followed by a much longer phase, spanning much the greater part of the British Neolithic, when contact appears to have been either much reduced, or to have had much less impact on the currency of monument forms. In this context, concepts of 'transmission' and 'translation' may provide a useful way of thinking about the changing relationships (Figure 6.1).

Northern France in the 5th and 4th millennium BC: standing stones, long mounds and passage tombs

The starting point is the sequence of monuments types current in northern France during the later 5th and 4th millennium, the period relevant to the earliest monuments of southern Britain. This sequence has been the subject of some controversy, partly owing to problems in establishing an absolute chronology, and partly through the variety of assumptions that have guided the modelling of monument sequences. Chronology has been rendered particularly difficult in the key areas of north-western France by the geology of the Armorican massif with its acid soils. Human skeletal remains do sometimes survive, but many of the available radiocarbon dates are based on charcoal, and in a number of cases it is unclear how the death of the sample relates to the structure or event one is seeking to date.

Across northern France an early series of monuments appear in the middle centuries of the 5th millennium BC. These include long linear funerary mounds or enclosures, and early (and often decorated) standing stones. The latter are best represented in southern Brittany but are inherently difficult to date. The six radiocarbon dates from the sockets of the Grand Menhir alignment at Locmariaquer, for example, range from 5,300–5,002 (Ly-2508) to 4,344–4,053 cal BC (Ly-2509), but half are on charcoal, two on carbonised hazelnut, and one on wheat grain (Cassen *et al.* 2009, 753, table 2). A *terminus ante quem* is provided by the reuse of several of these early decorated stelae in passage tombs, the first of which, as we shall see, may have been built in the period 4,300–4,200 cal BC. The decorated stelae must hence pre-date the passage tombs in which they were re-incorporated, but by how many centuries it is very difficult to determine. Bayesian modelling of the Grand Menhir sequence indicated only that those standing stones can be placed within the bracket 5,315–4,050 cal BC at 95% confidence (Cassen *et al.* 2009, 759). There are hints from two other locations in southern Brittany that stone rows may have been standing by 4,700 BC (Hoedic: Large and Mens 2009; Belz: Hinguant and Boujot 2009), but that requires confirmation from further field investigations and secure chronological indicators.

Available AMS dates on human bone from four Brittany passage tombs give poor resolution for Bayesian modelling. They are consistent with previous suggestions of an origin around 4,300–4,200 cal BC (Boujot and Cassen 1992 1993) although an earlier

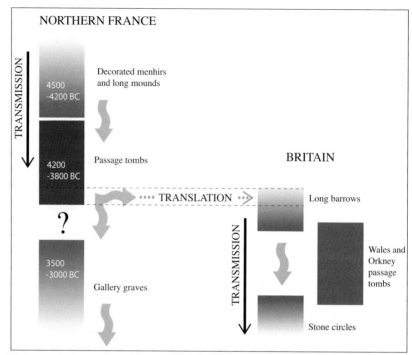

Figure 6.1. Transmission and translation of megalithic architectures in Britain and France, 4,500–2,500 BC.

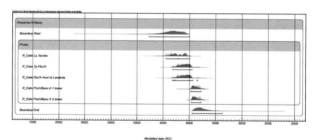

Figure 6.2. Bayesian analysis of radiocarbon dates from four passage tombs in Brittany. Data from Giot et al. 1994 and Schulting 2005. All dates on human skeletal material deposited within the passages or chambers. The two dates from Port-Blanc are for the lower layer of inhumations; the single date from the later upper layer has been excluded from this analysis. Results indicate a boundary start at 4,780–4,000 cal BC and a boundary end at 3,950–3,370 cal BC (95% probability). The poor level of precision reflects the small numbers of dates and the large standard errors associated with them. At this coarse level of analysis they are consistent with the evidence from Normandy (see Figure 6.3). Calibration and Bayesian analysis using OxCal 4.2 and IntCal09: Bronk Ramsey 2009 and Reimer et al. 2009.

date cannot be excluded (Figure 6.2). The passage tombs of Brittany can be related to the broader family of passage tombs in north-west France, and more specifically to those of immediately adjacent regions of limestone geology to the east and the south. A more secure chronological model is provided by the accumulating corpus of radiocarbon dates on human skeletal material from passage tombs in western Normandy, and from analogies with similar structures in limestone territory south of the Loire. The latter region has controversial early dates from Bougon in Poitou (Mohen and Scarre 2002), but reliable AMS results from Prissé-la-Charrière indicate the construction of passage tombs from *c*. 4,300–4,200 cal BC (Scarre *et al*. 2003).

More directly relevant in the present context are the passage tombs of western Normandy, which geography suggests might have provided the closest inspiration for the southern British series. No passage tombs are known to the east of the Caen plain. AMS dates on human remains from passage tombs of western Normandy indicate an origin between 4,410–4,180 cal BC (at 95% probability) (Figure 6.3). These passage tombs form a distinctive group, characterised by a preference for circular chambers and circular cairns (Figure 6.4). They were predominantly of dry-stone construction, with corbelled vaults covering the chambers (Ghesquière and Marcigny 2011, 173–175). Occasionally, circular chambers are grouped together in pairs or in larger numbers within a single cairn, notably at La Hogue and La Hoguette where as many as twelve circular chambers are found arranged in a radial manner within a sub-rectangular cairn (Coutil 1918; Caillaud and Lagnel 1972).

New passage tombs may have continued to be built in Normandy during the second quarter of the 4th millennium BC, although the latest dates might represent a tail or correspond to the later reuse of earlier chambers. It is most likely that new construction ceased by around 3,900 BC or possibly 3,800 BC. Bayesian analysis of AMS dates on human remains indicates a boundary end between 3,920 and 3,710 cal BC (at 95% probability) (Figure 6.3). This is an important point for the key theme of this paper, the parallel or divergent trajectories either side of the Channel, since it would suggest that the chronological overlap between the passage tombs of northern France and those of southern Britain was relatively short, indeed perhaps less than a century.

The British sequence: monument traditions of the earlier 4th millennium BC

The chronology of the earliest Neolithic monuments in southern Britain has been considerably clarified by the work of Alex Bayliss and Alasdair Whittle and their team in two successive projects. The first focussed on a group of southern English long mounds (Bayliss and Whittle 2007), the second on causewayed enclosures, but extending to include other categories of evidence (Whittle *et al*. 2011). Broadly speaking the funerary monuments of southern Britain fall into three geographical groups. The largest category are the long mounds of the central sector, some preceded by timber mortuary houses, others containing megalithic chambers (i.e. the Cotswold-Severn group) (Darvill 2004). They bear a superficial resemblance in their form and linearity to some of the 5th millennium long mounds and Passy type structures of northern France, but in construction they are quite distinct, and the chronologies do not support a direct connection. The first long mounds of central southern England were built probably in the 39th century cal BC, with new examples continuing to be added until at least the 35th century cal BC (Whittle *et al*. 2011, 723–724).[1]

Notably early dates have been suggested for two specific sites to the east and west of this distribution: Coldrum in Kent and Broadsands in Devon (Figure 6.5). The Coldrum site, one of the Medway tombs, consists of a small box-like chamber surrounded by a rectangular cairn

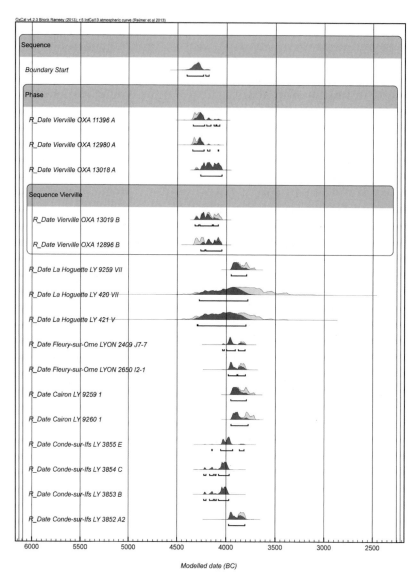

Figure 6.3. Bayesian analysis of radiocarbon dates from passage tombs in Lower Normandy and the Channel Islands. Data from Verron 2000; Schulting et al. *2010; Marcigny* et al. *2007; Ghesquière & Marcigny 2011; and Cyril Marcigny pers. comm. All dates on human skeletal material deposited within the passages or chambers. An earlier date of OxA 11395 5690±45 BP is considered unreliable and has been excluded from the analysis (Cyril Marcigny, pers. comm.); as has Gif Tan 90046: 4840±150 BP for the burial of a dwarf in the chamber of the passage tomb of Derrière-les-Près at Ernes. The latter is approximately contemporary with Gif 8798: 4880±70 BP for two bovid vertebrae in the external massif which represents a later addition to the chamber (San Juan & Dron 1997, 211), and hence may not be a primary interment. Analysis indicates a boundary start for this group of passage tomb burials at 4,410–4,180 cal BC and a boundary end at 3,920–3,710 cal BC (both at 95% probability). Calibration and Bayesian analysis using OxCal 4.2 and IntCal09: Bronk Ramsey 2009 and Reimer* et al. *2009.*

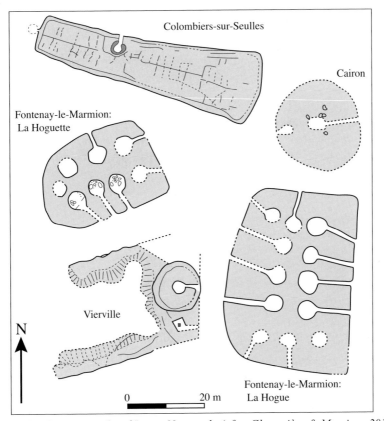

Figure 6.4. Passage tombs of Lower Normandy (after Ghesquière & Marcigny 2011).

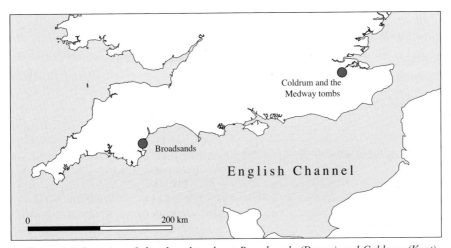

Figure 6.5. Location of chambered tombs at Broadsands (Devon) and Coldrum (Kent).

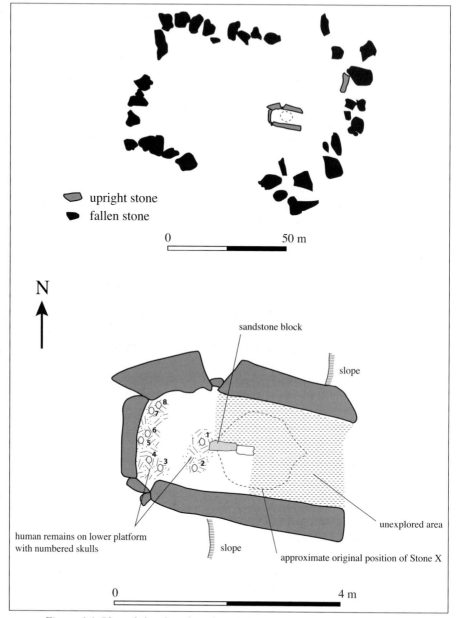

Figure 6.6. Plan of chambered tomb at Coldrum (Kent) (after Bennett 1913).

edged by a discontinuous monolithic kerb (Bennett 1913; Keith 1913; Ashbee 2005) (Figure 6.6). Within the chamber, disarticulated human skeletal remains were present, reportedly in two separate layers. Bayesian analysis of the 27 available radiocarbon dates indicates that the earlier deposit dates probably to between 3,980/3,800 cal BC and 3,930/3,750 cal BC (95%

probability) (Wysocki *et al.* 2013, 13). That would make Coldrum contemporary with the latest passage tombs of Normandy, but morphologically the Medway tombs are unlike any of those in northern France. Indeed, as recent reviews observe, "[t]he stone box at Coldrum is not easily paralleled" and earlier proposals for Scandinavian or north European parallels are now unlikely on chronological grounds (Whittle *et al.* 2011, 872; Wysocki *et al.* 2013, 3). Geographically the Medway, and Kent more generally, is relatively distant from the passage tombs of Normandy whose distribution, as we have noted, does not extend further east than the Caen plain. The absence of Continental parallels that are close either morphologically or geographically suggests that the builders of Coldrum may have espoused, or brought with them, the concept of collective burial in a megalithic structure, but had no specific model near to hand. It is really a rather remarkable indication of shared traditions widely held by early farming communities on both sides of the Channel.

A better candidate for direct Continental ancestry may be the chambered tomb of Broadsands in Devon (Figure 6.7). This was excavated rather poorly in the 1950s and the report is not at all points clear or reliable (Ralegh Radford 1958). The tomb survives as a small heavily disturbed megalithic chamber within a hedge line overlooking Torbay. Remains of a cairn were found around the foot of the chamber, and disturbed paving and human remains within the chamber. The argument for an early date rests on a combination of chronology and morphology. Four dates on human bone give the range 3,894–3,708 cal BC, and Bayesian modelling suggested tomb construction between 4,121–3,712 cal BC (95% probability) (Sheridan *et al.* 2008). The presence of carinated bowl pottery also fits comfortably with an early 4th millennium BC date. As at Coldrum, the dates overlap with the Normandy passage tomb sequence and the isolated character of Broadsands – it currently has no close regional parallels within south-west Britain – would be consistent with direct contact from Normandy. Indeed, "the fact that Broadsands stands alone in the south-west peninsula as an isolated example of a French-style passage tomb could be taken to indicate that we are dealing with a small-scale, one-off episode of settlement" (Sheridan *et al.* 2008 19).

This is an interesting argument but there are a number of uncertainties that merit further investigation. The quality of the excavation of the Broadsands tomb was poor, and ambiguities and errors are present in the recording of the human bone material. It is at least possible that some of the human remains were buried beneath the chamber rather than within it. One sherd of carinated bowl and several of the human bones were trampled into the ground below the paving slab (Sheridan *et al.* 2008, 15). It is not certain that the construction of the chamber was the first activity at this location.

The shape of the cairn also demands confirmation. Was it really circular, like the passage tombs of western Normandy? We are told that on the northern side the cairn had been truncated by the construction of a road, and on the south it had been undermined by the formation of a negative lynchet. On the west the mound had originally extended more than the 6ft beyond the chamber that was preserved (Ralegh Radford 1958, 157–158). The excavators report "no trace of a kerb" on the south-east and that "further search for the southern limit of the mound would be fruitless" (Ralegh Radford 1958, 157). On the northern side, "[t]he edge of the mound was established only for a short distance north of the entrance [to the passage]" (Ralegh Radford 1958, 158). The limited evidence and poor preservation did not however deter Radford from concluding that "The mound . . . was probably round, some 40

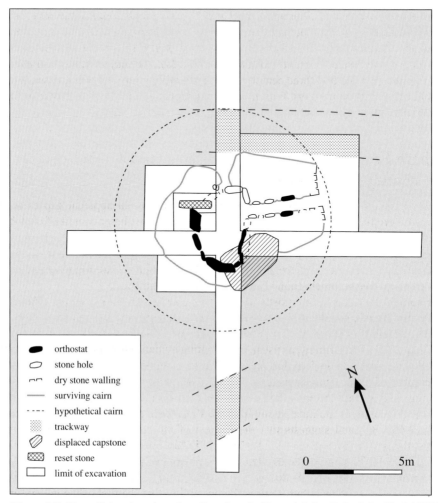

Figure 6.7. Plan of chambered tomb at Broadsands (Devon) (after Ralegh Radford 1958).

ft. in diameter" (Ralegh Radford 1958, 163). Whether indeed it was originally circular in form, and whether Broadsands can be considered a French style tomb on the Devon coast, remain open to question.

Nonetheless, Coldrum and Broadsands taken together suggest that cross-Channel connections within the first two or three centuries of the 4th millennium introduced the concept, and perhaps the practice, of megalithic funerary architecture to southern Britain. There are no close Continental parallels for Coldrum, and the claimed parallels for Broadsands remain to be confirmed, so that neither in itself lends any weight to variant proposals for the point and direction of contact. One persuasive scenario envisages "a small founder pool, operating say over only one or two generations, making a planned Channel crossing over its narrowest point and into the Greater Thames estuary" (Whittle *et al*. 2011, 861). An alternative view posits multiple axes of connection, some of them linking Brittany to the Irish Sea and beyond (Pailler and Sheridan 2009). Yet another recent proposal suggests "the earliest Neolithic monuments in Britain drew their inspiration from diverse sources, and mixed structural elements together creatively in order to achieve effects that were appropriate in the insular context." (Thomas 2013, 320). We may accept, at all events, a period of contact in the first three centuries of the 4th millennium BC, when passage tombs were still being built in northern France. But what happened to cross-Channel connections in the centuries that followed?

Northern France in the late 4th millennium BC: the second cycle of megalithic monuments

The last passage tombs of northern France are followed by an apparent gap of several centuries before the next major category of tomb appears. The latter consist of chambered tombs that would earlier have been classified as 'galleries' or 'gallery graves' (Forde 1929; Daniel 1941), with elongated, parallel-sided chambers opening from either one of the ends or from an entrance in one of the sides. Some of the structures are of stone (megalithic blocks in many cases); others (notably in Picardy) are of timber.

The north French tombs fall mostly into the category known today as *allées sépulcrales* but they also include *sépultures à entrée latérale* (lateral entry graves) and other types with elongated chambers such as angled passage tombs and V-shaped tombs (cf. L'Helgouach 1965; Scarre 2011). In Brittany, as usual, direct dating evidence is scarce. In the Paris basin, the chalk and limestone geology has preserved large quantities of human skeletal material, and a number of radiocarbon dates are available. The majority probably date to the late 4th millennium and perhaps the early 3rd millennium. A recent review of the evidence, however, places the beginning of the Late Neolithic in the Paris basin and the area up to the Channel coast at 3,600 BC, and suggests that the earliest of the collective tombs belong within the same timeframe (Salanova *et al.* 2011). This is based on new dates from the rock-cut hypogée II du Mont-Aimé à Valdes-Marais, along with early dates from Vignély-La Porte aux Bergers and Bury (*ibid,*. 78–80). Only a multiplication of further dates will resolve the chronology with confidence, but it raises the possibility that the first of the gallery graves followed the last of the passage tombs directly.

Were they then both parts of a single continuous tradition? The issue is complicated by the fact that the distribution of gallery graves in northern France overlaps with passage tombs only at its western end (in Brittany and western Normandy); and that it is here, in the area of overlap, that the evidence for dating gallery graves is most limited.

Rather than deriving gallery graves from passage tombs, we might alternatively consider a domestic parallel in the large timber halls of the same late 4th millennium period (Tinévez 2004; Praud *et al.* 2007; Joseph *et al.* 2011) (Figure 6.8). Some have been dated by dendrochronology, and it is interesting to note the contemporaneity between the date for the timber *allée sépulcrale* of La Croix-Saint-Ouen (wiggle-matched to 3,010–2,952 BC) and the long timber hall of Houplin-Ancoisne in north-eastern France (wiggle-matched to 3,111–2,930 BC) (Bernard *et al.* 1998; Praud *et al.* 2007) (Figure 6.9). The dating of the Houplin-Ancoisne structure has, however, been disputed, since AMS dates for 13 houses in northern France, on a variety of materials (charcoal, animal bone, charred cereals) fall within the range 2,883–2,349 BC (Joseph *et al.* 2011, 267). Furthermore the long timber

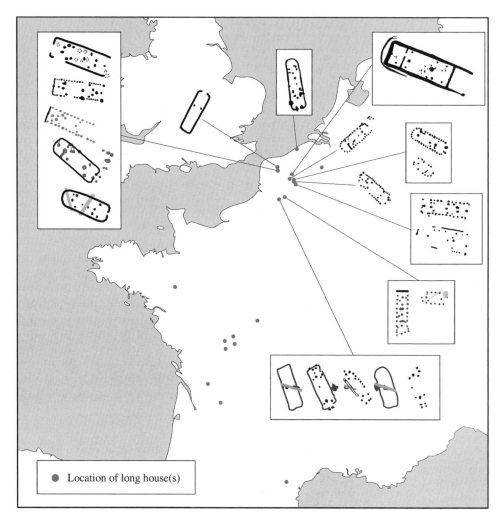

Figure 6.8. Distribution and plans of Late and Final Neolithic long houses in France (after Praud et al. 2007 and Joseph et al. 2011).

halls of Pléchâtel in central Brittany, which may form part of the same series, have been securely dated to the 28th and 27th centuries BC (Tinévez 2004, 134–139). Hence it is unlikely, on current evidence, that the long timber houses provided models for the gallery graves of northern France; if anything, rather the reverse.

Luc Laporte has highlighted the parallel in plan between these long rectangular halls and the contemporary chambered tombs (Laporte 2012; Laporte and Tineevez 2005). Thus the Pléchâtel houses with their long lateral corridors fit fairly neatly over the plan of the megalithic tomb of Goërem in the southern Morbihan. Laporte has even suggested that the Pléchâtel 'houses' might in reality be timber funerary structures, the acid soils destroying any human remains that had been deposited within them (Laporte 2012, 125). The elongated chamber, however, is not only found in northern France at this period, but also in northern

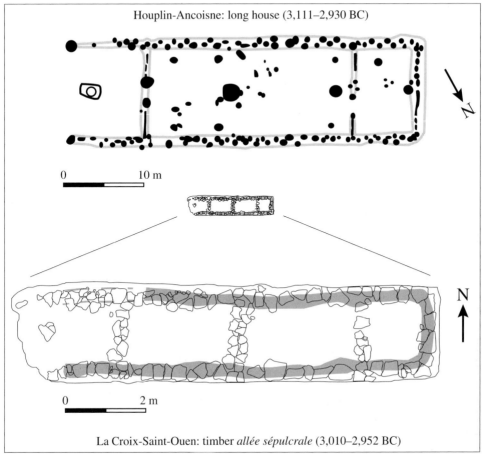

Houplin-Ancoisne: long house (3,111–2,930 BC)

0   10 m

0   2 m

La Croix-Saint-Ouen: timber *allée sépulcrale* (3,010–2,952 BC)

Figure 6.9. Comparison of the long house at Houplin-Ancoisne (3,111–2,930 BC; after Praud et al. 2007) and the timber allée sépulcrale at La Croix-Saint-Ouen (3,010–2,952 BC; after Bernard et al. 1998). Note the difference in scale between the two structures.

Europe. From Drenthe to the Polish frontier, there are large numbers of T-shaped passage tombs, along with gallery graves in the Halle region of Germany. Dating of birch bark within the dry-stonework of a number of Danish tombs indicates that these were built in the period of a century or two between 3,200 BC and 3,000 BC (Dehn and Hansen 2006; Scarre 2010). This would make them approximately contemporary with the north French gallery graves.

Parallels between late 4th millennium elongated chamber tombs of northern France and those of northern Europe have previously been proposed and are still occasionally entertained (L'Helgouach 1966; Briard *et al.* 1985; Laporte 2012, 129). Just as the French gallery graves may relate (and possibly derive from) contemporary long houses, so too might those of northern Europe. There is the potential for parallel, convergent development between these regions. One other feature, however, is consistent with a link between northern France and northern Europe: the distribution of the collared flasks known as '*bouteilles à collerette*' or '*Kragenflaschen*'. The earliest of these have been found in central Poland, but also cluster around the Dutch/German frontier, with a few outliers in Brittany, where they occur in gallery graves (notably, but not exclusively, lateral entry graves) and in reused passage tombs (L'Helgouach 1966; Huysecom 1976). The examples from Breton gallery graves have been assigned to Group 1 horizon C, with a chronology in the range 3,400–3,100 BC, continuing perhaps to 2,800 BC (Huysecom 1976 206–207). Do they testify to maritime connections down the North Sea coasts and English Channel in the late 4th or early 3rd millennium BC? If so, then they conspicuously avoid southern Britain and, like the tradition of long megalithic chambers, remain a purely continental phenomenon.

Southern Britain in the late 4th and 3rd millennium BC: splendid isolation?

Looking northwards across the Channel, the monument traditions of southern Britain in the late 4th and 3rd millennium BC are diverse in form and content, but entirely different from those of the continental mainland. In the Irish Sea province and in northern Britain, passage tombs of various kinds were built during the later 4th millennium: chronologies are now relatively well established for Irish court cairns and passage tombs, the smaller but perhaps related passage tombs of Wales, and the Orkney tombs (Burrow 2010; O'Sullivan and Bayliss 2013; Schulting *et al.* 2010 2011). These do not find close analogies on the continent at this period, but must refer back to continental forms of earlier centuries. The character of that ancestral reference has yet to be explored in detail.

Other features of the British monument tradition that find few parallels in adjacent areas of northern France are the great stone circles. None of the stone 'enclosures' of Brittany, such as those at the end of some of the Carnac avenues, are circular in form (and indeed many of them appear to be horseshoes rather than complete circuits). Furthermore the Carnac examples, such as Er Lannic, had probably been standing for more than a millennium by this period (Scarre 2011, 117). There is nothing to parallel Stonehenge or Avebury in northern France; although interestingly, the stone circle tradition does extend into northern and western Britain, and is not simply (or even perhaps predominantly) a southern phenomenon. Thus Britain from 3,500 BC, if not before, presents an increasingly insular image. Indeed, already by the middle of the 4th millennium there were already striking differences in the way monumental landscapes were composed on opposite sides of the Channel.

This impression of isolation is reinforced by the evidence of houses, ceramic styles and axehead flows. Grooved Ware, for example, is found throughout Britain from Orkney to Wessex, and is present in Ireland, but does not appear to have crossed the Channel. The house types represented at Orkney sites such as Skara Brae and echoed in the recent discoveries at Durrington Walls seem also to have been an exclusively insular tradition (Thomas 2010). It has even been proposed that Grooved Ware and small rectangular houses can be grouped with the construction and elaboration of Stonehenge to argue for "unification, bringing together groups with different ancestries in a coalition that encompassed the entirety of southern Britain, if not the entire island" (Parker Pearson 2012, 328). There are no long houses of the kind built during the 3rd millennium BC in northern and western France. The large-scale production of dolerite axeheads at Plussulien in Brittany made little impact in southern Britain (Figure 6.10). Only half a dozen examples have been identified (Group X: "[e]xtremely abundant in north-west France but exceedingly rare in Britain": Clough and

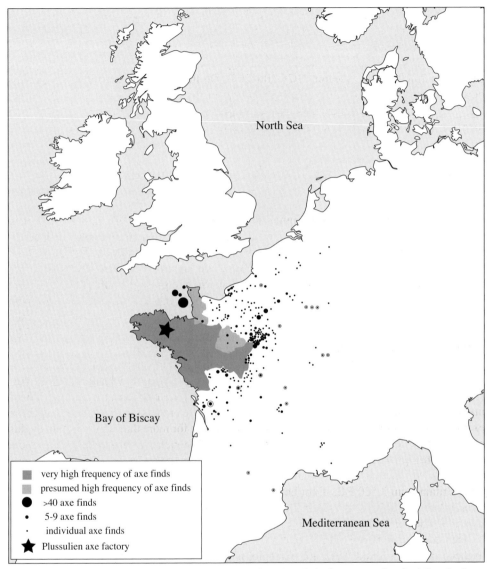

Figure 6.10. Distribution of Plussulien (Type A dolerite) polished stone axeheads (after Le Roux 1999). Approximate locations are circled.

Cummins 1988, 8). They represent only 0.2% of the 2381 axes examined by the Implement Petrology Group up to 1988 (Le Roux 1999, 186). Axe production at Plussulien began in the late 5th millennium BC and continued into the 3rd millennium BC, and at least one of the examples from southern Britain is of the relatively late 'hache à bouton' type (Le Roux 1999, 146; 2002, 111). This scarcity of Plussulien material can be contrasted with the 103 axes of Alpine greenstone known from Britain (Sheridan *et al.* 2011) (Figure 6.11). These were probably produced in the late 5th millennium BC and although some attribute them

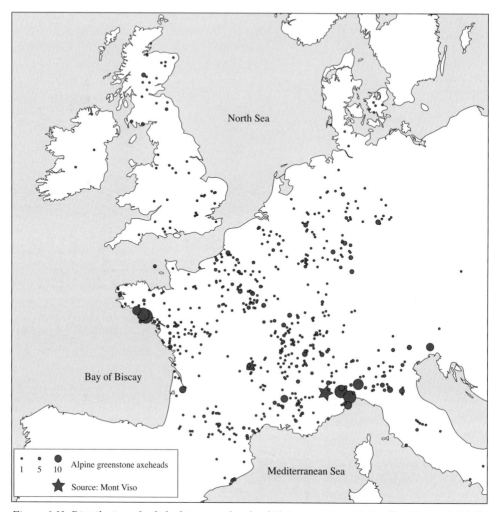

Figure 6.11. Distribution of polished stone axeheads of Alpine greenstone (after Sheridan et al. *2011).*

to Mesolithic interactions (Thomas 2013, 276–283) others argue that they came to Britain around the time of the Neolithic transition (Pétrequin *et al.* 2011; Sheridan *et al.* 2011, 415; Anderson-Whymark and Garrow, this volume). If that is the correct reading of the evidence, then the axes, like the monuments, suggest an early period of contact followed by several centuries of relative isolation.

Conclusion: transmission and translation

We are left, then, with more points of divergence than of convergence. The earliest Neolithic of Brittany with its decorated menhirs, its long mounds, and its stone rows had come and gone before the first Neolithic appeared in southern Britain, if we place the latter in the 41st century BC as recently proposed (Whittle *et al.* 2011, 800). There may be some overlap in time between the passage tomb tradition of northern France and that of southern Britain, but if so I suggest it was of relatively short duration. Most of the British passage tombs (including in that category the chambered long cairns) fall in the period after the last of the Normandy passage tombs, indeed at a time that may have coincided with a temporary hiatus in the construction of major monuments in northern France. That gap might be filled, if the results of further dating programmes prolong the construction of passage tombs in Normandy into the 36th century, and confirm the suggested early origin in that same century of *allées sépulcrales* and related gallery graves in central northern France (Salanova *et al.* 2011, 77). The two 'cycles' of megalithic funerary monuments in northern France – passage tombs and gallery graves – might then become chronologically successive, the second derived from the first. The broader perspective, however, opens up interesting potential connections with northern Europe, and the morphological similarities between the long megalithic chambers and the long houses of the North French Late Neolithic are also suggestive.

It is particularly striking that Britain does not appear to participate in the 'second cycle' of long megalithic chambers that became widespread in adjacent parts of the Continent in the late 4th millennium. In Britain, by contrast, this was a period when large stone circles came to be built which in turn have no analogies on the near Continent. That is not to deny the likelihood of contacts across the Channel throughout this period. Yet the differences in the trajectories suggest that the early stage contacts that presumably brought the Neolithic and, perhaps at a slightly later stage, chambered tombs and ditched enclosures to southern Britain were only transitory in character.

There is, however, a more fundamental issue to consider. That is the contrast between processes that could be termed 'transmission' and others that might be described as 'translation'. By transmission I mean the specific contacts that carried new artefacts, traditions and perhaps people from one region to another. For this process archaeology can provide material evidence, whether it be through the movement of materials or individual objects, or through techniques of manufacture (e.g. methods of pottery production). At some stage in the future, cross-Channel displacement of people at this period may be documented through stable isotope analysis, in the manner illustrated by the later 3rd millennium 'Amesbury Archer' (Fitzpatrick 2011, 234). There can also be morphological parallels so close as to be consistent with direct contact or transfer. So for example, the presence of Alpine jadeitite axes in Britain indicates cross-Channel contact (though it does not resolve the rather perplexing chronology).

But the danger here is that we end up chasing narratives of origin and ignore the more interesting and more obvious issue of differences, of the changes that take place once the new ideas or artefacts (or people) have arrived: of their 'translation' within the new context.

In the case of the monuments discussed above, the issue of translation may briefly be reviewed under three headings. First, there is morphology. How closely do the tomb morphologies match on either side of the Channel? One feature that is missing from southern Britain is the circular chamber with corbel vault that is a specific feature of the passage tombs of western Normandy. Furthermore, leaving aside the questionable evidence of Broadsands, none of the early passage tombs of southern Britain are encased within circular mounds or cairns like those of Normandy. Still more puzzling, the British monument with the very earliest dates, Coldrum, has no close continental parallels in either a morphological or a geographical sense.

Second, there is the arrangement of tombs within the landscape. The pattern of dispersed individual long mounds found for example in the Avebury area (Gillings *et al.* 2008, 186), or the Wylye valley of northern Wiltshire (Field 2006, 119) does not seem to have been present in northern France. In western Normandy, by contrast, many of the passage tombs are clustered in small groups or cemeteries: six cairns at Condé-sur-Ifs, seven at Bellengreville-Chicheboville, five at La Hoguette (Ghesquière and Marcigny 2011, 173). This does not emerge as a common characteristic of southern British chambered cairns. Long mounds frequently occur in groups, arranged for example along a ridge as at Skendleby in Lincolnshire (Field 2006, 107), but not tightly clustered as at Condé-sur-Ifs in Normandy nor as at Bougon in Poitou-Charentes.

Third, there is the issue of numbers. We need to exercise caution in comparing present distribution and frequency with past distribution and frequency, but it is interesting nonetheless to note the relatively high densities of chambered cairns in (particularly) central southern Britain compared to those in Normandy. Even Brittany has fewer sites than one might suppose, and those are very much clustered in the coastal zone. Contrasts can be drawn between tomb frequencies on the Channel Islands and on the Normandy mainland. On Guernsey, for example, place name evidence indicates 68 megalithic sites and 39 menhirs, and it has been suggested that Jersey and Guernsey each lost some 40–50 sites in the period from the late 18th up to the end of the 19th century. That compares with the 30 or so monuments that survive on each of the islands today (Hibbs 1986). Of those, fifteen are passage tombs. By contrast, the whole of Normandy has fewer than 30 passage tombs. That much thinner distribution is given added weight by the complete absence of such monuments in the eastern half of the region, and is difficult to explain by differential processes of destruction or discovery.

Britain, on the other hand, has rather larger numbers of monuments. In England alone one recent count gave some 538 definite and probable long barrows plus 102 mortuary enclosures and 14 bank barrows (Field 2006, 22). Scotland offers a similar number of recorded tombs (444 sites listed in Henshall 1972; 625 sites classified as 'chambered cairn' by Canmore, but not all of those of Neolithic date). But these numbers are modest compared with the enormous numbers of megalithic chambered tombs built in northern Europe during the second half of the 4th millennium BC: an estimated 25,000 in Denmark alone with over 7,000 sites recorded or extant, and probably more than 40,000 in northern Europe as a whole (Midgley 2008, 29–31). The substantial differences in monument numbers must surely indicate that the monuments played very different roles in the different Neolithic societies.

The extension of the Neolithic monument tradition to Britain is thus to be understood as part of a more widespread phenomenon, and not simply in terms of a short cross-Channel hop. Furthermore, whatever the argument about the timing and nature of the initial moment of contact – the 'transmission' of the tradition to southern Britain – subsequent histories on the opposite sides of the Channel were widely divergent. Focusing too much on origins risks obscuring that. There may very well have been continuing contacts in the centuries following the introduction of farming, but what is most striking is the insularity of the British tradition from the middle of the 4th millennium onwards. It is the 'translation' of these initial ideas as much as their inception that we should be seeking to follow, and that means exploring the British and French developments in the perspective of their respective counterparts.

Acknowledgements

I am grateful to Hugo Anderson-Whymark, Duncan Garrow and Fraser Sturt for inviting me to the conference at which a preliminary version of this paper was delivered; to Kate Sharpe for assistance with bibliography, for preparing the diagrams and for the Bayesian analyses; to Cyril Marcigny for permission to cite unpublished radiocarbon dates for Normandy passage tombs; and to Andrew Millard for helpful comments on an earlier version of this text.

Note

1 The early AMS dates from the Cotswold-Severn long cairn of Burn Ground overlap (with one exception) in the 39th/38th century BC and are consistent with this conclusion; the single outlier requires confirmation and may be on curated bone reburied here from another context (Whittle *et al.* 2011, 468; Smith and Brickley 2006; but see also Thomas 2013, 318).

References

Ashbee, P. 1998. Coldrum revisited and reviewed. *Archaeologia Cantiana* 118, 1–43.

Bayliss, A. and O'Sullivan, M. 2013. Interpreting chronologies for the Mound of the Hostages, Tara, and its contemporary context. In M. O'Sullivan, M. Doyle and C. Scarre (eds), *Neolithic and Bronze Age Ireland in Tara – from the past to the future. Towards a new research agenda*, 26–104. Dublin: Wordwell.

Bayliss, A. and Whittle, A. (eds). 2007. *Histories of the Dead: building chronologies for five southern British long barrows*. Cambridge: *Cambridge Archaeological Journal* 17(1) (Supplement).

Bennett, F. 1913. Coldrum monument and exploration 1910. *Journal of the Royal Anthropological Institute of Great Britain and Ireland* 43, 76–85.

Bernard, V., Billand, G., Guillot, H. and Le Goff, I. 1998. Première datation dendrochronologique d'une sépulture collective à La Croix-Saint-Ouen (Oise). In X. Gutherz and R. Joussaume (eds), *Le Néolithique du Centre-Ouest de la France. Actes du XXIe colloque inter-régional sur le Néolithique, Poitiers, 14, 15 et 16 octobre 1994*, 403–6. Chauvigny: Association des Publication Chauvinoises.

Bertrand, A. 1864. De la distribution des dolmens sur la surface de la France. *Revue Archéologique* 10, 144–54.

Bonstetten, B. 1865. *Essai sur les dolmens*. Geneva: Jules-Guillaume Fick.

Boujot, C. and Cassen, S. 1992. Le développement des premières architectures funéraires monumentales en France occidentale. In C.-T. Le Roux (ed.), *Paysans et Bâtisseurs. Actes du 17e Colloque Interrégional sur le Néolithique, Vannes 1990* 195–211. Rennes: Revue Archéologique de l'Ouest, supplément no.5.

Boujot, C. and Cassen, S. 1993. A pattern of evolution for the Neolithic funerary structures of the west of France. *Antiquity* 67, 477–91.

Briard, J., Gautier, M. and Leroux, G. 1995. *Les Mégalithes et les tumulus de Saint-Just, Ille-et Vilaine*. Paris: Comité des Travaux Historiques et Scientifiques.

Bronk Ramsey, C. 2009. Bayesian analysis of radiocarbon dates. *Radiocarbon* 51, 337–60.

Burrow, S. 2010. Bryn Celli Ddu passage tomb, Anglesey: alignment, construction, date, and ritual. *Proceedings of the Prehistoric Society* 76, 249–70.

Caillaud, R. and Lagnel, E. 1972. Le cairn et le crématoire néolithiques de La Hoguette à Fontenay-le-Marmion (Calvados). *Gallia Préhistoire* 15, 137–97.

Cassen, S., Lanos, P., Dufresne, P., Oberlin, C., Delqué-Kolic, E. and Le Goffic, M. 2009. Datations sur site (Table des Marchands, alignement du Grand Menhir, Er Grah) et modélisation chronologique du Néolithique morbihannais. In S. Cassen (ed.), *Autour de la Table. Explorations archéologiques et discours savants sur des architectures néolithiques à Locmariaquer, Morbihan (Table des Marchands et Grand Menhir)* 737–68. Nantes: Université de Nantes.

Caylus, A. comte de, 1766. *Recueil d'Antiquités Égyptiennes, Etrusques, Grecques, Romaines et Gauloises, Tome VI,* Paris.

Childe, V. G. 1950. *Prehistoric Migrations in Europe.* London: Kegan Paul.

Clough, T. and Cummins, W. (eds). 1988. *Stone Axe Studies, volume 2: The petrology of prehistoric stone implements from the British Isles.* London: Council for British Archaeology.

Collard, M., Edinborough, K., Shennan, S. and Thomas, M. 2010. Radiocarbon evidence indicates that migrants introduced farming to Britain. *Journal of Archaeological Science* 37, 866–70.

Coutil, L. 1918. Le tumulus de la Hogue à Fontenay-le-Marmion (Calvados). (Etude des tumulus néolithiques du Calvados et de l'Orne). *Bulletin de la Société Préhistorique Française* 15, 65–138.

Daniel, G. 1941. The dual nature of the megalithic colonisation of prehistoric Europe. *Proceedings of the Prehistoric Society* 7, 1–49.

Darvill, T. 2004. *Long Barrows of the Cotswolds and Surrounding Areas.* Stroud: Tempus.

Dehn, T. and Hansen, S. 2006. Birch bark in Danish passage graves. *Journal of Danish Archaeology* 14, 23–44.

Dron, J.-L., Le Goff, I. and Hänni, C. 1996. Approches architecturale, anthropologique et génétique d'un ensemble de tombes à couloir: La Bruyère-du-Hamel à Condé-sur-Ife (Calvados). *Bulletin de la Société Préhistorique Française* 93, 388–95.

Fergusson, J. 1872. *Rude Stone Monuments in All Countries; their Ages and Uses.* London: John Murray.

Field, D. 2006. *Earthen Long Barrows: the earliest monuments in the British Isles,* Stroud: Tempus.

Fitzpatrick, A. 2011. *The Amesbury Archer and the Boscombe Bowmen. Bell Beaker Burials on Boscombe Down, Amesbury, Wiltshire.* Salisbury: Wessex Archaeology.

Forde, C. 1929. The megalithic gallery in Brittany. *Man* 29, 105–9.

Ghesquière, E. and Marcigny, C. (eds). 2011. *Cairon. Vivre et mourir au Néolithique. La Pierre Tourneresse en Calvados.* Rennes: Presses Universitaires de Rennes.

Gillings, M., Pollard, J., Wheatley, D. and Peterson, R. 2008. *Landscape of the Megaliths: excavation and fieldwork on the Avebury monuments 1997–2003.* Oxford: Oxbow Books.

Giot, P.-R., Marguerie, D. and Morzadec, H. 1994. About the age of the oldest passage-graves in western Brittany. *Antiquity* 68, 624–6.

Guyodo J.-N. 2005. Les assemblages lithiques de la fin du Néolithique ancien et du Néolithique moyen sur le Massif armoricain et ses marges. In G. Marchand and A. Tresset (eds), *Unité et diversité des processus de néolithisation sur la façade atlantique de l'Europe (6è – 4è millénaires avant J.-C.) Actes de la table-ronde de Nantes, 26–27 avril 2002,* 213–24. Société Préhistorique Française 36.

Henshall, A. 1972. *The Chambered Tombs of Scotland, Volume 2.* Edinburgh: Edinburgh University Press.

Hinguant S. and Boujot C. 2009. Les pierres couchées de Belz ou la découverte d'un ensemble mégalithique. In J.-P. Demoule (ed.), *La révolution néolithique dans le monde, actes du colloque international «la révolution néolithique dans le monde. Aux origines de l'emprise humaine sur le vivant»,* 383–97. Inrap et Cité des sciences et de l'industrie, Paris, 2–4 Oct. 2008, CNRS éditions.

Joseph, F., Julien, M., Leroy-Langelin, E., Lorin, Y. and Praud, I. 2011. L'architecture domestique des sites du IIIe millénaire avant notre ère dans le Nord de la France. In F. Bostyn, E. Martial and I. Praud (eds), *Le Néolithique du Nord de la France dans son contexte européen: habitat et économie aux 4e et 3e millénaires avant notre ère. Actes du 29e colloque interrégional sur le Néolithique, Villeneuve-d'Ascq 2009,* 249–73. Revue Archéologique de Picardie, numéro spécial 28.

Joussaume, R. 2006. Les tumulus de Champ-Châlon à Benon (Charente-Maritime). *Bulletin du Groupe Vendéen d'Études Préhistoriques* 42, 1–90.

Keith, A. 1913. Report on the human remains found by F. J. Bennett, Esq., F.G.S., in the central chamber of a megalithic monument at Coldrum, Kent. *Journal of the Royal Anthropological Institute of Great Britain and Ireland* 43, 86–100.

Kerdivel, G. 2012. *Occupation de l'Espace et Gestion des Ressources a l'Interface Entre Massifs Primaires et Bassins Secondaires et Tertiaires au Néolithique. S*2383. Oxford: Archaeopress.

Laporte, L. 2012. Dépôts de mobilier, architectures et pratiques funéraires dans l'ouest de la France, au cours du Néolithique récent et final. In M. Sohn and J. Vaquer (eds), *Sépultures collectives et mobiliers funéraires de la fin du Néolithique en Europe occidentale*, 113–45. Toulouse: École des Hautes Études en Sciences Sociales.

Laporte, L. and Tinévez, J.-Y. 2005. Neolithic houses and chambered tombs of western France. *Cambridge Archaeological Journal* 14, 217–34.

Large, J.-M. and Mens, E. 2009. The Douet alignment on the island of Hoedic (Morbihan): new insights into standing stone alignments in Brittany. *Oxford Journal of Archaeology* 28, 239–54.

L'Helgouach 1965. *Les Sépultures Mégalithiques en Armorique*. Rennes: Travaux du Laboratoire d'Anthropologie Préhistorique de la Faculté des Sciences.

Le Roux, C.-T. 1999. *L'outillage de pierre polie en métadolérite du type A: les ateliers de Plussulien (Côtes-d'Armor): production et diffusion au Néolithique dans la France de l'ouest et au delà.* Rennes: Université de Rennes.

Leclerc, J. and Masset, C. 2006. L'évolution de la pratique funéraire dans la sépulture collective néolithique de La Chaussée-Tirancourt (Somme). *Bulletin de la Société Préhistorique Française* 103, 87–116.

Marcigny, C., Ghesquière, E. and Desloges, J. (eds). 2007. *La Hache et la Meule. Les premiers paysans du Néolithique en Normandie*. La Havre: Muséum d'Histoire Naturelle du Havre.

Marcigny, C., Ghesquière, E., Juhel, L. and Charraud, F. 2010. Entre Néolithique ancien et Néolithique moyen en Normandie et dans les îles anglo-normandes. Parcours chronologique. In C. Billard and M. Legris (eds), *Premiers Néolithiques de l'Ouest. Cultures, réseaux, échanges des premières sociétés néolithiques à leur expansion*, 117–62. Rennes: Presses Universitaires de Rennes.

Midgley, M. 2008. *The Megaliths of Northern Europe*. London: Routledge.

Mohen, J.-P. and Scarre, C. 2002. *Les Tumulus de Bougon. Complexe mégalithique du Ve au IIIe millénaire*. Paris: Errance.

Pailler, Y. and Sheridan, A. 2009. Everything you always wanted to know about . . . la néolithisation de la Grande-Bretagne et de l'Irlande. *Bulletin de la Société Préhistorique Française* 106, 25–56.

Parker Pearson, M. 2012. *Stonehenge. Exploring the Greatest Stone Age Mystery*. London: Simon and Schuster.

Pétrequin, P., Sheridan, A., Cassen, S., Errera, M., Gauthier, E., Klassen, L., Le Maux, N., Pailler, Y., Pétrequim, A.-M. and Rossy, M. 2011. Eclogite or jadeitite: the two colours involved in the transfer of alpine axeheads in western Europe. In V. Davis and M. Edmonds (eds) *Stone Axe Studies III*, 55–82. Oxford: Oxbow Books.

Praud, I., Bernard, V., Martial, E. and Palau, R. 2007. Un grand bâtiment du Néolithique final à Houplin-Ancoisne «Le Marais de Santes» (Nord, France). In M. Besse (ed.), *Sociétés néolithiques. Des faits archéologiques aux fonctionnements socio-économiques. Actes du 27e colloque interrégional sur le Néolithique (Neuchâtel, 1 et 2 octobre 2005)*, 445–60. Lausanne: Cahiers d'archéologie romande 108.

Ralegh Radford, C. A. 1958. The chambered tomb at Broadsands, Paignton. *Proceedings of the Devon Archaeological Exploration Society* 5, 147–66.

Reimer, P., Baillie, M., Bard, E., Bayliss, A., Beck, J., Blackwell, P., Bronk Ramsey, C., Buck, C. E., Burr, G. S., Edwards, R. L., Friedrich, M., Grootes, P. M., Guilderson, T. P., Hajdas, I., Heaton, T. J., Hog,g A. G., Hughen, K. A., Kaiser, K. F., Kromer, B., McCormac, F. G., Manning, S. W., Reimer, R. W., Richards, D. A., Southon, J. R., Talamo, S., Turney, C. S. M., van der Plicht, J. and Weyhenmeyer, C. E. 2009. IntCal09 and Marine09 radiocarbon age calibration curves, 0–50,000 years cal BP. *Radiocarbon* 51, 1111–1150.

Salanova, L., Brunet, P., Cottiaux, R., Hamon, T., Langry-François, F., Martineau, R., Polloni, A., Renard, C. and Sohn, M. 2011. Du Néolithique récent à l'âge du Bronze dans le Centre Nord de la France: les étapes de l'évolution chrono-culturelle. In F. Bostyn, E. Martial and I. Praud (eds), *Le Néolithique du Nord de la France dans son contexte européen: habitat et économie aux 4e et 3e millénaires avant notre ère. Actes du 29e colloque interrégional sur le Néolithique, Villeneuve-d'Ascq 2009*, 77–101. Revue Archéologique de Picardie, numéro spécial 28.

San Juan, G. and Dron, J.-L. 1997. Le site néolithique moyen de Derrière-les-Prés à Ernes (Calvados). *Gallia Préhistoire* 39, 151–237.II

Scarre, C. 2010. Stone people: monuments and identities in the Channel Islands. In M. Furholt, F. Lüth and J. Müller (eds), *Megaliths and identities: early monuments and neolithic societies from the Atlantic to the Baltic*, 95–104. Bonn: Dr Rudolf Habelt.

Scarre, C. 2011. *Landscapes of Neolithic Brittany.* Oxford: Oxford University Press.

Scarre, C., Laporte, L. and Joussaume, R. 2003. Long mounds and megalithic origins in western France: recent excavations at Prissé-la-Charrière. *Proceedings of the Prehistoric Society* 67, 235–51.

Schulting, R. 2005. Comme la mer qui se retire: les changements dans l'exploitation des resources marines du Mésolithique au Néolithique en Bretagne. In G. Marchand and A. Tresset (eds), *Unité et diversité des processus de néolithisation sur la façade atlantique de l'Europe (6e–4e millénaires avant J.-C.)*, 163–71. Paris: Société Préhistorique Française.

Schulting, R., Sebire, H. and Robb, J. 2010. On the road to Paradis: new insights from AMS dates and stable isotopes at Le Déhus, Guernsey, and the Channel Islands Middle Neolithic. *Oxford Journal of Archaeology* 29, 143–79.

Sheridan, A. 2003. French Connections I: spreading the *marmites* thinly. In I. Armit, E. Murphy, E. Nelis and D. Simpson (eds), *Neolithic Settlement in Ireland and Western Britain*, 3–17. Oxford: Oxbow Books.

Sheridan, A. 2007. From Picardie to Pickering and Pencraig Hill? New information on the 'Carinated Bowl Neolithic' in northern Britain. In A. Whittle and V. Cummings (eds), *Going Over. The Mesolithic-Neolithic Transition in North-West Europe*, 441–92. Oxford: Oxford University Press.

Sheridan, A., Pailler, Y., Pétrequin, P. and Errera, M. 2011. Old friends, new friends, a long-lost friend and false friends: tales from Projet JADE. In V. Davis and M. Edmonds (eds), *Stone Axe Studies III*, 411–26. Oxford: Oxbow Books.

Sheridan, A., Schulting, R., Quinnell, H. and Taylor, R. 2008. Revisiting a small passage tomb at Broadsands, Devon. *Proceedings of the Devon Archaeological Society* 66, 1–26.

Smith, M. and Brickley, M. 2006. The date and sequence of use of Neolithic funerary monuments: new AMS dating evidence from the Cotswold-Severn region. *Oxford Journal of Archaeology* 25, 335–55.

Thomas, J. 2013. *The Birth of Neolithic Britain. An Interpretive Account.* Oxford: Oxford University Press.

Tinévez, J.-Y. (ed.) 2004. *Le site de La Hersonnais à Pléchâtel (Ille-et-Vilaine): un ensemble de bâtiments collectifs du Néolithique final.* Paris: Société Préhistorique Française.

Tresset, A. 2003. French connections II: of cows and men. In I. Armit, E. Murphy, E. Nelis and D. Simpson (eds), *Neolithic Settlement in Ireland and Western Britain*, 18–30. Oxford: Oxbow Books.

Verron, G. 2000. *Préhistoire de la Normandie.* Rennes: Éditions Ouest-France.

Westendorp, N., 1822. *Verhandeling ter beantwoording der Vrage: welke volkeren hebben de zoogenoemde hunebedden gesticht? In welke tijden kan man onderstellen, dat zij deze oorden hebben bewoond?* Groningen: Oomkens.

Whittle, A. 2007. The temporality of transformation: dating the early development of the southern British Neolithic. In A. Whittle and V. Cummings (eds), *Going Over. The Mesolithic-Neolithic Transition in North-West Europe*, 377–98. Oxford: Oxford University Press.

Whittle, A., Healy, F. and Bayliss, a. 2011. *Gathering Time. Dating the Early Neolithic enclosures of southern Britain and Ireland.* Oxford: Oxbow Books.

What was and what would never be: changing patterns of interaction and archaeological visibility across north-west Europe from 2,500 to 1,500 cal BC

Neil Wilkin and Marc Vander Linden

Introduction

Identifying and explaining interaction across large spaces during prehistory has as long a history as the discipline itself. During the first half of the 20th century, similarities in the archaeological record were typically interpreted in terms of shared social and ethnic identities (see Jones 1997, 15–39). Material patterns became archaeological cultures, themselves the unquestionable traces of past tribes whose movements could be mapped across vast territories, sometimes across the Channel (e.g. Childe 1957; Butler 1963). The culture-historical view soon became taboo in English-writing academic circles under the aegis of processual – and later post-processual – archaeology, although seamless 'chest of drawers' models of archaeological theoretical developments should be treated with a note of caution, and interaction continued to be perceived as a driving socio-cultural force (see Roberts and Vander Linden 2011; Vander Linden and Roberts 2011). Artefact similarities across space and time were still recognised, but were expressed in other, economically and (particularly) socially formulated terms; thus their Continental typo-chronological affinities were rarely expanded upon, becoming abstract and static concepts within social and cosmological readings of the evidence (e.g. Thorpe and Richards 1984; Thomas 1991).

In the past decade or so there has been a resurgence of new work explicitly focused on the question of the contacts between Britain, Ireland and the near Continent (e.g. Needham 2000; 2006; 2009; Bourgeois and Talon 2009; Moore and Armada 2011). New archaeological and scientific data, and a 'material culture turn', in reaction to some of the idealistic excesses of post-processual landscape and monument based studies, are largely responsible for this recent burst of publications, research projects, exhibitions and conferences (e.g. Clark 2004; 2009; Fitzpatrick 2011; Lehoerff 2012). Despite this, relatively little direct collaboration has taken place between researchers with their origins on either side of the Channel. This contribution responds to several of the shortcomings we both perceive in the current treatment of earlier Bronze Age relations between Britain, Ireland and north-west Europe.

There has traditionally been a compulsion (still felt today) to relate British and European artefacts or else face the charge of insularity – a kind of archaeological 'Euroscepticism' and a failure of academic reach. While a parochial outlook is certainly unhelpful, so too is an unqualified stress placed on cross-Channel connections in order to justify the international 'impact' of archaeological objects and research. We would contend that the overuse of the notion is as misleading – in terms of the variety and complexity of the evidence – as the over-emphasis of notions of 'insularity', and has contributed to a decontextualized appreciation of their role in the wider system of changing relations. There has also been a paucity of research into Irish-British relations during the Bronze Age, possibly as a continuation of the old notion of *ex oriente lux*. It has also helped to sustain the implicit socio-evolutionary idea that, as soon as they were suitably sophisticated, British and Irish communities would have naturally sought Continental fashions and technologies. The coincidence of stronger relations between Southern England and the Continent during the later phases of the Bronze Age (*c.*1,000–800 cal BC: O'Connor 1980), and apparent changes in seafaring technology (Cunliffe 2009, 84; cf. Van de Noort 2009), has helped to give the impression that the earlier Bronze Age can be understood as the formative period in a relatively simplistic long-term narrative of trade and exchange (e.g. Brun 1998). The characteristics of relations – and the driving motivations that underlay them – were instead more contextually informed and constructed, with cosmological factors at times more significant than motivations geared around economic trade networks (cf. Needham 2000; 2006; 2009). This paper also aims to demonstrate that we can only properly evaluate the significance of Continental connections by also appreciating contacts across the Irish Sea. Indeed, the fuller maxim *ex oriente lux, ex occidente lex* ('from the East comes light, from the West law'), is more balanced given that Bronze Age Continental connections form part of a complex, integrated system. In this paper we consider these ideas for three major chronological phases: pre-2,500 cal BC; 2,500–2,300/2,200 cal BC; and 2,200–1,800 cal BC.

The period covered is beset by terminological uncertainty and variation, with, from one region to the other, references to it as Chalcolithic (Spain, Britain), Late Neolithic (Netherlands, Denmark), Final Neolithic (France), Bell Beaker Culture, Bell Beaker Phenomenon and Early Bronze Age (Bourgeois and Talon 2006, fig. 3.1; Roberts *et al.* 2013). For the sake of simplicity, we will refer here to the period between 2,500–2,300/2,200 cal BC as Bell Beaker Phenomenon (BBP hereafter), and to the following centuries up to 1,600/1,500 cal BC as Early Bronze Age (although these technically cover part of the Middle Bronze Age in some regions of north-west Europe: see *ibid.*, figs 2.1–2.5).

Before 2,500 cal BC: Insular worlds and 'invisible' dimensions

In order to understand more fully the development of the BBP, it is necessary to examine briefly the situation during the first half of the 3rd millennium cal BC. Broadly speaking, three main cultural blocks can be distinguished.

Britain and Ireland
Across Britain and Ireland interaction can be recognized in association with Grooved Ware, a ceramic style with a wide geographic distribution which encompasses all of Britain during the early 3rd millennium cal BC, as well as several Irish sites (e.g. Cleal and McSween

1999; Sheridan 2004; Carlin and Brück 2012, 203–7). Grooved Ware is found in a number of contexts but, throughout all of Britain and Ireland, there seems to be a preference for its deposition in various types of open-air, circular, non-funerary monuments such as henges, timber and stone circles. While the geographic distribution of each category of monuments overlaps rather than coincides, the collective effort put into the construction of such structures is another defining trait shared by Late Neolithic communities across Britain and Ireland (Figure 7.1, Nos 1–2). This collective ethos appears to have been associated with feasting events involving Grooved Ware pottery (Parker Pearson and Ramilisonina 1998; Rowley-Conwy and Owen 2011; Needham 2012, table 1.8). Jan Harding (2000; 2012) has argued for the importance of pilgrimages to henge monuments and ceremonial landscapes during this period. Recent research also provides evidence for the physical movement of various categories of goods, including animals (Viner *et al.* 2010).

The notion that life during this period in Britain was relatively static and lacked mobility and long-distance travel (particularly in contrast to the following BBP period) should therefore only be accepted with reservations. Exchanges of material culture and ideas regarding how to use and deposit them took place across the Irish Sea, and it may be noted that this degree of synchronicity in terms of ceramic *and* depositional practices between Ireland and Southern England was not seen again on a large-scale until the later phases of the Early Bronze Age, in association with the full adoption of cremation burial with Collared Urns and Cordoned Urn ceramics (see below). The key factors were the fixed, enduring nature of monuments, and the unifying effects of communal feasting events. The nature of feasting and monument construction would tend to bind those participating into acts of *communitas*, following Victor Turner's (1969) definition, in which the expression of individual identity or status were no longer relevant or appropriate. The fact that these practices did not have relevance on the opposite side of the North Sea/Channel despite the occurrence of the Grooved Ware/monument complexes on either side of the Irish Sea may be related to the existence and communal nature of pre-existing social relations and connections between those regions (e.g. in terms of shared traditions of megalithic architecture: cf. Sheridan 2004, 32–3), rather than the fundamental character of social interaction or any inherently 'insular' property of the Grooved Ware 'complex'. Issues of reception and the basic character of socio-ritual practices may be more significant than the frequency of interactions when seeking to understand the apparent 'insularity' of Late Neolithic Britain and Ireland.

Continental Europe
Along the Continental Atlantic façade, several local archaeological cultures (e.g. Artenac, Gord, Deûle-Escaut) are defined on the basis of numerous traits, especially pottery typology, but, at the same time, appear to be directly connected. Intensive and long distance contacts are attested by the distribution and use of Grand-Pressigny daggers. These impressive long flint blades were produced by skillful knappers in the French Touraine (Pélegrin 2002), although unfortunately little is known about the acquisition of raw material (Villes 2007). From the Touraine, daggers were moved across the Paris basin (Mallet *et al.* 2004) and beyond to reach the Morbihan coast to the west (Ihuel 2004), the shores of the French Jura lakes to the east (Mallet 1992), and the funerary mounds of the Dutch Single Grave Culture (SGC hereafter) to the North, sometimes in impressive quantities (Drenth 1989; see below). In addition to the movement of objects, there is also good evidence for the circulation of ideas.

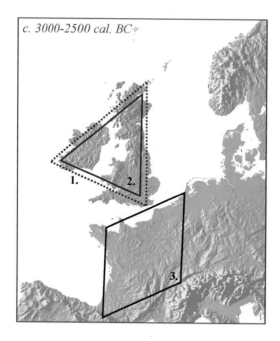

1. Grooved Ware pottery and evidence for communal feasting practices, long distance mobility and ?pilgrimages

2. Late Neolithic British & Irish architecture: including henges, hengiforms, timber circles, 'houses' and timber settings

3. Rectangular longhouse architecture

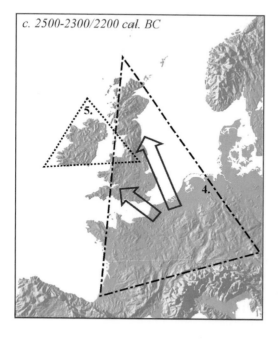

4. Bell Beaker network expands from Continental Europe

5. Ireland adopts Bell Beaker traits but not full 'package' of funerary rites

Figure 7.1. The changing cultural geography of north-west Europe, c.3,000–1,500 cal BC. Solid line: architecture; dashed line: material culture; dash-dot line: funerary practices.

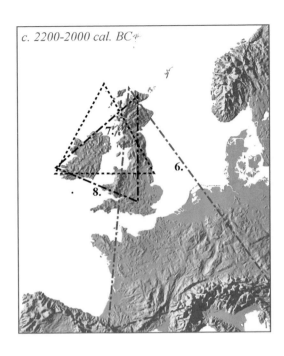

c. 2200-2000 cal. BC

6. *Fragmentation of the Bell Beaker network as local emphases come to the fore in various regions of Britain and North West Europe*

7. *Food Vessel funerary practices and other non-Beaker traditions (e.g. riveted daggers, jet ornament etc.).*

8. *Dominance of copper sources from SW Ireland*

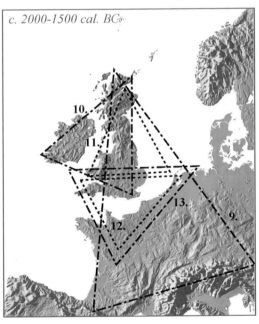

c. 2000-1500 cal. BC

9. *Increased importance of cremation burial as burial mode (Not associated with a pan-European package of practices and material culture)*

10. *Collared/Cordoned Urn use across Britain and Ireland*

11. *Welsh copper sources become more significant*

12. *Continental sources of copper supply southern England*

13. *Continental (cross-channel) two way exchange of material culture associated with funerary rites (e.g. precious cups and Armorican-Wessex relations)*

During the late 4th and early 3rd millennia cal BC, long rectangular buildings were erected in a vast area stretching from the Dordogne to the south and Flanders and Champagne to the north (Figure 7.1, No. 3; see also Vander Linden 2012). It is notable that, beyond their general rectangular appearance, each region presents its own coherent architectural tradition (e.g. Joseph *et al.* 2011; Laporte and Tivénez 2004).

North of the Rhine-Meuse estuary, the SGC corresponds to the western-most extension of the Corded Ware Complex (Drenth 2005). Its defining characteristic is, as its name suggests, the setting of single graves under round barrows, a novel feature in a north-western European context. Innovations also included the posture of the body and the character of the grave goods, with strict rules based around gender (Vander Linden 2003). The boundary between the SGC and the Continental Atlantic façade was far from impermeable as, in many cases, the weapon placed next to the dead was an imported Grand-Pressigny flint dagger (Drenth 1989).

While objects and ideas were moved and exchanged by communities across the near Continent, Britain and the Irish Sea, the archaeological record for the early 3rd millenium cal BC presents little evidence for cross-Channel contacts. Assessments of socio-cultural interaction should, therefore, not be predicated solely on cross-Channel/North Sea relations alone. This brief overview has also demonstrated the variation inherent in the available evidence. However, can we really hope to compare periods or regions dominated by evidence for monument construction with those in which artefacts are more useful without mismatching the evidence for social and ritual life at a very basic level? This issue is taken up in greater detail below. It is difficult to believe that the Channel was entirely devoid of seaborne traffic for several centuries. Rather, cross-Channel contacts were probably either minimal and/or of a character that does not lend itself to being preserved in the archaeological record. The latter may be more likely – and less of a case of special pleading – than has previously been realised, especially when we consider the rarity of certain categories of evidence (e.g. funerary contexts) during the Late Neolithic in Britain, Ireland and parts of the near Continent.

c. 2,500–2,300/2,200 cal BC: New networks and complex relations

The quantity and quality of connections between Britain, Ireland and the near Continent changed dramatically after 2,500 cal BC in association with the BBP (Figure 7.1, No. 4). As seminally argued by Abercromby (1902; 1912), the first clue to the re-opening of the interaction across the Channel lies in pottery typology and especially the eponymous Bell Beaker.

The BBP in Britain and Ireland sees dramatic changes in terms of trade and exchange networks and funerary practices. Metal was brought into Southern England from Continental Europe ('Bell Beaker metal': Rohl and Needham 1998; Needham 2004). Further north, important connections between Britain and Ireland were forged, as the mine at Ross Island provided copper ('A metal') for artefacts such as halberds and broad butted axes (Rohl and Needham 1998; Needham 2004, illus. 19.14; Bray and Pollard 2012). This relationship reflects a north/south division in the circulation of metal and the character of Continental connections that would endure for much of the Bronze Age.

Irish gold lunulae may be an important example of early connections in the opposite direction, although their dating is debated and there are only a small number from Britain (concentrated in Cornwall) and Continental Europe (concentrated in Brittany and Normandy) (Taylor 1980; Needham 2009, 31–4, fig. 2.9). The question of whether lunulae belong to the British and Irish Chalcolithic (*c.*2,500/2,400–2,200 cal BC), or straddle both, is an important but debated point due to the paucity of datable associations (see the pre- and post-2,200 cal BC radiocarbon dates for Beakers with similar motifs: Curtis and Wilkin 2012, 239–40). George Eogan (1994, 33–4) has argued that this type of neck ornament spread from Continental Europe and was later perfected by Irish goldworkers. Given the tenuous nature of the dating evidence and the concentration of examples in Ireland, it seems reasonable to question the direction of exchange and the presumption is likely to relate to the notion of *ex oriente lux* noted above.

Aside from the issues of exactly where lunulae sit in chronological terms, the connections they represent between Britain and Ireland involved a relatively restricted number of objects compared to the flow of copper alloy and ceramic influences after *c.* 2,200 cal BC (cf. Needham 2004; Bray and Pollard 2012). They could, therefore, represent an important initial period of contact associated with a developing trade and exchange of goldwork initiated by primary Beaker goldwork (cf. Needham 2011, 131–8), and during which time the inter-regional relationships that would flourish in the following centuries were established. Alternatively, their rarity may indicate the existence of a different, special relationship between particular regions of Britain and Ireland. Indeed, the relationship between Cornish and Irish lunulae is particularly noteworthy given the possible importance of Cornish sources of tin in the production of bronze after *c.* 2,200 cal BC. Even when our chronological resolution is problematic, differences in the quantity and character of metalwork may reflect very different kinds of socio-cultural relations, a point that can easily be overlooked in purely typological discussions.

Lunulae are remarkable not just because of their distinct form and decoration, but also because of the unusual use of Beaker design motifs (cf. Taylor 1970). The application of these motifs to objects that are rarely found in funerary contexts rather than ceramics closely associated with the dead reflects the wider, novel and productive attitude of Irish communities towards BBP practices. Neil Carlin (2012) has recently demonstrated that the character of Beaker deposition in Ireland differed from its outset from Britain and Continental Europe: deposits have been found at monuments, in scatters and pits rather than in 'traditional' Beaker funerary contexts (Figure 7.1, No. 5; cf. Carlin 2011; Brück and Carlin 2012). Innovation in funerary practices occurs, but is expressed in other terms with the development of a new type of megalithic construction, the wedge-tomb (O'Brien 2012). However, it is possible that Beakers were deposited in similar ways in at least some regions of Britain, notably as secondary deposits at Neolithic chambered tombs across northern and western Scotland (Wilkin in prep; cf. Bradley 2000; Sharples 2009). Indeed, the vast majority of the Beaker burials from northern Britain have been recovered from the east coast, with the North Sea playing a central role in connecting these regions to one another (cf. A. Shepherd 2012) and to Continental Europe (see below). To better appreciate Irish-British relations it is, therefore, important to appreciate the relationship between systems of interaction within the Irish Sea and the North Sea/Channel Zones.

In typical culture-historical fashion, David Clarke (1970) sought the sources of typological variation in putative geographical origins of Beaker types; his evocative terminology, embodying cross-Channel connections. The validity of Clarke's scheme was soon challenged by the Dutch scholars Jan Lanting and Johannes van der Waals (1972) who argued for an internal (regional) development of British Beakers following an initial period of introduction based on their work on the Dutch Beaker sequence. Both the regional emphasis and the central tenet of an exogenous origin followed by a local development still largely hold relevant today (e.g. I. Shepherd 1986; Needham 2005; Curtis and Wilkin 2012; A. Shepherd 2012), even if the typo-chronological dimension of their scheme has only been broadly demonstrated (with Steps 3–6 often difficult to untangle) (cf. Kinnes *et al.* 1991; Needham 2005; Sheridan 2007). A new body of work demonstrates that local types of Beakers (traditionally held to have late start dates) start being produced at a relatively early in the overall chronology of Beaker use in Britain (Curtis and Wilkin 2012; Healy 2012; Parker Pearson *et al.* in prep.).

It is noticeable that Continental Bell Beaker sequences present a similar pattern to the one outlined for Britain. For the Netherlands, several competing typological schemes exist, but all agree as to highlight the continuity from the SGC to the BBP and beyond, during the Early Bronze Age (e.g. Lanting and van der Waals 1976; Drenth and Hogestijn 2001; Lanting 2007/8; see review in Beckerman 2011/2). A recent assessment of typological and radiocarbon record by Beckerman confirms the validity of this overall scheme (Beckerman 2011/2), with the SGC lasting from the 28th until the 25th centuries cal BC, whilst the BBP occurs between the 26th century cal BC and the turn of the 3rd millennium cal BC. As for Britain, both AOO and maritime (i.e. the supposedly early styles) stand early in the sequence, as does the local Veluwe style whose earlier occurrences date to the 25th century cal BC. Likewise, in the Paris basin, typological and radiocarbon analysis indicate an early BB phase between 2,550 and 2,450 cal BC, dominated by AOO ceramic production, quickly followed by a second, longer phase between 2,450 and 2,150 cal BC, characterised by the development of local production and the incorporation of various external influences (Salanova 2011; Salanova *et al.* 2011). All across north-west Europe, ceramic typology tells the same story of introduction of new ceramic style in the local repertoires, leading to a rapid, if not immediate, appropriation by local potters.

The same largely holds for Beaker stone bracers, which are intricately associated with Europe-wide Bell Beaker funerary practices. Direct imports from the Continent cannot be ruled out, as for the case of the 'Amesbury Archer', and other early examples (Woodward and Hunter 2011, 110–15). However, locally sourced raw materials were clearly important, most notably Langdale (Group VI) greenstone, a type of rock used to make widely traded and prized axes during the Neolithic (Bradley and Edmonds 1993). Indeed, as Woodward and Hunter (2011) have demonstrated, the vast majority of bracers were manufactured in specific local raw materials, seemingly from a relatively early date (Woodward 2011, table 7.1), the Continental influence was thus rendered in material that had a long running local significance. More than mere imported commodities, bracers were instrumental for communities across Britain, as testified by the range of technical skills invested in their production.

Whilst copper metallurgy had been practiced for several centuries in several parts of western Europe prior to the development of the BBP, the situation markedly differs in Britain and Ireland. Indeed, the introduction of copper metallurgy was closely associated with the BBP. For most of the second half of the 3rd millennium cal BC, all copper in use in Britain and Ireland had been extracted and processed in a single place, the site of Ross Island in south-west Ireland (O'Brien 2004). Yet, as noted in above, the adoption of the BBP in Ireland was extremely distinctive and selective. This suggests that despite the existence of visible 'economic' contacts (i.e. a thriving trade in metal: Needham 2004), the key elements of the cultural contact and shared ritual practice cannot be seen (cf. the Grooved Ware tradition of the Late Neolithic: Sheridan 2004).

The BBP is also linked to a major change in funerary practices, with the normative nature of single graves, characterised by gender-based rules regarding the deposition of the bodies in the graves and the selection of grave goods (e.g. the complementary opposition in the body posture of male and female burials and patterns of grave good association), all practices which find their direct counterpart across north-western and central Europe (Vander Linden 2003). BBP graves were often placed under barrows, a continuation of a common feature of SGC phase burials in Continental Europe (Bourgeois 2013). There is however much regional variation; in the Netherlands for instance, SGC barrows were often distributed in lines stretching across the landscape, a pattern rarely encountered during the BBP (Bourgeois 2013). The funerary Bell Beaker corpus for northern and central France remains limited. However, the extensive re-use of megalithic monuments has been documented for a long time (Brittany: L'Helgouach 2001; Paris basin: Salanova 2004; southern Belgium: Cauwe *et al.* 2001), and recent development-led work has widened the range of mortuary practices, especially regarding individual burials (see contributions in Salanova and Tchérémissinoff 2011). Bell Beaker barrows *per se* are absent during the BBP in northern and central France, but numerous examples point to the existence of funerary architecture. At La Folie, close to Poitiers, a central grave pit was circled by a post palisade, a configuration not unlike several Dutch examples (Tchérémissinoff *et al.* 2011). The site of La Folie is radiocarbon dated to *c.* 2,400–2,200 cal BC, and indeed other examples of funerary buildings are encountered throughout the duration of the BBP in the area. For instance, at both Ciry-Salsogne – Bouche à Vesle (*c.* 2,550–2,450 cal BC: Hachem *et al.* 2011) and Gurgy – Nouzeau (*c.* 2,300–2,130 cal BC: Meunier *et al.* 2011), individual burials were associated with four corner postholes, likely part of a wooden chamber (see also site of Mondelange – La Sente: Lefebvre 2010). Two examples from Lorraine deserve particular attention. At Hatrize – Le Gond des Près (Lefebvre *et al.* 2011), excavations conducted in 2003 have revealed, along the individual burial of an adult male, a funerary chamber containing the remains of an adult male, a child and a and cremated adult. The adult and the child were buried simultaneously, while the cremation was undertaken elsewhere (cf. the absence of any charcoal). At Pouilly – ZAC Chèvre Haie (*ibid.*), amongst a total of ten Bell Beaker graves, one larger funerary chamber covered by a small cairn contained the remains of two individuals: a child buried in primary position with, by his/her side, the disconnected remains of an adult woman which were probably stored in a little wooden box. These last two examples remind us that, whilst individual primary burial dominates the record, post-depositional manipulation of human remains and multiple burials were consistent features on both sides of the Channel (e.g. the site of Niersen in the Netherlands: Bourgeois *et al.* 2009; for Britain, see Petersen 1972; Gibson 2007).

So far, we have resorted to 'classical' categories of evidence but the major, new area of development in Bell Beaker studies concerns stable isotopes. The stimulus for renewed interest in the period amongst British archaeologists was the discovery of the 'Amesbury Archer', close to Stonehenge. This is an exceptional discovery in many respects: chronologically speaking, it lies early in the sequence, and it is the most richly furnished Bell Beaker grave yet found. Furthermore, strontium isotopic signals suggest that this individual was not born on the British chalklands, but rather was a migrant from the continent, with the outskirts of the Black Forest being a possible origin point (Fitzpatrick 2011). Comparable examples seem to exist, although not backed by isotope measurements, as several sites look 'out of place' in their local environment but rather echo other areas, such as Sorisdale on Coll, in the Western Isles of Scotland (Sheridan 2008), or the aforementioned site of La Folie in Poitiers. The significance of such finds must however be set in its proper context. Indeed, there is also a growing body of data showing mobility on a smaller scale: unearthed in the close vicinity of the Amesbury archer, the multiple grave of individuals collectively known as the 'Boscombe Bowmen' also comprised non-local individuals, although in this case, their origins are probably to be sought in Wales rather than on the Continent (Evans *et al.* 2006; Fitzpatrick 2011). On the other side of the Channel, the closest example of strontium studies is the Tumulus des Sables, a collective grave in the French Médoc (Boel 2011). In this case, because of the limits inherent to the Sr technique, it was only possible to identify the possible presence of non-local individuals, probably coming from a nearby region. Further away, work conducted by Price *et al.* (2004) in central Europe also identified human mobility between early childhood and death, although there was no patterning in terms either of geographical range, or of gender/age identity of the migrants. Thus discussions on Bell Beaker mobility should not be shadowed by outstanding discoveries such as the Amesbury Archer, but rather consider an element of human mobility as a necessary term in the social and cultural equation (Vander Linden 2007).

By presenting several key and intriguing ingredients spread over a wide geographical area: pots, elaborate motifs, hunting/archer 'gear' and complementary but opposing patterns of body posture, the BBP phenomenon has become one of the most frequently and hotly debated issues in prehistoric archaeology (see e.g. papers in Nicolis 2001). Part of their appeal lies in the repetition of features but also in terms of the themes that they seem to present, in terms of ritualised consumption (of alcoholic beverages?), a warrior/hunter ethos, individuality and gender relations. The simplicity and clarity of these themes may underlie both their popularity today *and* the wide geographical uptake during the BBP period. Indeed, it could be argued that the popularity of BBP studies shares some important points in common with the myriad of studies of Shakespeare's plays and sonnets. Jonathon Bate (1998, 34–64) has noted that Shakespeare's sonnets have an 'extraordinary capacity to elicit categorical statements from their interpreters…partly because of what they leave out…[they] imply a plot without actually spelling it out…[and thus] leave interpretative space for the audience' (*ibid.*, 34). The implied narratives of the sonnets therefore have a 'cunning reticence which allows our fantasies to run riot' (*ibid.*, 43). The BBP appears to have similar characteristics, guaranteeing its pervasiveness in the past and in academic research. The notion that there should be a definitive answer to the meaning of the BBP rather misses the point: their compelling, 'cunning reticence' and 'interpretative space' is to some degree the point and the feature that allowed them to have a wide geographical spread, crossing much of north-west Europe. Such characteristics do not follow the rules of social and economic development in any simple sense but may be prerequisites of the kind of pan-European connections identified during the period 2,500–2,300/2,200 cal BC.

Are we comparing like-with-like?

Before 2,500 cal BC, we have noted the existence on the Continent and in Britain of several, distinct regional entities, within and between which objects and ideas flowed, but were not successfully transmitted across the Channel. However, the character of the evidence for ceremonial complexes in Britain during this period is also different in kind, stressing communal enterprise, and stands in stark contrast to the single grave tradition from the BBP onwards. This has created the impression that comparing the evidence for monument complexes and Beaker burials is a comparison of like-with-like. Rather, communal ceremony and highly normative burial could form part of a single, dialectic system and reflect very different dimensions of social life. One way to understand the differences is to evoke Victor Turner's (1969) notion of structure and anti-structure:

> 'The first [structure] is of society as a structured, differentiated, and often hierarchical system of politico-legal-economic positions with many types of evaluation, separating men in terms of "more" or "less". The second [anti-structure], which emerges recognizably in the liminal period, is of society as an unstructured or rudimentarily structured and relatively undifferentiated *comitus*, community, or even communion of equal individuals who submit together to the general authority of the ritual leaders.' (*ibid.*, 96)

Significantly, for Turner (*ibid.*, 97) the two were invariably related and dialectical rather than exclusive. Previous models that perceive the Late Neolithic and BBP evidence as standing in stark but related opposition (e.g. Thorpe and Richard 1984; Shennan 1986) have therefore overlooked the very different character of ceremonial and funerary practices and regional variation in the evidence (cf. Garwood 2011, 411–2). The temptation to do so is considerable and on some occasions it may be necessary. The near mutually exclusive distribution of henge monuments and Beaker heartlands in Eastern Scotland is striking (Curtis and Wilkin 2012). However, we should note that we know relatively little about funerary practices in these 'henge' zones during this period and that the refusal to adopt Beaker burial on a wide scale is not evidence for an entirely different social structure. This point is demonstrated by the probable spatial and chronological overlap of recumbent stone circles (built on a far smaller scale and with greater spatial density than large henge monuments and Late Neolithic ceremonial complexes) and early Beaker burials in north-east Scotland (Welfare 2011). Although these two strands of evidence appear to have rarely coincided (*ibid.*, 145–53), that is probably because they related to different dimensions of social and ritual life, as Turner's theory of dialectic of structure and anti-structure suggests. The key point to take is that the Late Neolithic left a variety of legacies that later communities adopted and adapted in various ways, and that the abstract notion of a 'clash' of world-views is too simplistic. A more useful question may be: why did certain communities at particular times invest varying degrees of time and energy in structured, normative actions rather than communal enterprises while others did the opposite or else struck a more balanced middle ground? The foregoing discussion suggests that social contacts and connections and the pre-conditions of social and ritual development are the largely invisible but critical elements needed to answer such questions. Once the great monuments have been built, once trade routes have been forged through an ingenious and attractive ideology, there is no turning back and socio-political change can only come from reacting to what has already been. The important point is that this does not require us to think in binary terms, but rather to think of changing emphases promoted for their novelty and agency within complex 'historical' contexts.

2,300/2,200–1,500 cal BC: Regionality and the allure of the tangible

The centuries following the expansion of the BBP present a complicated and fragmented picture across north-west Europe, despite or, as we shall argue, *because* of the particular cosmological and ideological characteristics of the BBP, and the networks of interactions that it helped to establish (Figure 7.1, No. 6). The structure of this overview follows the preceding section in considering the situation within and between Britain and Ireland before comparing it to the evidence from Continental Europe.

Britain and Ireland

The relationship between Britain and Ireland changed quite considerably around 2,200 cal BC and changed again on several occasions before 1,500 cal BC: from a situation in which funerary practices were divergent to one in which they were essentially synchronous. It was also during this period that inhumation became increasingly rare and cremation became the dominant mode of burial.

To understand the process of change, we can consider the role of both Food Vessels and the trade and exchange of copper alloy (Figure 7.1, Nos 7–8). During the first centuries of the period (*c.* 2,200/2,100–1,900 BC), there is a relatively strong connection between the Food Vessels of western Scotland and Ireland, indicated by the influence of certain decorative motifs, techniques and morphological attributes and generally weakening with distance from the Irish Sea (e.g. false relief, comb impression, and Bowl-forms: cf. Simpson 1965; Pierpoint 1980). Exploitation of Ross Island copper appears to have come to a close around 2,000/1,900 cal BC (Bray and Pollard 2012, 857), contemporary with important changes in the character of funerary practices, as cremation burial became more significant, associated with the adoption of both Collared Urns and Cordoned Urns (Figure 7.1, Nos 9–11; Longworth 1984; Waddell 1995). Although it may at first appear contradictory, it is only with the use of cinerary urns that widespread parallelism is evident in the funerary practices of Britain and Ireland. This helps to demonstrate that metal was not the sole driving force of social and cultural exchange. Funerary and ceramic practices existed in a separate sphere that may – but need not – have overlapped with other social and economic networks, and each region and period (however defined in our accounts) has to be assessed on its own merits.

In an influential recent paper, Stuart Needham (2005, 205–6) defined a 'fission horizon' from *c.* 2,200 cal BC, during which time the number of Beaker and other grave goods types available to British communities expanded considerably. This involved the introduction of non-Beaker funerary traditions not found in Continental Europe: Food Vessels, jet necklaces, and British style flint and flat bronze daggers. Seemingly implicit within the concept of the 'fission' horizon is an understanding that the primary, more European character of Beaker burials was being altered by the omission of Beaker vessels (*ibid.*, 209), and that more local influences were associated with these changes (*ibid.*, 206, Figure 13). The temptation to see these burials as 'insular' because they do not follow Continental traditions should be resisted as they could involve complex networks of trade and exchange: as noted above in relation to Irish copper and Food Vessel influences and in the case of Whitby jet spacer plate necklaces, which are distributed in distant parts of Britain, despite the source of jet lying exclusively in small coastal areas of North Yorkshire (Shepherd 1981; Sheridan and Davis 2002; Frieman 2012, 89–115).

It is tempting to link these changes to the trade and exchange of copper alloy along networks established by Beaker using communities. By weaving new social networks prior to *c.* 2,200 cal BC, the communities who formed the Beaker network unwittingly sowed the seeds of its own competition. Once Ross Island copper started to flow through these interlinked communities and regions it was probably inevitable that the ideological connections that sustained them would be undermined and that new symbols, ideas and cultural groups would emerge. For much of the Early Bronze Age, the metalwork evidence demonstrates a considerable localism: local traditions and craft specialisation are also features of grave good traditions, including jet and jet-like ornaments and small batches of high quality Food Vessels (often carrying exotic Irish and ancient Beaker attributes) (Manby 1994; Pierpoint 1980, 119–21). Perhaps while these object types and knowledge were being developed there was no need to look for continental inspiration: the ideological and technological know-how of Beaker cultural practices had been replaced by more tangible, local material resources of the copper circulation. Only after this period of British and Irish innovation had run for some centuries do we see a re-engagement with Continental practices, and then only between Southern Britain and Continental Europe, as symbolised by the 'precious cups' of the English Channel maritime region (or 'maritory') during the period *c.* 1,900–1,700 cal BC (Needham 2006; 2009). This renewed connection notably begins only after the period of considerable synchronicity between Britain and Ireland (Figure 7.1, Nos 12–13). As was the case for periods of cultural fusion during the Late Neolithic (associated with ceremonial complexes and Grooved Ware) and the pre-2,200 cal BC Beaker networks change was highly likely in the face of social and political change through time.

In reviewing the evidence for the connections traditionally held to have existed between the south coast of England, Wessex and the near Continent during the period 2,000–1,700 cal BC (e.g. Piggott 1938), Needham (2000; 2006; 2009) has demonstrated that, although links were increasing during this period, they were still relatively limited (Needham 2006, 75; 2009, fig. 2.8). Furthermore, he has raised the significance of cosmological – rather than purely economic – motivations for the acquisition of materials and objects from the Continent. In the case of the 'precious cups' of *c.* 1,900–1,550 cal BC, Needham suggests they functioned as a '*specific* mechanism' (2006, 81, original emphasis) within the evidence for cross-Channel trade and exchange. Likewise, the connections evident in Wessex graves relate to a very specific connection between that region and Armorica (Needham 2000).

The specificity and cosmological readings of these connections are significant as they suggest that not all the evidence can be grouped together, and, rather, that different motivations, related to chronology and regionality were important. The reduction in the scale and change in the character of these relations (vis-à-vis the BBP) is notable. After the widespread and relatively normative character of the BBP across north-west Europe, material connections became more varied and complex. For instance, in describing the Wessex-Armorican connections, Needham (*ibid.*, 184) notes the 'lack of conformity' and the existence of a 'medley of old traditions and new concepts'. This observation is significant in terms of the successful spread of beliefs and practices at a pan-European scale, a point we return to below.

Continental Europe
As in Britain, several cracks also appear in the relative uniformity of the BBP on the Continent by 2,300/2,200 cal BC. Diversity is noticeable in various traits, especially ceramics, with increasingly regional Beaker styles (e.g. Barbed Wire style in the Netherlands: Beckerman 2011/2), as well as other Early Bronze Age ceramic traditions which owe little to Beaker typology (e.g. Groupe des Urnes à décor plastique in northern and central France: Salanova *et al.* 2011).

In terms of funerary practices, the stage largely remains set according to the options laid down during the preceding centuries. Barrows are a defining feature of the landscape in the North Sea basin, with various concentrations scattered from the Somme valley to Jutland. When reviewed in detail, the picture is one of considerable variation. In the Netherlands, scarcely any barrows were built during the local Early Bronze Age (2,000–1,800 cal BC), but this was followed by a busy period of construction during the earlier stages of the Middle Bronze Age ('MBA A' in the Dutch sequence) from 1,800 until *c.* 1,500 cal BC. Parallel to this fluctuating intensity, the relationship between barrows and the surrounding landscape also underwent various changes (Bourgeois 2013). Immediately south in the Belgian Flanders, hundreds of ring-ditches have been recognised through systematic aerial photographic recording run by the University of Ghent (e.g. De Reu *et al.* 2011; De Reu and Bourgeois 2013). In the Netherlands, barrow construction reaches its peak between *c.* 1,700–1,400 cal BC, then comes to an abrupt end, although older monuments were still re-used (De Reu and Bourgeois 2013). A general preference for placing barrows in topographic elevations is noticeable (De Reu *et al.* 2011), but the high rate of destruction because of erosion and ploughing, and the low proportion of excavated sites prevent any further in-depth assessment of potential chronological trends. Barrow groups are also known along the French Channel coast (e.g. Toron 2006) and further south along the Atlantic façade. Barrows and flat graves are both recorded in the Paris basin, possibly in association (e.g. site of Marolles-sur-Seine – La Croix de la Mission: Peake and Delattre 2005). Further east in Lorraine, from 2,200 cal BC onwards, small cemeteries of flat graves organised in rows become the norm, and clear gender-based rules regarding body posture were still relevant (Lefebvre 2010). Similar spatial arrangements of graves occur in the Rhine valley in Alsace (e.g. sites of Rixheim – ZAC du Petit Prince and of Eckbolsheim – Zénith), although at a slightly later date as evidence for the earliest phase of the Early Bronze Age is currently absent in this area, reflecting the past reality of biases in preservation and discovery (Denaire and Croutsch 2010; Jeunesse and Denaire 2010). The concurrence of row-arranged cemeteries, strict gender-based rules and specific ceramic types (see Salanova 2011) all point to close links with central Europe.

As in Britain and Ireland, a gradual but steady shift from inhumation to cremation can also be observed through the course of the Early Bronze Age in several areas of Continental north-west Europe. In the Netherlands, as well as in northern Belgium, cremation already occurs during the BBP. Its practice has been suspected for a long time on the site of Kruishoutem (De Laet and Rogge 1972), and several examples have recently been directly dated by radiocarbon to the BBP – and in once case to the SGC – in the Netherlands (Beckerman 2011/2). Cremation burials are widely encountered across several regions of France during the Late Neolithic, including the Paris basin (Gatto 2007), but, after the dominance of inhumation associated with the BBP, it is only in the course of the Early and Middle Bronze Age that cremations appear more regularly in the archaeological record. In several instances, cremations and inhumations co-exist on the same site, as in Fresnes-lès-Montauban – Motel (Desfossés and Masson 1992), and Coquelles – RN1 (Bostyn *et al.* 1992), both located in Nord-Pas-de-Calais, or in Saint-Martin-de-Fontenay – La Grande Chasse, Normandy (Germain-Vallée, 2005).

As metal was flowing in various quantities and over various distances across north-west Europe, a certain element of human mobility must have occurred at the turn of the 3rd and 2nd millennium cal BC. It is however unclear whether or not this mobility corresponded to short trading trips, or led to lifelong relocation of individuals. The latter possibility has been suggested for a long time on the basis of similarities in the archaeological record between distinct regions of Europe such as Wessex, Brittany and southern Germany. Yet, the only isotopic study of mobility available for the period indicates a very low, if not complete absence, of such relocation. A recent multi-isotopic (Sr, O, C, N) analysis of the Early Bronze Age cemetery of Singen in South-West Germany did not produce evidence for migration, including from the remains of a man buried with a dagger of Atlantic type. As far as the precisions of the method allow, it appears that all the sampled individuals were born within a 25km radius of the cemetery where they were eventually buried (Oelze *et al.* 2012).

When compared to the previous period, two elements are quite striking: whilst the movement of goods increases during the Early Bronze Age, the cultural map conversely becomes more fragmented. There seems to be an element of dissociation here between both facets of the archaeological record and, in general, it appears as if the extreme level of interaction and normative ritual practices that characterised the BBP is not sustained. Quite the contrary, each region, whilst aware of and clearly in contact with its neighbours, follows its own particular direction. Although at first sight these points appear contradictory, the divergent trajectories stem from shared BBP backgrounds, thus giving the general impression of similarity resulting less from horizontal transmission through space than from vertical transmission through time.

Faced with the task of upholding the normative character of Beaker burial practices, we instead appear to see different communities addressing the question of how best to move forward using the ideas they inherited in the context of changing social and economic networks. It is tempting to see this as a shift from a European 'union' sustained by ideas and beliefs associated with the BBP to a different world in which more tangible and 'real' material were flowing. By its success the BBP altered networks of trade and exchange and the fragmentation of that very network can in fact be better understood as the product of that success.

Conclusions

This paper has presented some of the key changing spatial patterning of the archaeological record on either side of the Channel/North Sea from the mid-3rd millennium cal BC to the mid-2nd millennium cal BC and sought to understand some of the reasons why these changes occurred.

Prior to 2,500 cal BC in Britain and Ireland, the Grooved Ware/ceremonial monument complexes involved feasting, communal efforts of construction and ceremonies which did not spread to the Continent, perhaps because of the structure (or, rather, communal 'anti-structure') of the social and ritual practices involved. This does not necessarily reflect the entire tapestry of the social and political life of the period and is therefore not necessarily entirely at odds with what followed or from Continental practices (*pace* Thorpe and Richards 1984), rather it appears to have reflected the dominant beliefs and mode of socialising captured by the archaeological record for this period in time. Relatively long distance movement and sea voyages were involved, but typically between communities who already had connections in the cumbersome form of architectural traditions in stone and wood (cf. Sheridan 2004; Bradley 2013), reflecting practices that could not be moved so quickly as those that underpinned the BBP.

Along the Continental Atlantic façade, several local cultural groups were noted, but it was also noted that there was a widespread trade and exchange of Grand-Pressigny flint daggers that linked these groups. The overlap highlights the importance of recognising complexity and context in interactions (Vander Linden 2012; cf. Bradley 2013, 12). North of the Rhine-Meuse the single grave culture was dominant at this period but Grand-Pressigny daggers also found their way into these territories and were incorporated within funerary practices. There are, therefore, important differences between various regions but also in the kind and complexity of evidence that is available to discuss interactions.

The situation on both sides of the Channel/North Sea changes considerably in the course of two or three centuries with the introduction of the BBP: the movement of goods, ideas and people all contribute to the making and short term maintenance of an impressive and unique interaction sphere. The unusual nature of the BBP cannot be stressed enough and was arguably the result of a combination of seductive elements and alluring simplicity that could be successfully integrated within a number of pre-existing (or desired) social and ideological regimes. Indeed, in Britain and Ireland, local elements appear to have been incorporated within the BBP relatively rapidly.

The BBP was followed by a more substantial period of 'fragmentation' from 2,300/2,200 cal BC, which occurred across north-west Europe, despite a likely rise in the flow of goods at several scales. This period has often been misunderstood because of its apparently contradictory character: demonstrating evidence for increased trade/exchange but greater regional variability in burial mode and associated grave good traditions. It was argued that the misunderstanding results from the expectation that the remarkably structured and normative BBP should persist into later centuries, when in fact it is a novelty when viewed in a wider 'historical' context. Furthermore, we suggested that the links that were established during the BBP sowed the seeds of its demise by forging a new set of relations and more tangible connections that could then be pursued in funerary practices and other spheres of life (e.g. metalworking and craft specialisation).

The overall impression – with the notable exception of a remarkable century or two at the start of the BBP – is that each region flowed along its own path: neither the Channel nor Atlantic supported the notion of an isolated *or* open-ended period or episode of cultural interaction. Indeed, the entire system of relationships between types of evidence (monuments, burials, metalwork) and networks or interaction can be seen to be related, with one informing the other. The complicating factor is that the visibilities of dimensions of the evidence are frequently low or entirely absent. This situation is inevitable given the nature of prehistoric archaeology and the potential for variation in depositional practices. It is also preferable to the foregoing alternative of assuming that the archaeological record reflects an accurate representation of cross-Channel/North Sea relations through time without reference to the relationship between contacts and the ritual and depositional practices through which they actually became inscribed in the archaeological evidence.

Acknowledgements

We would like to thank the conference organisers, Hugo Anderson-Whymark, Duncan Garrow and Fraser Sturt for inviting one of us (MVL) to speak at the original conference from which this volume stems, and for their patience in waiting for the manuscript. The argument presented here greatly benefited from discussions with several colleagues and friends, namely Jody Joy; Ben Roberts; Neil Carlin and Paul Garwood. As always, we remain the only ones to blame for any factual mistakes and interpretations to be found in the contents of this contribution.

References

Abercromby, J. 1902. The oldest Bronze Age ceramic type in Britain, its close analogies on the Rhine, its probable origin in central Europe. *Journal of the Royal Anthropological Institute* 32, 373–397.

Abercromby, J. 1912. *A Study of the Bronze Age Pottery of Great Britain and its associated Grave Goods*. Oxford: Clarendon Press.

Bate, J. 1998. *The Genius of Shakespeare*. London: Picador.

Beckerman, S. 2011/2. Dutch Beaker chronology re-examined. *Palaeohistoria* 53–4, 25–64.

Boel, C. 2011. *Identifying Migration: strontium isotope studies on an Early Bell Beaker population from le Tumulus des Sables, France*. Unpublished Thesis, Australian National University.

Bourgeois, J. and Talon, M. 2009. From Picardy to Flanders: Transmanche connections in the Bronze Age. In P. Clark (ed.), *Bronze Age connections. Cultural contacts in Prehistoric Europe*, 38–59. Oxford: Oxbow Books.

Bourgeois, Q. 2013. *Monuments on the Horizon. The Formation of Barrow Landscape Throughout the 3rd and 2nd Millennium BC*. Leiden: Sidestone Press.

Bourgeois, Q., Amkretuz, L. and Panhuysen, R. 2009. The Niersen beaker burial: a renewed study of a century-old excavation. *Journal of Archaeology of the Low Countries* 1 (2), 83–105.

Bostyn, F., Blancquaert, G. and Lanchon, Y. 1992. Les enclos funéraires de l'Âge du Bronze de Coquelles « RN 1 » (Pas-de-Calais). *Bulletin de la Société Préhistorique Française* 89, 413–28.

Bradley, R. 2000. *The Good Stones: A New Investigation of the Clava Cairns*. Edinburgh: Society of Antiquaries of Scotland.

Bradley, R. 2005. *Ritual and Domestic Life in Prehistoric Europe*. London: Routledge.

Bradley, R. 2013. Houses of Commons, Houses of Lords: domestic dwellings and monumental architecture in prehistoric Europe. *Proceedings of the Prehistoric Society* 79, 1–17.

Bradley, R. J. and Edmonds, M. 1993. *Interpreting the Axe Trade: production and exchange in Neolithic Britain*. Cambridge: Cambridge University Press.

Bray, P. and Pollard, A. 2012. A new interpretative approach to the chemistry of copper-alloy objects: source, recycling and technology. *Antiquity* 86, 853–867.

Brun, P. 1998. Le complexe culturel atlantique: entre le cristal et la fumée. *Trabalhos de Arqueologia* 10, 40–51.

Butler, J. 1963. Bronze Age connections across the North Sea: a study in prehistoric trade and industrial relations between the British Isles, the Netherlands, North Germany and Scandinavia, c. 1700–700 B.C. *Palaeohistoria* 9.

Carlin, N. 2011. Into the west: placing Beakers within their Irish contexts. In A. M. Jones, and G. Kirkham (eds), *Beyond the Core: Reflections on Regionality in Prehistory*, 87–100. Oxford: Oxbow Books.

Carlin, N. 2012. *A Proper Place for Everything: The Character and Context of Beaker Depositional Practice in Ireland*. Unpublished PhD thesis, University College Dublin.

Carlin, N. and Brück, J. 2012. Searching the Chalcolithic: continuity and change in the Irish Final Neolithic/Early Bronze Age. In M. Allen, J. Gardiner and A. Sheridan (eds), *Is there a British Chalcolithic? People,Place and Polity in the Later 3rd Millennium*, 193–201. Oxford: Oxbow Books/Prehistoric Society Research Papers.

Cauwe, N., Vander Linden, M. and Vanmontfort, B. 2001. The Middle and Late Neolithic. *Anthropologica et Praehistorica* 112, 77–89.

Childe, V. G. 1957. *The Dawn of European Civilization.* St. Albans: Paladin.

Clark, P. (ed.). 2004. *The Dover Bronze Age Boat in Context: society and water transport in prehistoric Europe.* Oxford: Oxbow.

Clark, P. (ed.) 2009. *Bronze Age Connections: cultural contact in prehistoric Europe.* Oxford: Oxbow.

Clarke D. 1970. *Beaker Pottery of Great Britain and Ireland.* Cambridge: Cambridge University Press.

Cleal, R. and MacSween, A. (eds). 1999. *Grooved Ware in Britain and Ireland.* Oxford: Oxbow.

Cunliffe, B. 2009. Looking forward: maritime contacts in the first millennium BC. In P. Clark (ed.), *Bronze Age Connections: cultural contact in prehistoric Europe*, 80–93.Oxford: Oxbow Books.

Curtis, N. and Wilkin, N. 2012. The regionality of Beakers and bodies in the Chalcolithic of North-East Scotland. In M. Allen, J. Gardiner and A. Sheridan (eds), *Is there a British Chalcolithic? People, Place and Polity in the Later 3rd Millennium*, 237–56. Oxford: Oxbow Books/ Prehistoric Society Research Papers.

De Laet, S. and Rogge, M. 1972. Une tombe à incinération de la civilisation aux gobelets campaniformes trouvée à Kruishoutem (Flandre orientale). *Helinium* 12, 209–224.

Denaire, A. and Croutsch, C. 2010. Du Campaniforme à la fin du Bronze ancien en Alsace: essai de synthèse chronologique. In C. Jeunesse and A. Denaire (eds). *Du Néolithique final au Bronze Ancien dans le Nord-Est de la France. Actualité de la recherche.* 165–186. Zimmersheim: Association pour la Promotion de la Recherche Archéologique en Alsace.

De Reu, J., Bourgeois, J., De Smedt, P., Zwertvaegher, A., Antrop, M., Bats, M., De Maeyer, P., Finke, P., Van Meirvenne, M., Verniers, J. and Crombé, P. 2011. Measuring the relative topographic position of archaeological sites in the landscape, a case study on the Bronze Age barrows in northwest Belgium. *Journal of Archaeological Science* 38, 3435–3446.

De Reu, J. and Bourgeois, J. 2013. Bronze age barrow research in sandy Flanders (NW Belgium): an overview. In D. Fontijn, A.J. Louwen, S. van der Waart and K. Wentink (eds), *Beyond Barrows. Current Research on the Structuration and Perception of the Prehistoric Landscape through Monuments*, 155–193. Leiden: Sidestone Press.

Desfossés, Y. and Masson, B. 1992. Les enclos funéraires du « Motel » à Fresnes-lès-Montauban (Pas-de-Calais). *Bulletin de la Société Préhistorique Française* 89, 303–42.

Drenth, E. 1989. Een onderzoek naar aspecten van de symbolische betekenis van Grand-Pressigny en Pseudo-Grand-Pressigny dolken van de Enkelgrafcultuur in Nederland. In A. Niklewicz-Hokse and C. Lagerwerf (eds), *Bundel van de Steentijddag (Groningen, 1 April 1989)*, 100–121. Groningen: Biologisch-Archaeologisch Instituut.

Drenth, E. 2005. Het Laat-Neolithicum in Nederland. In J. Deeben, E. Drenth, M.-F. van Oorsouw and L. Verhart (eds), *De Steentijd van Nederland. Archeologie* 11/12, 333–365.

Drenth, E. and Hogestijn, W. 2001. The Bell Beaker culture in the Netherlands: the state of research in 1998. In F. Nicolis (ed.), *Bell Beakers today. Pottery, people, culture, symbols in prehistoric Europe. Proceedings of the International Colloquium, Riva del Garda (Trento, Italy), 11–16 May 1998*, 309–332. Trento: Ufficio Beni Archeologici.

Eogan, G. 1994. *The Accomplished Art: Gold and Gold-working in Britain and Ireland during the Bronze Age.* Oxford: Oxbow.

Evans, J., Chenery, C. and Fitzpatrick, A. 2006. Bronze age childhood migration of individuals near Stonehenge, revealed by strontium and oxygen isotope tooth enamel analysis. *Archaeometry* 48(2), 309–321.

Fitzpatrick, A. 2011. *The Amesbury Archer and the Boscombe Bowmen. Early Bell Beaker Burials at Boscombe Down, Wiltshire, Great Britain.* Salisbury: Wessex Archaeology.

Frieman, C. 2012. *Innovation and Imitation: Stone Skeuomorphs of Metal from 4th–2nd Millennia BC Northwest Europe*. Oxford: British Archaeological Report S2365. Oxford: Archaeopress.

Garwood, P. 2011. Making the dead. In G. Hey, P. Garwood, M. Robinson, A. Barclay and P. Bradley (eds), *The Thames Through Time: volume 1, section 2; earlier prehistory*, 383–432. Oxford: Oxford Archaeology.

Gatto, E. 2007. La crémation parmi les pratiques funéraires du Néolithique récent-final en France Méthodes d'étude et analyse de sites. *Bulletins et mémoires de la Société d'Anthropologie de Paris* 19 (3–4). Available online at http://bmsap.revues.org/5013.

Germain-Vallée, C. 2005. RD 562. Saint-Martin-de-Fontenay. La Grande Chasse. *Bilan Scientifique Régional Basse-Normandie* 2004, 57–59.

Gibson, A. 2007. A Beaker veneer? Some evidence from the burial record. In M. Larsson and M. Parker Pearson (eds), *From Stonehenge to the Baltic. Living with Cultural Diversity in the Third Millennium BC*, 47–64. Oxford: British Archaeological Report S1692. Oxford: Archaeopress.

Hachem, L., Allard, P., Convertini, F., Robert, B., Salanova, L., Sidéra, I. and Thevenet, C. 2011. La sépulture campaniforme de Ciry-Salsogne « la Bouche à Vesle » (Aisne), France. In L. Salanova and Y. Tchérémissinoff (dir.) *Les sépultures individuelles campaniformes en France, XLIe supp. Gallia Préhistoire*, 21–35. Paris: CNRS.

Harding, J. 2000. Later Neolithic ceremonial centres, ritual, and pilgrimage: the monument complex of Thornborough, North Yorkshire. In A. Ritchie (ed.), *Neolithic Orkney in its European Context*, 31–46. Cambridge: McDonald Institute for Archaeological Research.

Harding, J. 2012. Henges, rivers and exchange in Neolithic Yorkshire. In A. Jones, J. Pollard, M. Allen and J. Gardiner (eds), *Image, Memory and Monumentality. Archaeological Engagements with the Material World: a Celebration of the Academic Achievements of Professor Richard Bradley*, 43–51. Oxford: Oxbow Books/Prehistoric Society Research Papers.

Healy, F. 2012. Chronology, corpses, ceramics, copper, and lithics. In M. Allen, J. Gardiner and A. Sheridan (eds), *Is there a British Chalcolithic? People, Place and Polity in the Later 3rd Millennium*, 144–163. Oxford: Oxbow Books/Prehistoric Society Research Papers.

Ihuel, E. 2004. *La diffusion du silex du Grand-Pressigny dans le massif armoricain au Néolithique. Supplément n° 2 au Bulletin de l'Association des Amis du Musée du Grand-Pressigny*. Paris: C.T.H.S.

Jeunesse, C. and Denaire, A. (eds). 2010. *Du Néolithique final au Bronze Ancien dans le Nord-Est de la France. Actualité de la recherche*. Zimmersheim: Association pour la Promotion de la Recherche Archéologique en Alsace.

Jones, S. 1997. *The Archaeology of Ethnicity. Constructing identities in the past and present*. London: Routledge.

Joseph, F., Julien, M., Leroy-Langevin, E., Lorin, Y. and Praud, I. 2011. L'architecture domestique des sites du IIIe millénaire avant notre ère dans le Nord de la France. In F. Bostyn, E. Martial, and I. Praud (eds), *Le Néolithique du Nord de la France dans son contexte européen: habitat et économie aux 4e et 3e millénaires avant notre ère. Actes du 29e colloque interrégional sur le Néolithique, Villeneuve-d'Ascq 2–3 octobre 2009. Revue archéologique de Picardie* 28, 249–273.

Kinnes, I., Gibson, A., Boast, R., Ambers, J., Leese, M. and Bowman, S. 1991. Radiocarbon dating and British Beakers. *Scottish Archaeological Review* 8, 35–68.

Lanting, J. 2007/08. De NO-Nederlandse/NW-Duitse Klokbeker-groep: culturele achtergrond, typologie van het aardewerk, datering, verspreiding en grafritueel. *Palaeohistoria* 49/50, 11–236.

Lanting, J. and van der Waals, J.D. 1972. British Beakers as seen from the Continent: a review article. *Helinium* 12, 20–46.

Lanting, J. and van der Waals, J. 1976. Beaker culture relations in the Lower Rhine basin. In J. Lanting and J. van der Waals (eds), *Glockenbecher Symposion. Oberried 1974*, 2–80. Haarlem, Fibula-Van Dishoeck.

Laporte, L. and Tinevez, J.-Y. 2004. Neolithic houses and chambered tombs of western France. *Cambridge Archaeological Journal* 14(2), 217–234.

Lefebvre, A. 2010. Les sépultures du Néolithique final / Bronze ancien en Lorraine: vers l'émergence de nouvelles problématiques. In C. Jeunesse and A. Denaire, A. (dirs), *Du Néolithique final au Bronze Ancien dans le Nord-Est de la France. Actualité de la recherche*, 103–118. Zimmersheim, Association pour la Promotion de la Recherche Archéologique en Alsace.

Lefebvre, A., Franck, J. and Veber, C. 2011. Les sépultures individuelles en Lorraine: l'exemple de Pouilly (Moselle) et d'Hatrize (Meurthe-et-Moselle). In L. Salanova and Y. Tchérémissinoff (dir.), *Les sépultures individuelles campaniformes en France. XLIe supp. Gallia Préhistoire*, 97–113. Paris: CNRS.

Lehoerff, A. (ed.) 2012. *Beyond the Horizon: Societies of the Channel and North Sea 3,500 Years Ago*. Paris: Somogy Editions d'Art.

L'Helgouach, J. 2001. Le cadre culturel du campaniforme armoricain. In F. Nicolis (ed.), *Bell Beakers Today. Pottery, people, culture, symbols in prehistoric Europe. Proceedings of the International Colloquium, Riva del Garda (Trento, Italy), 11–16 May 1998*, 289–299. Trento: Ufficio Beni Archeologici.

Longworth, I. 1984. *Collared Urns of the Bronze Age in Great Britain and Ireland*. Cambridge: Cambridge University Press.

Mallet, N. 1992. *Le Grand-Pressigny. Ses relations avec la civilisation Saône-Rhône*. Argenton-sur-Creuse, Les Amis du Musée de Préhistoire du Grand-Pressigny.

Mallet, N., Richard, G., Genty, P. and Verjux C. 2004. La diffusion des silex du Grand-Pressigny dans le Bassin parisien. *Anthropologica et Praehistorica* 115, 123–138.

Manby, T. 1994. Appendix: I Type 1 Food Vessels. *Yorkshire Archaeological Journal* 66, 48–50.

Meunier, K., Bonnardin, S., Chambon, P., Convertini, F., Renard, C. and Salanova, L. 2011. La sépulture campaniforme de Nouzeau (Gurgy, Yonne). In L. Salanova and Y. Tchérémissinoff (dir.), *Les sépultures individuelles campaniformes en France. XLIe supp. Gallia Préhistoire*, 63–77. Paris: CNRS.

Needham, S. 2000. Power pulses across a cultural divide: cosmologically driven acquisition between Armorica and Wessex. *Proceedings of the Prehistoric Society* 66, 151–207.

Needham, S. 2004. Migdale-Marnoch: sunburst of Scottish metallurgy. In I. A. G. Shepherd and G. J. Barclay (eds), *Scotland in Ancient Europe: The Neolithic and Early Bronze Age of Scotland in their European context*, 217–45. Edinburgh: Society of Antiquaries of Scotland.

Needham, S. 2005. Transforming Beaker Culture in north-west Europe; processes of fusion and fission. *Proceedings of the Prehistoric Society* 71, 171–217.

Needham, S. 2006. Networks of contact, exchange and meaning; the beginning of the Channel Bronze Age. In S. Needham, K. Parfitt and G. Varndell (eds), *The Ringlemere Cup. Precious Cups and the Beginning of the Channel Bronze Age*, 75–81. London: The British Museum Research Publication no. 163.

Needham, S. 2009. Encompassing the sea: 'maritories' and Bronze Age maritime interactions. In Clark, P. (ed.), *Bronze Age Connections. Cultural contacts in Prehistoric Europe*, 12–37. Oxford: Oxbow.

Needham, S. 2011. Basket-shaped ornaments and Primary Beaker Goldwork. In A. Fitzpatrick *The Amesbury Archer and the Boscombe Bowmen: Early Bell Beaker burials at Boscombe Down, Wiltshire, Great Britain*, 131–38. Salisbury: Wessex Archaeology.

Needham, S. 2012. Case and place for the British Chalcolithic. In M. Allen, J. Gardiner, and A. Sheridan (eds), *Is there a British Chalcolithic? People, Place and Polity in the Later 3rd Millennium*, 1–26. Oxford: Oxbow Books/Prehistoric Society Research Papers.

Nicolis, F. (ed.) 2001. *Bell Beakers Today: pottery, people, culture, symbols in prehistoric Europe*. Trento: Officio Beni Archeologici.

Moore, T. and Armada, X-L. (eds) 2011. *Atlantic Europe in the First Millennium BC: Crossing the divide*. Oxford: Oxford University Press.

O'Brien, W. 2004. *Ross Island: mining, metal and society in early Ireland. Bronze Age Studies 6*. Galway: National University of Ireland.

O'Brien, W. 2012. The Chalcolithic in Ireland: a chronological and cultural framework. In M. Allen, J. Gardiner and A. Sheridan (eds) *Is there a British Chalcolithic? People, Place and Polity in the Later 3rd Millennium*, 211–25. Oxford: Oxbow Books/Prehistoric Society Research Papers.

O'Connor, B. 1980. *Cross Channel Relations in the Later Bronze Age*. Oxford: British Archaeological Report S91. Oxford: British Archaeological Reports.

Oelze, V. M., Nehlich, O. and Richards, M. P. 2012. There's no place like home – No isotopic evidence for mobility at the Early Bronze Age cemetery of Singen, Germany. *Archaeometry* 54(4), 752–778.

Parker Pearson, M. and Ramilisonina 1998. Stonehenge for the ancestors: the stones pass on the message. *Antiquity* 72, 308–26.

Parker Pearson, M., Richards, M., Chamberlain, A. and Jay, M. (eds) in prep. *The Beaker People: isotopes, mobility and diet in prehistoric Britain*. Oxford: Oxbow Books/Prehistoric Society Research Papers.

Peake, R. and Delattre, V. 2005. L'apport des analyses 14 C à l'étude de la nécropole de l'âge du Bronze de" La Croix de la Mission" à Marolles-sur-Seine. *Revue archéologique du Centre de la France* 44. Available online at http://racf.revues.org/index484.html.

Pélegrin, J. 2002. La production des grandes lames de silex du Grand-Pressigny. In J. Guilaine (ed.), *Matériaux, productions, circulations, du Néolithique à l'Âge du bronze*, 125–141. Paris: Errance.

Petersen, F. 1972. Traditions of multiple burial in later Neolithic and early Bronze Age England. *Archaeological Journal* 129, 22–55.

Piggott, S. 1938. The Early Bronze Age in Wessex. *Proceedings of the Prehistoric Society* 4, 52–106.

Pierpoint, S. 1980. *Social Patterns in Yorkshire Prehistory, 3500–750 BC*. British Archaeological Report 74. Oxford: British Archaeological Reports.

Price, T. D., Knipper, C., Grupe, G. and Smrcka, V. 2004. Strontium isotopes and prehistoric human migration: the Bell Beaker period in central Europe. *European Journal of Archaeology* 7(1), 9–40.

Roberts, B. and Vander Linden, M. 2011. Introduction. In B. Roberts and M. Vander Linden (eds), *Investigating archaeological cultures. Material culture variability and transmission*, 1–21. New-York, Springer.

Roberts, B., Uckelmann, M. and Brandherm, D. 2013. Old Father Time: The Bronze Age Chronology of Western Europe. In H. Fokkens and A. Harding (eds), *The Oxford Handbook of the European Bronze Age*, 17–46. Oxford: Oxford University Press.

Rohl, B. and Needham, S. 1998. *The Circulation of Metal in the British Bronze Age: the Application of Lead Isotope Analysis*. British Museum Occasional Paper 102. London: British Museum.

Rowley-Conwy, P. and Owen, A. 2011. Grooved Ware feasting in Yorkshire: Late Neolithic animal consumption at Rudston Wold. *Oxford Journal of Archaeology* 30(4), 325–67.

Salanova L., 2004. The frontiers inside the western Bell Beaker block. In J. Czebreszuk (ed.), *Similar but Different. Bell Beakers in Europe*, 63–75. Poznań: Adam Mickiewicz University.

Salanova, L. 2011. Chronologie et facteurs d'évolution des sépultures individuelles campaniformes dans le Nord de la France. In L. Salanova and Y. Tchérémissinoff (dirs), *Les sépultures individuelles campaniformes en France. XLIe sup. Gallia Préhistoire*, 125–142. Paris: CNRS.

Salanova, L. and Tchérémissinoff, Y. (dir.). 2011. *Les sépultures individuelles campaniformes en France. XLIe sup. Gallia Préhistoire*. Paris: CNRS.

Salanova, L., Brunet, P., Cottiaux, R., Hamon, T., Langry-François, F., Martineau, R., Polloni, A., Renard, C. and Sohn, M. 2011. Du Néolithique récent à l'Age du Bronze dans le Centre Nord de la France: les étapes de l'évolution chrono-culturelle. In F. Bostyn, E. Martial and I. Praud (eds), *Le Néolithique du Nord de la France dans son contexte européen: habitat et économie aux 4e et 3e millénaires avant notre ère. Actes du 29e colloque interrégional sur le Néolitique, Villeneuve-d'Ascq 2–3 octobre 2009. Revue archéologique de Picardie* 28, 77–102.

Sharples, N. 2009. Beaker settlement in the Western Isles. In M. Allen, N. Sharples and T. O'Connor (eds.) *Land and People. Papers in Honour of John G. Evans,* 147–58. Oxford: Oxbow Books/ Prehistoric Society Research Papers.

Shennan, S. 1986. Interaction and change in the third millennium BC western and central Europe. In C. Renfrew and J. F. Cherry (eds) *Peer Polity Interaction and Socio-political Change*, 137–48. Cambridge: Cambridge University Press.

Shepherd, I. 1981. Bronze Age jet working in Northern Britain. *Scottish Archaeological Forum* 11, 43–51.

Shepherd, I. 1986. *Powerful Pots: Beakers in north-east prehistory*. Aberdeen: Anthropological Museum, University of Aberdeen.

Shepherd, A. 2012. Stepping out together: men, women and their beakers in time and space. In M. Allen, J. Gardiner and A. Sheridan (eds.) *Is there a British Chalcolithic? People, Place and Polity in the Later 3rd Millennium*, 257–80. Oxford: Oxbow Books/Prehistoric Society Research Papers.

Sheridan, A. 2004. Going round in circles? Understanding the Irish Grooved Ware 'complex' in its wider context. In H. Roche, E. Grogan, J. Bradley, J. Coles and B. Raftery (eds), *From megaliths to Metal. Essays in honour of George Eogan*, 26–37. Oxford: Oxbow Books.

Sheridan, A. 2007. Scottish Beaker dates: The good, the bad and the ugly. In M. Larsson and M. Parker Pearson (eds), *From Stonehenge to the Baltic: Living with cultural diversity in the third millennium BC*, 91–123. British Archaeological Report S1692. Oxford: Archaeopress.

Sheridan, A. 2008. Upper Largie and Dutch-Scottish connections during the Beaker period. *Analecta Praehistorica Leidensia* 40, 247–260.

Sheridan, A. and Davis, M. 2002. Investigating jet and jet-like artefacts from prehistoric Scotland: the National Museums of Scotland project. *Antiquity* 76, 812–25.

Simpson, D. 1965. Food Vessels in south-west Scotland. *Transactions of the Dumfries and Galloway Natural History and Antiquarian Society* 42, 25–50.

Taylor, J. 1970. Lunulae reconsidered. *Proceedings of the Prehistoric Society* 36, 38–81.

Taylor, J. 1980. *Bronze Age Goldwork of the British Isles*. Cambridge: Cambridge University Press.

Tcheremissinoff, Y., Convertini, F., Fouere, P. and Salanova, L. 2011. La sépulture campaniforme de La Folie (Poitiers, Vienne). In L. Salanova and Y. Tchérémissinoff (dirs), *Les sépultures individuelles campaniformes en France. XLIe sup. Gallia Préhistoire*, 11–19. Paris: CNRS.

Thomas, J. 1991. Reading the body: Beaker funerary practices in Britain. In P. Garwood, F. Jenning, R. Skeates, and J. Toms (eds), *Sacred and Profane. Proceedings of a Conference on Archaeology, Ritual and Religion, Oxford: 1989*, 33–42. Oxford: Oxford University Press.

Thorpe, I. and Richards, C. 1984. Ritual, power and ideology: a reconstruction of Earlier Neolithic rituals in Wessex. In R. Bradley and J. Gardiner (eds) *Neolithic Studies: A Review of Some Recent Research*, 67–84. British Archaeological Report 133. Oxford: British Archaeological Reports.

Toron, S. 2006. De la Picardie aux Flandres belges: une approche comparative des enclos circulaires de l'âge du Bronze ancien et moyen. *Lunula. Archaeologia Protohistorica* 14, 71–76.

Turner, V. 1969. *The Ritual Process. Structure and Anti-Structure*. Brunswick/London: Aldine.

Van de Noort, R. 2009. Exploring the ritual of travel in prehistoric Europe: the Bronze Age sewn-plank boats in context. In P. Clark (ed.), *Bronze Age Connections: cultural contact in prehistoric Europe*, 159–75. Oxford: Oxbow Books.

Vander Linden, M. 2003. Competing cosmos. On the relationship between Corded Ware and Bell-Beaker mortuary traditions. In J. Czebreszuk and M. Szmyt (eds), *The Northeast Frontier of Bell Beakers, Proceedings of the symposium held at the Adam Mickiewicz University Poznań, May 26–29 2002*, 11–19. Oxford: British Archaeological Report S1155. Oxford: Archaeopress

Vander Linden, M. 2007. What linked the Bell Beakers in the third millennium Europe? *Antiquity* 81, 343–352.

Vander Linden, M. 2012. The importance of being insular. British Isles in the context of continental north-western Europe during the 3rd millennium BC. In M. Allen, J. Gardiner and A. Sheridan (eds), *Is there a British Chalcolithic? People, Place and Polity in the Later 3rd Millennium, Prehistoric Society Research Paper No 4*, 69–82. Oxford: Oxbow Books/Prehistoric Society Research Papers.

Vander Linden, M. and Roberts, B. 2011. A Tale of two countries: contrasting archaeological culture history in British and French archaeology. In B. Roberts and M. Vander Linden (eds), *Investigating Archaeological Cultures. Material Culture, Variability, and Transmission*, 23–40. New York: Springer.

Villes, A. 2007. Où en sommes-nous des recherches au Grand-Pressigny (Indre-et-Loire)? In F. Le Brun-Ricalens, F. Valotteau and A. Hauzeur (eds), *Relations interrégionales au Néolithique entre Bassin parisien et Bassin rhénan. Actes du 26e colloque interrégional sur le Néolithique. Luxembourg, 8 et 9 novembre 2003*, 383–39. *Archeologia Mosellana* 79.

Viner, S., Evans, J., Albarella, U. and Parker Pearson, M. 2010. Cattle mobility in prehistoric Britain: strontium isotope analysis of cattle teeth from Durrington Walls (Wiltshire, Britain). *Journal of Archaeological Science* 37, 2812–2820.

Waddell, J. 1995. The Cordoned Urn tradition. In I. Kinnes and G. Varndell (eds), *Unbaked Urns of Rudely Shape: essays on British and Irish Pottery for Ian Longworth*, 113–22. Oxford: Oxbow Books.

Welfare, A. 2011. *Great Crowns of Stone. The Recumbent Stone Circles of Scotland.* Edinburgh, Royal Commission on the Ancient Historical Monuments of Scotland.

Wilkin, N. in prep. Pursuing the Penumbral: The deposition of Beaker pottery at Neolithic Monuments in Chalcolithic and Early Bronze Age Scotland.

Woodward, A. 2011. Chronology, In A. Woodward and J. Hunter (eds) *An Examination of Prehistoric Stone Bracers from Britain*, 86–95. Oxford: Oxbow Books.

Woodward, A. and Hunter, J. (eds) 2011. *An Examination of Prehistoric Stone Bracers from Britain.* Oxford: Oxbow Books.

8

Rethinking Iron Age connections across the Channel and North Sea

Leo Webley

Introduction

Britain has long had a marginal status in the study of the European Iron Age. The dominant narrative holds that the beginning of the Iron Age was marked by a sharp decline in contacts between Britain and the near Continent, with the breakdown of the long-distance networks of metal exchange that had been so important during the Bronze Age. Contacts are thought to have remained fairly limited up until the last two centuries of the pre-Roman Iron Age, when there was a resurgence of cross-Channel 'trade'. This presaged the Roman conquest which brought (southern) Britain into a new European system.

I will argue here that this narrative is misleading. The impression of limited cross-Channel contact through most of the Iron Age comes from a narrow focus on the evidence of portable material culture, and certain kinds of 'high-status' artefacts in particular. This skews our perspective towards particular kinds of interactions. When we consider a broader range of Iron Age practices, connections between the communities either side of the Channel and North Sea become more evident. Britain was firmly embedded in the wider European Iron Age.

A point about frameworks of analysis should be made at the outset. By setting up 'Britain' and 'the Continent' as opposing and coherent entities, and then taking the interactions between them as a discrete subject of study, we may predispose ourselves to reach particular conclusions. Taking a holistic view of the interactions that occurred at varying scales within and between Britain, Ireland and Continental north-west Europe would allow us to better understand the significance of those interactions that happened to cross the Channel or North Sea. Providing that wider picture is beyond the scope of this paper, though a forthcoming book will attempt to address the issue (Bradley *et al.* forthcoming). In line with the theme of this volume, I will limit myself to discussing connections and patterns of similarity and difference between pre-Roman Iron Age communities in Britain and the nearest Continent (*c.* 800 BC to mid-1st century AD: Table 8.1). The undoubtedly significant connections between Britain and Ireland will not be discussed.

I will begin by briefly outlining the historical development of perspectives on Britain's place within the European Iron Age, before surveying the evidence of portable material culture, which has been so central to previous discussions. I will then go on to compare other aspects of Iron Age life in Britain and on the near Continent, such as the ways that people

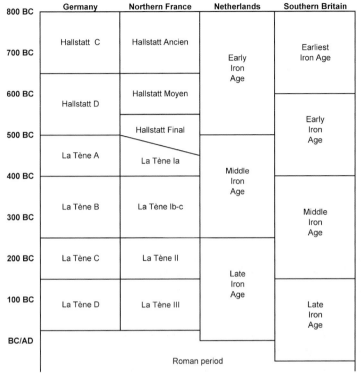

	Germany	Northern France	Netherlands	Southern Britain
800 BC				
700 BC	Hallstatt C	Hallstatt Ancien	Early Iron Age	Earliest Iron Age
600 BC	Hallstatt D	Hallstatt Moyen		
500 BC		Hallstatt Final		Early Iron Age
400 BC	La Tène A	La Tène Ia	Middle Iron Age	
300 BC	La Tène B	La Tène Ib-c		Middle Iron Age
200 BC	La Tène C	La Tène II	Late Iron Age	
100 BC	La Tène D	La Tène III		Late Iron Age
BC/AD				
	Roman period			

Table 8.1. Schematic chart of chronological schemes used in north-west Europe.

engaged with the landscape, ordered their settlements and treated their dead. Evidence from recent excavations has revealed more similarities in these practices than were evident before.[1]

Changing perspectives

In British Iron Age studies, as in prehistoric studies as a whole, the early to mid-20th century was an era of culture-historical narratives in which invasions or migrations of people from the Continent played a dominant role (Cunliffe 2005, 3–20). Such folk movements were invoked to explain the spread of new artefact styles, technologies and burial practices, as well as the Celtic languages. The possibility that innovations could also have spread in the other direction – from Britain to Continental Europe – was barely discussed. This approach reached its apogee in Hawkes' 'ABC' scheme for the British Iron Age, based on the premise of three major successive waves of migration from the Continent, representing the Hallstatt, early La Tène and late La Tène cultures (Hawkes 1959). It was assumed that between these episodes of migration British communities were essentially static and isolated.

The 'invasion hypothesis' underwent sustained critique from the 1960s onwards, notably by Hodson and Clark, who demolished the slender evidence base for most of the supposed folk movements (Hodson 1964; Clark 1966). Migration did continue to be discussed as an explanation for the appearance of two geographically restricted traditions of apparently 'Continental-style' burial – the 'Arras culture' inhumations of middle/late Iron Age East Yorkshire and the 'Aylesford-Swarling culture' cremations of late Iron Age south-east England – though even here there was increasing scepticism. New theoretical perspectives developed in the 1960s and '70s placed more emphasis on the internal workings of social systems. This went in parallel with increased interest in issues such as settlement forms, agriculture and the environment, for which the relevance of overseas contacts was less obvious. The application of radiocarbon dating also meant that there was less need to invoke Continental parallels to construct chronologies, though it should be said that radiocarbon has never been as important to the Iron Age as it is to earlier periods of prehistory.

Theoretical trends from the late 1980s onwards have reinforced these inward-looking tendencies. New approaches to past identities have led many to question the assumption that Iron Age communities in Britain, Ireland and large areas of the Continent shared a common 'Celtic' culture or ethnicity (James 1999; Collis 2003). The view that the emergence and spread of the Celtic language group took place before rather than during the Iron Age has also become more popular (Koch 2013). Though not motivated by any desire to emphasise the separateness of Britain, these arguments have hardly encouraged British researchers to engage more with the Iron Age archaeology of the near Continent. At the same time, the 'post-processual' emphasis on agency, context and the micro scale has led to a focus on defining local differences within the British Iron Age, rather than super-regional patterns. These developments have also created a divide in theoretical concerns between archaeologists working in Britain and those in many other European countries. This has hampered dialogue, exacerbating the divisions created by differences in language and by varying national archaeological traditions (Haselgrove *et al.* in prep.; Moore and Armada 2012b).

Over the last four decades, then, work on the British Iron Age has been largely characterised by insularity. Equally, Britain has tended to play a peripheral role in accounts of the European Iron Age produced by Continental writers (e.g. Brun 1987). Though a few authors have highlighted the existence of contacts across the Channel (Champion 1975; 1994; Cunliffe 1990; 2005; Haselgrove 2001; 2002), in practice the archaeological record of Iron Age Britain has been discussed with little reference to its wider European context, with two main exceptions. The first is work by specialists in decorated metalwork, 'Celtic art' and coinage, for whom Continental parallels have always played a central role (see Joy, this volume). These specialists to some extent work within their own discrete sub-disciplines, and the objects that they study are themselves often dissociated from the rest of the archaeological record, limiting their influence on wider archaeological thought. The second theme has been work on cross-Channel 'trade' and engagement with the expanding Roman world during the closing stages of the Iron Age (discussed below). These late developments were essentially limited to southern England, and have sometimes been viewed more as a prelude to the Roman period than as part of the Iron Age 'proper' (Bradley 2007, 271).

During the last few years there have been welcome signs of a renewed interest in situating the British Iron Age in its European context (e.g. Bradley *et al.* forthcoming; Hamilton 2007; Hunter and Carruthers 2012, 107–15; Marcigny and Talon 2009; Moore and Armada 2012a). There have even been some suggestions that Iron Age communities either side of the Channel could have shared a common culture. Cunliffe (2001) and Henderson (2007) outline an Atlantic Iron Age incorporating maritime western Britain, Ireland, western France and north-west Iberia, defined mainly by comparisons of settlement forms. This marks a return to the mid-20th-century interest in the 'western seaways' (Bowen 1972) as a conduit for prehistoric culture contact. Cunliffe (2009) has also recently referred to a 'Southern North Sea cultural zone' during the 6th to 4th centuries BC, evinced by similarities in pottery styles between south-east England and neighbouring areas of northern France. It should however be stressed that this new interest in cross-Channel relationships remains patchy, and opposing perspectives are still widespread (e.g. Sharples 2010b, 115, 311). This stands in contrast with the more extensive recent work on the Channel Bronze Age. Attempts to develop comparable maritime perspectives on the Channel Iron Age have been hindered by the fact that remains of undisputed seagoing boats are still unknown from this period in either Britain or the near Continent, and even depictions of boats are largely absent (van de Noort 2011; Hill and Willis 2013).

Material culture and exchange, *c.* 800–150 BC

Portable artefacts – and in particular certain kinds of elaborate artefact such as decorated metalwork and fine pottery – have traditionally been accorded a privileged role in defining relationships between Britain and the Continent during the Iron Age. The focus has been on identifying imports, and locally made artefacts that mimic foreign styles (e.g. Cunliffe 2005, 446–84; 2009). Where imported or foreign-style 'prestige' objects occur, this has generally been explained in terms of exchanges or emulation between elite individuals on either side of the Channel, or by the sharing of knowledge between skilled craft specialists. Cunliffe (1995, 17) has for example referred to "diplomatic gifts" of fine metalwork during the early Iron Age. It is often implied that only elite *men* would have had agency in these contacts, even when 'female' items were imported. Thus it is claimed to be "quite likely" that early Iron Age brooches in the Continental Hallstatt style "were brought into Britain on the dress of women arriving in the islands to sustain alliances through marriage" (Cunliffe 2009, 84).

Based on this approach, the standard narrative is that following the breakdown of long-distance networks of bronze exchange around 800 BC contacts between Britain and the near Continent were relatively limited, until cross-Channel 'trade' decisively reopened during the late 2nd to early 1st century BC. Some similarities in metalwork and ceramics did continue during the earliest Iron Age (*c.* 800–600 BC), though to some extent this may simply reflect shared inheritance of late Bronze Age styles (Gerloff 2004). For the period following *c.* 600 BC, studies of styles of decorated artefacts tend to stress increasing regional diversity on both sides of the Channel. Some clear similarities have however been recognised between ceramics in south-west England and Brittany (Cunliffe 1990), and those in Kent and the areas on the opposite side of the Dover Strait (Champion 2011, 223; Cunliffe 2009). Small numbers of fine Greek and Italic ceramic vessels were imported into Britain, focusing around the 6th to 5th centuries BC, a period when such objects were widely distributed across western Europe (Bradley and Smith 2007). Metalwork from Britain also shows some contact with wider European trends, notably with the introduction of La Tène ('Celtic art') styles from the 5th/4th century BC, though these styles then followed their own insular path of development after *c* 300 BC. Few actual imports of metalwork – travelling in either direction – can be confidently identified (see Joy, this volume). The coral used as inlays on some metal objects

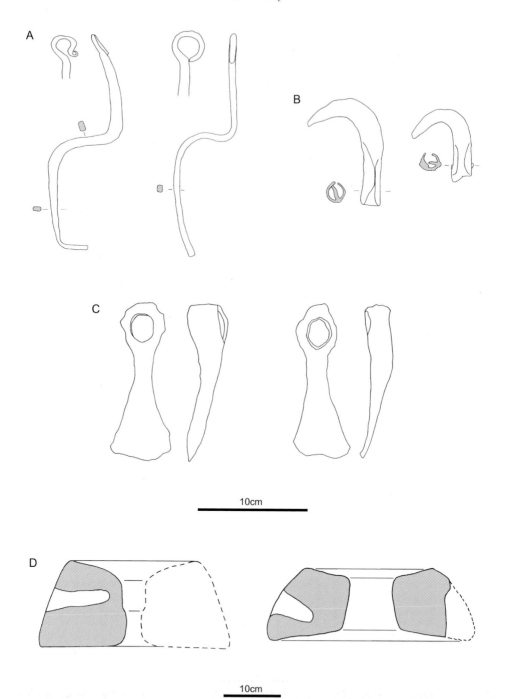

Figure 8.1. Domestic objects of iron and stone from Iron Age sites in northern France (left in each pair) and southern Britain (right in each pair). A: latch lifters; B: reaping tools; C: adzes; D: rotary quern upper stones. Redrawn after Cunliffe 1987; Cunliffe and Poole 1991; Malrain and Pinard 2006; Vauterin et al. 2011.

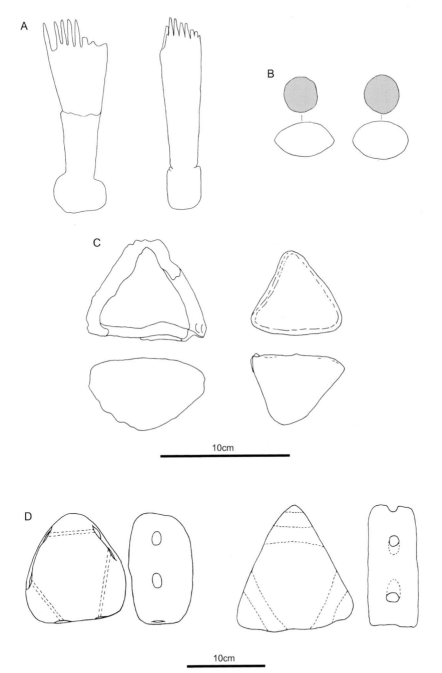

Figure 8.2. Domestic objects of bone and fired clay from Iron Age sites in northern France and the Netherlands (left in each pair) and southern Britain (right in each pair) A: bone/antler 'weaving' combs; B: fired clay sling bullets; C: crucibles; D: fired clay loomweights. Redrawn after Blancquaert and Desfosses 1994; Cunliffe 1987; Cunliffe and Poole 1991; Fell 1990; Malrain and Pinard 2006; van Heeringen 1987.

found in Britain must however derive from the Mediterranean. It is also possible that some coins arrived in Britain from Continental Europe and the Mediterranean as early as the 3rd century BC, though none of these are from datable contexts (de Jersey 1999; Haselgrove 1999; Holman 2005). Meanwhile, armrings made from Kimmeridge shale from Dorset have been identified in graves dating from the 6th/5th century BC onwards in Switzerland and at Manching in Bavaria from the 3rd century BC onwards (Teichmüller 1992). Put together, the evidence of fine metalwork and other decorated artefacts shows that contacts did exist between Britain and the Continent throughout the early and middle Iron Age, but it leaves the door open for arguments that these contacts were not particularly intensive or sustained.

The focus on elaborate artefacts to define cross-regional interactions has its limitations, however. First of course there is the well-recognised issue that the distributions of such objects may reflect regional differences in practices of their deposition – such as whether they were used as grave goods – more than their actual pattern of circulation. More fundamentally, an emphasis on 'high-status' material culture may skew our perspective towards particular kinds of interactions at the expense of others.

Looking also at more quotidian artefacts may help to provide a more balanced view. It is not widely appreciated that much of the domestic material culture of Iron Age Britain can be directly paralleled on the other side of the Channel (Figures 8.1 and 8.2). For example, a wide range of iron tool and implement types developed during the second half of the 1st millennium BC take identical forms on either side of the Channel. Triangular fired-clay loomweights appear in Britain and the Low Countries around the middle of the 1st millennium BC, spreading to northern France from *c.* 250 BC (Gautier and Annaert 2006, 39; Malrain and Pinard 2006; Wilhelmi 1977). Long-handled bone or antler 'weaving' combs – in use in Britain from the later Bronze Age – occur sporadically from Picardy to the Netherlands from *c.* 500 BC onwards (Malrain and Pinard 2006; Tuohy 1999). Rotary querns are a further case in point. The earliest known examples in Europe appear in eastern Iberia and southern Britain during the 5th century BC, but they only reached northern France in the 3rd or even early 2nd century BC, and the Low Countries even later (Wefers 2011). It is unclear whether the idea spread from Iberia to Britain, or vice versa, or was independently invented in each region. I would however suggest that the rotary quern could well have been introduced into northern France from Britain, reversing the usual assumption of a south to north spread of innovations. Notably, the earliest examples in northern France seem more similar to the bun- or beehive-shaped forms of Britain than the flatter forms of southern France and the Mediterranean (Boyer and Buchsenschutz 1998; Pommepuy 1999). Given the geological similarities between southern Britain and northern France, actual imports of simple stone and ceramic objects would be easy to miss.[2] Alongside new domestic and agricultural artefact types, it is of course possible that new crop varieties and breeds of livestock were exchanged across the Channel. Certainly, the chicken was first introduced to south-east Britain during the early Iron Age (Champion 2011).

The material culture of the communities on either side of the Channel and North Sea from the 8th to 2nd centuries BC thus presents a complex picture. Often we see an emphasis on distinctive local identities expressed through media such as styles of personal equipment and decoration on pottery. At the same time, cross-regional connectivity throughout the period is implied by the sharing of new technologies and artefact types. This was not a time of isolation for Britain, nor were contacts limited to elite levels of society.

Material culture and exchange, *c.* 150 BC–AD 43

Cross-Channel exchange during the last two centuries of the Iron Age has been intensively discussed (e.g. Carver 2001; Cunliffe 1988a; Cunliffe and de Jersey 1997; Daire 2002; Fitzpatrick 1989; 2001; 2003; Haselgrove 1995; Macready and Thompson 1984; Morris 2010; Trott and Tomalin 2003). From the late 2nd to early 1st century BC maritime exchange networks between north-west France and the coasts of Wessex and south-west England become more visible. Recognisable imports brought to southern Britain via these western networks included Italian wine amphorae, Armorican pottery and some Armorican coins. Evidence for the movement of British artefacts such as pottery and coinage in the other direction is much more limited (Cunliffe and de Jersey 1997). Recent scientific analysis has however confirmed that Kimmeridge shale was transported to north-west France at this time (Baron 2012). This includes a vase from a grave at Saint-Gatien-des-Bois near the mouth of the Seine (Paris *et al.* 2000) and probably the assemblage of roughouts for armrings from the harbour site at Urville-Nacqueville on the Cotentin peninsular, where recent excavations have also uncovered a group of roundhouses (Lefort 2008; 2010; 2011; see below for discussion of roundhouses).

These western cross-Channel contacts were preferentially focused on specific harbour sites in southern Britain, notably Hengistbury Head and Poole Harbour in Dorset, and possibly also the Isle of Portland (Taylor 2001) and Mount Batten in Plymouth Sound (Cunliffe 1988b). These have been described as 'ports-of-trade', acting as centres for exchange and the redistribution of imports (Cunliffe 1987; 1988a). Notably though, a substantial proportion of the amphorae and other imports seem to have travelled no further than the harbour sites or their immediate hinterlands. In fact, the large majority of late Iron Age Armorican pottery found in Britain comes from Hengistbury alone. It is of course possible that wine and foodstuffs were decanted at the harbour side from amphorae into other containers for distribution inland (Cunliffe 1994), but it seems less plausible that fine, decorated Armorican bowls were transported across the Channel merely as packaging. It may be better to see these harbour sites not merely as intermediate nodes in a trading network, but as places that were to some extent destinations in their own right. In other words, they could have served as places of contact between communities on either side of the Channel, circumscribed areas where activities (festivities?) involving the deployment of exotic goods could take place. These sites may have been selected for their geographically and socially liminal positions. Hengistbury was a headland cut off by ramparts and lay at a cultural boundary zone (Sharples 1990), while the sites at Poole Harbour (Green Island/Furzey Island), on the Isle of Portland and on Mount Batten all occupied insular or virtually insular locations.

More visible exchange relationships also developed between south-east England and northern France around the mid-2nd century BC with the import of 'Gallo-Belgic' gold coins, similar British gold issues beginning around the same time or soon after (Haselgrove 1999). From the mid-1st century BC – around the time of the Roman conquest of Gaul and Caesar's expeditions to Britain – exchange links following this eastern axis became more prominent while those across the western Channel declined. Imports during this period included amphorae containing wine and olive oil, and a few elaborate metal vessels of Italian origin. From *c.* 20/10 BC, 'Gallo-Belgic' and Mediterranean tableware pottery was imported and imitated. British societies were clearly being selective in their adoption of Continental goods, and those chosen embody an ideological emphasis on feasting and hospitality. This is underlined by the recent identification of exotic foods including olive, coriander and celery in pre-conquest deposits at Silchester (University of Reading 2012). There is little evidence that exchange networks to south-east England after *c.* 50 BC were mediated through ports-of-trade similar to Hengistbury Head, though a recently investigated site at Folkestone may be a candidate (Parfitt 2012). Rather than being concentrated on a few coastal sites, imports were now more widely distributed inland and were often placed in graves. This suggests that the mechanisms and social context for exchange had changed. As before, there is rather less evidence for British objects reaching the Continent, other than small numbers of coins and items of metalwork (Gruel and Haselgrove 2007; Guillaumet and Eugène 2009). It is often assumed that these goods must have taken an archaeologically invisible form, with Strabo's contemporary reference to British exports of grain, cattle, gold, silver, iron, slaves and hunting dogs routinely invoked (Cunliffe 2005, 478). More likely perhaps is that much of the movement of objects to Britain embodied social and kinship ties across the Channel, and was not predicated on a 'balance of trade' (Fitzpatrick 2001).

Cross-Channel contacts during the late Iron Age led to the adoption of new technologies such as coin minting and the use of the potter's wheel in southern Britain. There is also limited evidence for the adoption of literacy at the very end of the Iron Age, in the form of inscriptions on coins and graffiti on pottery. Contacts with the Continent have also been seen as bound up with broader social changes during the 1st century BC and early 1st century AD. Social hierarchy and political centralisation became more visible in southern and eastern Britain, for example in the appearance of rich burials and the major focal sites traditionally referred to as 'oppida'. There may have been increasing links between the Roman rulership and the emerging British elites, with the formation of client kingdoms before the conquest (Creighton 2000). How these various phenomena were related is a contentious issue. Was the construction of trading and political links across the Channel driven by the needs of the expanding Roman world, or should we also acknowledge the agency of the British partners in these exchanges (Fitzpatrick 2001)? And can we accept the argument that these contacts were critical in stimulating social change in late Iron Age southern Britain (Cunliffe 1988a)? While the availability of exotic goods and exposure to (Gallo-)Roman customs and ideas would certainly have provided new opportunities for social differentiation, the numbers of imports actually found in Britain are modest (Fitzpatrick 2001). Many recent authors thus instead prefer to emphasise indigenous social developments with their roots in the middle Iron Age (Haselgrove 1995; Hill 1995).

These arguments need not be recapitulated here. It can though be noted that those on both sides of the debate have often assumed that cross-Channel exchange was essentially a new phenomenon in the late Iron Age. As we have seen, there is in fact abundant evidence for the sharing of artefact types between Britain and the near Continent in the centuries before *c.* 150 BC. What changed therefore was not the fact of contact but the nature of the objects exchanged and the ways in which these were used. Gaulish- and Roman-style decorated objects and customs of feasting, drinking and hospitality now played an important role in the ways that (some) people presented themselves and their relationships to others. It is relevant to note that the 2nd to 1st centuries BC was also a time of increasing internationalisation of decorated material culture and 'elite' practice in many other regions of temperate Europe (cf. Fitzpatrick 1993). This went beyond contacts between indigenous Iron Age societies and the Mediterranean world. Roymans (2007) and Brandt (2001) have for example made important studies of the contacts and exchanges between the La Tène 'core' of Gaul and central Europe on the one hand and the 'Germanic' regions of the Lower Rhine and northern Germany on the other. They show that the import and emulation of non-local material culture and customs was a selective and creative process, just as it was in Britain. Not just new objects were introduced but also new ideas and values, providing the possibility of changed social relationships. Developments in Britain should be seen within the context of this wider pattern of cross-regional interaction at the close of the pre-Roman Iron Age.

Dwelling

For many years it was seen as fundamental to the distinctiveness of Iron Age Britain and Ireland that houses on these islands were mainly round. In contrast to the various forms of rectangular house used across most of the Continent (Webley forthcoming). In recent years this distinction has been blurred by the discovery of roundhouses at more than 30 sites in northern France dating from the mid-2nd millennium BC to the end of the Iron Age (e.g. Dechezleprêtre and Ginoux 2005; Figure 8.3), suggesting that we are in fact dealing with an Atlantic tradition also encompassing the circular buildings of north-west Iberia. The French roundhouses share some specific similarities with those in Britain, such as the fact that many have entrances facing east or south-east. Of course, as roundhouses were used either side of the Channel already during the Bronze Age they do not necessarily evince

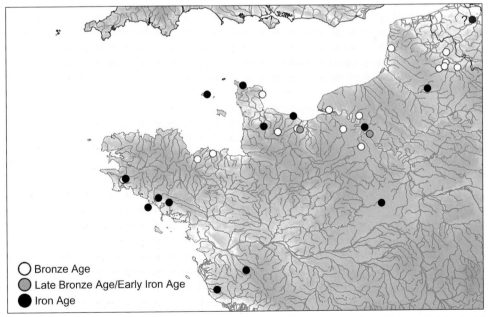

Figure 8.3. Distribution of Bronze Age and Iron Age roundhouses in northern France, Belgium and the Channel Islands.

contacts during the Iron Age, though their presence at the late Iron Age 'harbour' site of Urville-Nacqueville is certainly suggestive (Lefort 2010). The prevalence of roundhouses in Iron Age northern France should also not be overstated. Convincing examples are essentially confined to maritime areas from Picardy to Vendée, where they only form a small minority of total known houses. Even on individual sites circular buildings are sometimes outnumbered by rectangular houses, contrasting with the situation in the later Bronze Age when whole villages of roundhouses were present in Lower Normandy. Why this combination of house forms occurred within single communities – whether for example it embodied social distinctions – remains to be investigated.

There are also further well-known similarities in settlement forms between north-west France and south-west Britain from around 500 BC onwards (Arbousse Bastide 2000; Henderson 2007). 'Cliff castles' are a distinctive form of enclosure found along the coasts of both areas. Souterrains were also used for storage and other purposes in settlements in Brittany, Lower Normandy, west Cornwall and Scilly. Claims of a discrete Atlantic cultural zone defined by settlement forms and extending also to Scotland and Ireland (Henderson 2007) seem questionable, however. As Sharples (2010a) points out, during the later pre-Roman Iron Age Atlantic Scotland is set apart by the emphasis on monumental roundhouses rather than enclosures, while in Ireland recent excavation has shown that occupation sites were typically unenclosed and ephemeral (Corlett and Potterton 2012). And while souterrains do occur in Scotland, they are also found outside the 'Atlantic zone' in Jutland (Webley 2008, 115–6).

Perhaps it would be useful to focus less on typologies of settlement features than on ways of dwelling. The results of recent large-scale excavation suggest that broadly comparable developments in settlement patterns – albeit with significant local variations in timing and expression – occurred during the Iron Age across a region stretching from northern France to the Low Countries, north-west Germany and southern Scandinavia, and also parts of southern and eastern England and the Midlands (Bradley *et al.* forthcoming). To summarise, during the earlier Iron Age settlements were often unenclosed and loosely structured, and in some cases underwent frequent shifts in location. During the later Iron Age, there was a trend towards more stable and ordered settlement. Enclosure became more common, with a broad trend over time to increasingly rectilinear enclosure. In some areas – notably parts of northern France and Britain – enclosed settlements could be embedded in extensive complexes of field systems and trackways by the end of the Iron Age. Comparable trends in settlement dynamics either side of the Channel and North Sea could simply have been a case of parallel development of communities that found themselves faced with similar circumstances. Equally, it could be that shared ideas developed concerning land tenure, generational succession, and the relationship between people and place.

Hillforts

Hillforts first appeared in Britain and north-west Continental Europe during the late Bronze Age, but further waves of construction occurred at various stages of the Iron Age. Their distribution during the Iron Age was very uneven, with marked concentrations in some areas but few or none in others (notably Ireland and the longhouse-using areas of the Low Countries and lowland northern Germany). The scarcity of large-scale excavations of hillfort interiors

Figure 8.4. Schematic map showing the main distribution of different traditions of metalwork deposition in early Iron Age north-west Europe.

means the roles these sites played remain poorly understood. In Britain it has been argued that sites labelled as hillforts were used in widely varying ways (Hill 1995) – some contained substantial settlements, while others have little or no evidence for permanent occupation and may have served for periodic gatherings or rituals. In some cases the ramparts would have provided a meaningful defensive barrier, in others not. The same range of variability has also been identified on the near Continent (e.g. Schulze-Forster 2007). Perhaps the common thread linking the Iron Age hillforts of north-west Europe is that they acted as foci for and symbols of the communities that lived in and around them. There is little evidence that they were elite residences or centres of coercive power, in contrast to hillforts in some other parts of Europe, notably the so-called *Fürstensitze* of central France and south-west Germany during the 6th to 5th centuries BC.

Ritual in the landscape

A recently recognised feature of the Bronze Age to Iron Age transition in southern Britain is the occurrence of extensive or even monumental midden sites. These typically contain much animal dung, and were foci for the deposition of large quantities of artefacts and animal bone, and often also human remains. They may have served as places for collective gatherings, feasting and ritual. While these midden sites have been discussed as an insular phenomenon, they share features with some sites on the other side of the Channel. Most notable is Mez-Notariou on the island of Ouessant, off the west coast of Brittany, where a substantial midden deposit made up of shell, bone and artefacts lay at the edge of a settlement dated to around the 8th to 6th centuries BC (Le Bihan and Méniel 2002; Le Bihan *et al.* 2007). A striking feature of this deposit is that the animal remains show a strong emphasis on right forequarters. This selective depositional pattern is mirrored by the midden at Llanmaes in south Wales (Madgwick *et al.* 2012), where Armorican axeheads were found. Another practice seen at Mez-Notariou – the deposition of miniature bronze axeheads, some with deliberate perforations – can be paralleled at a number of British midden sites (Sharples and Waddington 2011, 35). Milcent (2009) suggests that the enigmatic site at Les Huguettes on Alderney is also comparable to the British middens, though this seems less certain.

Ritual practices involving the deposition of metalwork in the landscape, which had been so important during the later Bronze Age, reduced dramatically after *c.* 800 BC across north-west Europe. They did not disappear entirely, however. Swords continued to be placed in rivers around the southern North Sea basin – including the Thames, Seine and Rhine – and also in Ireland (Milcent 2009, fig. 12; O'Connor 2007, fig. 5). In contrast, in north-west France and (on a smaller scale) Wessex and south-west Britain, dry land hoards of bronze axeheads occur instead of these riverine deposits (Figure 8.4). While this has long been seen as a late continuation of Bronze Age hoarding traditions, recent work has shown that almost all of the French axe hoards date to around the 7th century BC, following a hiatus of a century when metal deposits of any kind virtually ceased (Gomez de Soto *et al.* 2009). Reassessment of the dating of the British hoards will now be needed.

During the last few centuries of the Iron Age, the quantity and range of metal artefacts deposited in the landscape increased again across much of north-west Europe, including Britain. This included not only weapons, coins and elaborate decorated objects, but also simpler iron tools and 'currency bars'. A variety of locations were chosen for these deposits, including rivers and other wet places, isolated dry land sites, and boundaries surrounding settlements and hillforts. A broad distinction continued between an emphasis on rivers and wet places in eastern Britain and the facing areas of the near Continent, and an emphasis on dry locations in central-southern England and north-west France (Haselgrove and Hingley 2006; Kurz 1995).

In south-east Britain and the near Continent as far north as the Rhine, certain places that became foci for repeated ritual deposits during the late Iron Age have been described as 'shrines', 'temples' or 'sanctuaries'. As well as coins and other metalwork, these deposits could include human and animal remains. In some cases the rituals simply took place in the open air, in others they were focused within or around an enclosure or building. The classic image of a late Iron Age temple is of a rectangular compound with a central building or unroofed structure, though only a minority of sites conform to this pattern (as for example at Hayling Island in Hampshire and Martberg bei Pommern in western Germany). The desire to formalise and separate sacred space at this time could perhaps have been associated with the emergence of a distinct class of ritual specialists.

The dead and the living

The treatment of the dead has long been seen as a distinctive aspect of the insular Iron Age. A contrast is often drawn between the apparent scarcity of 'formal' burials in Britain and the more abundant evidence for cemeteries on the Continent. This now requires reassessment. On one hand, increasing numbers of unaccompanied inhumations have been identified in several parts of Britain in recent years (e.g. Sharples 2010b), thanks in part to more widespread use of radiocarbon dating, though their distribution remains very patchy. On the other hand, it has also become clear that several parts of the near Continent lack formal burials for at least part of the period. In coastal areas of the Netherlands they are essentially absent throughout the 1st millennium BC (Hessing 1993). In many parts of northern France, they are scarce during particular stages of the Iron Age, as in Picardy from *c.* 800–500 BC, Nord-Pas-de-Calais, Somme and Seine-Maritime between *c.* 500–250 BC, and Brittany from the 4th century BC onwards (Brun *et al.* 2005; Desenne *et al.* 2009b; Oudry-Braillon 2009; Villard-Le Tiec *et al.* 2010). After *c.* 250 BC, wide areas of the near Continent have few or no cemeteries (Roymans 2007, fig. 1). Further afield, in north-west Iberia burials disappear after the late Bronze Age and only reappear during the Roman period (Parcero Oubiña and Cobas Fernández 2004). Arguments that cemeteries have somehow been missed are now untenable given the huge amount of recent fieldwork in many of these areas. Rather, we are seeing the outcome of particular attitudes to the dead that were shared by many (but not all) communities either side of the Channel and North Sea.

In those areas where formal cemeteries are lacking, this does not imply an absence of human remains. Across north-west Europe, human skeletons, partial skeletons and individual bones are commonly found in settlements and hillforts, in features such as pits and ditches. They are particularly common in disused grain storage pits across a region stretching from southern Britain to northern France, western Germany and Switzerland, up until the 1st century BC when they largely disappeared (e.g. Baray and Boulestin 2010; Cunliffe 1992; Hansen and Meyer 2006). Cunliffe (2009, 85) has suggested that pit deposits and formal cemeteries were mutually exclusive traditions, but in fact both practices were common in many parts of France and Germany.

In Britain, the frequent occurrence of disarticulated bone has often been explained with the argument that mortuary rites for much of the population involved excarnation. After exposure of the body, selected bones could be recovered and ultimately deposited in settlement contexts. Sharples (2010b) has however suggested another possible source for these disarticulated remains, highlighting evidence from Wessex for the deliberate reopening of Iron Age burials to recover bones. This practice is also well attested on the near Continent (e.g. Diepeveen-Jansen 2001), suggesting that in both regions the ancestral dead played an active role in the lives of the living.

A further tradition found in several parts of north-west Europe is the deposition of corpses or body parts in natural places such as rivers, lakes or caves. The best known examples are the 'bog bodies' found across a region stretching from Ireland and northern Britain to the Netherlands, northern Germany and southern Scandinavia – a complementary distribution to that of storage pit burials. While bog bodies on the Continent largely belong to the pre-Roman and Roman Iron Age, few of the British examples have been dated, though at least some are from around the 1st century AD (van der Sanden 1996).

Standing out from the background of few formal cemeteries, three burial traditions with suggested Continental affinities emerged in discrete areas of Britain during the middle and late Iron Age. Firstly, there is a group of inhumation burials within stone cists in south Devon, Cornwall and Scilly, probably dating to between the 4th/3rd century BC and 1st century AD. These have been compared to contemporary cist cemeteries on Guernsey and uncertainly dated examples from Brittany (Burns *et al.* 1996; Henderson 2007), though similarities beyond the use of stone-lined graves are not obvious. Secondly, there are the inhumation burials of the so-called 'Arras culture' in east Yorkshire, dating to around the 4th to 2nd centuries BC. These show a number of parallels with north Gaulish traditions, including the use of barrows surrounded by square ditched enclosures, and the presence of chariots in a few of the richest graves. Immigration from northern France was for a long time invoked to explain the introduction of this burial rite, though the consensus today is that if such a population movement occurred at all it is likely to have been on a small scale. Detailed examination of the 'Arras culture' burial rite shows that it combines traits derived from various different parts of northern Gaul with indigenous elements such as the dominance of crouched interments (Anthoons 2007). Furthermore, Bayesian modelling of radiocarbon dates from the chariot burials suggests that they belong to a short period around 200 BC (Jay *et al.* 2012), by which time they had gone or were going out of fashion on the Continent. Isotopic analysis has failed to provide clear evidence for individuals born overseas (see below). The third regional tradition of 'formal' burial is the cremation rite of south-east England during the 1st century BC and 1st century AD, which shows close similarities to contemporary practices in northern France. In both regions small groups of flat burials were the norm, sometimes associated with square enclosures or buildings. A similar range of ceramics and metal artefacts were used as grave or pyre goods, and pork and chicken were preferentially selected as food offerings (Desenne *et al.* 2009a; 2009b; Fitzpatrick 1997).

Alongside these three regional burial traditions, there is a sparser scattering of accompanied burials in other parts of Britain during the second half of the 1st millennium BC. The most spectacular recent find is the chariot burial at Newbridge on the east coast of Scotland, dating to the 5th/early 4th century BC. Carter *et al.* (2010) argue that the burial rite is paralleled by though not identical to contemporary practices in Champagne and the Belgian Ardennes, while the vehicle itself was probably of British manufacture. There are also further inhumation burials dotted around Britain with weapons (Hunter 2005) or other artefacts that belong broadly within the European La Tène tradition. The scattered distribution of accompanied burials has made them easy to ignore as aberrations, but as we have seen the occurrence of formal, accompanied burials is also patchy across much of the near Continent during this period. Communities on both sides of the Channel selectively and creatively drew on elements of wider traditions.

Isotopic evidence for mobility

Few isotopic analyses investigating human mobility have yet been carried out on Iron Age skeletal material either in Britain or on the Continent. The technique will no doubt make an increasingly important contribution in future, as long as it is recognised that the results of isotopic analyses must be assessed as carefully and critically as other sources of evidence. The one study to argue for cross-Channel movement is a strontium/oxygen analysis of a cemetery at Cliffs End Farm on the Isle of Thanet (McKinley *et al.* 2013). This site has burials radiocarbon dated to the late Bronze Age, 5th century cal BC and 4th to 3rd century cal BC. In all three periods it is claimed that some individuals were local while others had been born in Scandinavia. Some of the late Bronze Age individuals and one from the later Iron Age group are argued to have come from Iberia or the Mediterranean. The burial rites – crouched unaccompanied inhumation and deposits of disarticulated bone – are however consistent with indigenous customs; cremation was the norm in Scandinavia at this time. A recurring pattern of migration to this locality over many centuries would be remarkable, and the issue must remain open pending final publication of the excavation and isotopic analysis. Meanwhile, isotopic studies of 'Arras culture' burials from Yorkshire (Giles 2012, 116–7; Jay *et al.* 2013) have not produced clear evidence for individuals born overseas, though equally they do not exclude this.

Conclusion

It is time to discard the notion that contacts between Britain and the Continent were meagre before the closing stages of the Iron Age. This idea derives from a disproportionate focus on the movement or imitation of certain types of fine, decorated objects. When we consider a broader range of evidence – such as quotidian artefacts, settlement patterns, ritual practices and the treatment of the dead – connections become more apparent. Communities either side of the Channel and North Sea shared objects, technologies, ideas and practices throughout the Iron Age, with innovations travelling in both directions. The variety of connections that can now be identified moves us on from seeing contact merely in terms of exchange or emulation between high-status individuals or schools of metalworkers. A wider range of interactions can be envisaged, that may have involved various different sectors of society. Estimating the actual frequency of cross-Channel mobility is of course difficult, but we should not assume that it was *necessarily* lower during the early to middle Iron Age than in the later Bronze Age – it may simply be that the character of the contacts was different. Following the end of the Atlantic bronze exchange networks, displaying long-distance connections through media such as decorated metalwork was no longer as important in forming people's identity and status. The 2nd to 1st centuries BC marked another shift in the character of interaction. The forging of new kinds of links across the Channel at this time was closely bound up with the creation of new social relationships within southern British and northern Gaulish societies.

The axes of contact linking Britain to the Continent during the Iron Age present a complex picture. Unsurprisingly, Wessex and south-west Britain often had connections with north-west France, while south-east Britain tended to have closer links with northern France and the southern Low Countries. It is also no surprise that evidence for direct links following the more difficult crossing over the northern North Sea is more modest. Which axes come to prominence does however depend on which kinds of evidence (e.g. metalwork, everyday artefacts, burial practices) is considered. This implies that communities may have faced in different directions at once, varying according to the nature of the interaction and who within the community it involved. Thus although I see Britain as firmly embedded in the wider north-west European Iron Age, I would not follow Henderson (2007) and Cunliffe (2009) in arguing for cross-Channel cultural unities during this period. While that kind of approach may help to break down perceptions of British separateness, it runs the risk of creating new mental boundaries that are ultimately equally unhelpful. And in practice it is only possible to define such cultural blocs by emphasising certain aspects of the evidence and downplaying others. We have seen that the concept of a discrete and coherent Atlantic Iron Age (Henderson 2007) is open to question. While Scotland and Ireland may have had links with south-west Britain, Brittany and Iberia via the 'western seaways', it is not obvious that these links were more important than those with other parts of Britain and the near Continent (Sharples 2010a). Cunliffe's (2009) concept of a 'Southern North Sea cultural zone' seems even more tenuous, based as it is on similarities between particular types of pottery that form only a subset of the ceramic repertoires used on either side of the Channel narrows (cf. Couldrey 2007, 170). It is more realistic to see different practices as having cross-cutting, Venn-diagram-like distributions across north-west Europe, even if this is less satisfying than drawing lines around discrete territories on a map.

By highlighting connectivity in this paper, I do not wish to deny that there were concepts and practices that did not cross the Channel, or that apparently similar practices could have a different significance in different places. I also do not wish to downplay the meaningfulness of the regionality shown by some kinds of material culture, such as the forms and decoration of pottery or dress accessories, during certain stages of the Iron Age across north-west Europe. But as Hill (1995) points out, rather than being a sign of isolation a desire to display regional differences can in some cases be a response to high level of contact. Furthermore, as such episodes of regionality in Britain correspond to those on the near Continent, by expressing their distinctiveness British communities were paradoxically following wider European trends (Haselgrove 2001). Clearly, we should not focus our attention exclusively on either cross-regional commonalities or local variability; the interesting story will often lie in the interplay between the two.

Notes

1 Parts of this paper are based on research carried out for the project *The Prehistory of Britain and Ireland in their European Context*, led by Prof. Richard Bradley and Prof. Colin Haselgrove. The monograph publication of that project (Bradley *et al.* forthcoming) will develop some of the arguments presented here at greater length.
2 It has taken recent detailed scientific analysis to prove that puddingstone querns from Upper Normandy were transported to southern Britain during the Late Iron Age (Green and Peacock 2011).

References

Anthoons, G. 2007. The origins of the Arras Culture: Migration or elite networks? In R. Karl and J. Leskovar (eds), *Interpretierte Eisenzeiten. Fallstudien, Methoden, Theorie. Tagungsbeiträge der 2. Linzer Gespräche zur interpretativen Eisenzeitarchäologie*, Studien zur Kulturgeschichte von Oberösterreich 19, 141–52. Linz: Oberösterreichisches Landesmuseum.

Arbousse Bastide, T. 2000. *Les structures de l'habitat rural protohistorique dans le sud-ouest de l'Angleterre et le nord-ouest de la France*. British Archaeological Report S847. Oxford: Archaeopress.

Baray, L. and Boulestin, B. (eds). 2010. *Morts anormaux et sépultures bizarres: Les dépôts en fosses circulaires ou en silos du Néolithique à l'âge du Fer*. Dijon: Universitaires de Dijon.

Baron, A. 2012. *Provenance et circulation des objets en roches noires (« lignite ») à l'âge du Fer en Europe celtique (VIIIème–Ier s. av. J.-C.)*. British Archaeological Report S2453. Oxford: Archaeopress.

Blancquaert, G., and Desfosses, Y. 1994. Les établissements ruraux de l'âge du Fer sur le tracé de l'autoroute A 29 (Le Havre-Yvetot). In O. Buchsenschutz and P. Méniel (eds), *Les installations agricoles de l'âge du Fer en Île-de-France*, 227–54. Paris: Presses de l'École Normale Supérieure.

Bowen, E. 1972. *Britain and the Western Seaways*. London: Thames and Hudson.

Boyer, F. and Buchsenschutz, O. 1998. Les conditions d'une interprétation fonctionnelle des moulins "celtiques" rotatifs à mains sont-elles réunies?, *Revue Archéologique du Centre de la France* 37, 197–206.

Bradley, R. 2007. *The Prehistory of Britain and Ireland*. Cambridge: Cambridge University Press.

Bradley, R., Haselgrove, C., Vander Linden, M. and Webley, L. forthcoming. *The later Prehistory of Northwest Europe*. Oxford: Oxford University Press.

Bradley, R. and Smith, A. 2007. Questions of context: A Greek cup from the River Thames. In C. Gosden, H. Hamerow, P. de Jersey and E. Durham (eds), *Communities and Connections*, 30–42. Oxford: Oxford University Press.

Brandt, J. 2001. *Jastorf und Latène. Kultureller Austausch und seine Auswirkungen auf soziopolitische Entwicklungen in der vorrömischen Eisenzeit*, Internationale Archäologie 66. Rahden: Marie Leidorf.

Brun, P. 1987. *Princes et princesses de la Celtique: Le premier âge du Fer en Europe, 850–450 av. J.-C.* Paris: Errance.

Brun, P., Buchez, N., Gaudefroy, S. and Talon, M. 2005. Bilan de la protohistoire ancienne en Picardie. *Revue Archéologique de Picardie* 3–4, 99–127.

Burns, B., Cunliffe, B. and Sebire, H. 1996. *Guernsey: An island community of the Atlantic Iron Age*. Oxford: Oxford University Committee for Archaeology Monograph 43.

Carter, S., Hunter, F. and Smith, A. 2010. A 5th century BC Iron Age chariot burial from Newbridge, Edinburgh. *Proceedings of the Prehistoric Society* 76, 31–74.

Carver, E. 2001. *The Visibility of Imported Wine and its Associated Accoutrements in Later Iron Age Britain*. British Archaeological Report 325. Oxford: Archaeopress.

Champion, T. 1975. Britain in the European Iron Age. *Archaeologia Atlantica* 1, 127–45.

Champion, T. 1994. Socio-economic development in eastern England in the first millennium B.C. In K. Kristiansen and J. Jensen (eds), *Europe in the First Millennium B.C.*, 125–44. Sheffield: J. R. Collis.

Champion, T. 2011. Later prehistory. In P. Booth, T. Champion, S. Foreman, P. Garwood, H. Glass, J. Munby and A. Reynolds, *On Track. The Archaeology of High Speed 1 Section 1 in Kent*, 151–241. Oxford and Salisbury: Oxford Wessex Archaeology.

Clark, J. G. D. 1966. The invasion hypothesis in British archaeology. *Antiquity* 40, 172–89.

Collis, J. 2003. *The Celts: origins, myths and inventions*. Stroud: Tempus.

Corlett, C. and Potterton, M. (eds). 2012. *Life and Death in Iron Age Ireland in the Light of Recent Archaeological Excavations*. Dublin: Wordwell.

Couldrey, P. 2007. The late Bronze Age/early Iron Age pottery. In P. Bennett, P. Couldrey and N. Macpherson-Grant, *Highstead Near Chislet, Kent. Excavations 1975–1977*, 101–75. Canterbury: Canterbury Archaeological Trust.

Creighton, J. 2000. *Coins and Power in Late Iron Age Britain*. Cambridge: Cambridge University Press.

Cunliffe, B. 1987. *Danebury: an Iron Age hillfort in Hampshire. Volume 2. The excavations 1969–1978: the finds*, Council for British Archaeology Research Report 52. London: Council for British Archaeology.

Cunliffe, B. 1987. *Hengistbury Head, Dorset. Volume 1: the prehistoric and Roman settlement, 3500 BC–AD 500*, Oxford University Committee for Archaeology Monograph 13. Oxford: Oxford University Committee for Archaeology.

Cunliffe, B. 1988a. *Greeks, Romans and Barbarians: Spheres of interaction*. London: Batsford.

Cunliffe, B. 1988b. *Mount Batten, Plymouth: A prehistoric and Roman port*. Oxford: Oxford University Committee for Archaeology.

Cunliffe, B. 1990. Social and economic contacts between western France and Britain in the early and middle Le Tène period. In J. L'Helgouach (ed.), *La Bretagne et l'Europe préhistoriques*, 245–51. Revue Archéologique de l'Ouest Supplément 2.

Cunliffe, B. 1992. Pits, preconceptions and propitiation in the British Iron Age. *Oxford Journal of Archaeology* 11, 69–83.

Cunliffe, B. 1994. After hillforts. *Oxford Journal of Archaeology* 13, 71–84.

Cunliffe, B. 1995. *Iron Age Britain*. London: Batsford.

Cunliffe, B. 2001. *Facing the Ocean: the Atlantic and its peoples, 8000 BC–AD 1500*. Oxford: Oxford University Press.

Cunliffe, B. 2005. *Iron Age Communities in Britain* (4th edn). London: Routledge.

Cunliffe, B. 2009. Looking forward: Maritime contacts in the first millennium BC. In P. Clark (ed.), *Bronze Age Connections. Cultural Contact in Prehistoric Europe*, 80–93. Oxford: Oxbow Books.

Cunliffe, B., and de Jersey, P. 1997. *Armorica and Britain. Cross-Channel Relationships in the Late First Millennium BC*. Oxford: Oxford University Committee for Archaeology.

Cunliffe, B., and Poole, C. 1991. *Danebury: an Iron Age hillfort in Hampshire. Volume 5. The excavations 1979–1988: the finds*. London: Council for British Archaeology.

Daire, M.-Y. 2002. Armorica in the context of Atlantic and cross-Channel contacts during the La Tène period. In A. Lang and V. Salač (eds), *Fernkontakte in der Eisenzeit*, 160–72. Prague: Archäologisches Institut der Akademie der Wissenschaften der Tschechischen Republik.

Dechezleprêtre, T., and Ginoux, N.-C. 2005. Les constructions circulaires de la moitié nord de la France: État de la question. In O. Buchsenschutz and C. Mordant (eds), *Architectures protohistoriques en Europe occidentale du Néolithique final à l'âge du Fer*, 77–87. Paris: Comité des Travaux Historiques et Scientifiques.

de Jersey, P. 1999. Exotic Celtic coinage in Britain. *Oxford Journal of Archaeology* 18, 189–216.

Desenne, S., Auxiette, G., Demoule, J.-P., Gaudefroy, S., Henon, B. and Thouvenot, S. 2009a. Dépôts, panoplies et accessoires dans les sépultures du second âge du Fer en Picardie. *Revue Archéologique de Picardie* 2009 (3–4), 175–86.

Desenne, S., Blancquaert, G., Gaudefroy, S., Gransar, M., Hénon, B. and Soupart, N. 2009b. Implantation et occupation des espaces funéraires au second âge du Fer en Picardie. *Revue Archéologique de Picardie* 2009 (3–4), 25–45.

Diepeveen-Jansen, M. 2001. *People, Ideas and Goods. New perspectives on 'Celtic barbarians' in western and central Europe (500–250 BC)*, Amsterdam Archaeological Studies 7. Amsterdam: Amsterdam University Press.

Fell, V. 1990. *Pre-Roman Iron Age metalworking tools from England and Wales: Their use, technology, and archaeological context*. PhD thesis, University of Durham (http://etheses.dur.ac.uk/6610/).

Fitzpatrick, A. 1989. *Cross-Channel relations in the British later Iron Age*. PhD thesis, University of Durham (http://etheses.dur.ac.uk/949/).

Fitzpatrick, A. 1993. Ethnicity and exchange: Germans, Celts and Romans in the late (pre-Roman) Iron Age. In C. Scarre and F. Healy (eds), *Trade and Exchange in Prehistoric Europe*, 233–44. Oxford: Oxbow.

Fitzpatrick, A. 1997. *Archaeological investigations on the route of the A27 Westhampnett bypass, West Sussex, 1992. Volume 2: The late Iron Age, Romano-British and Anglo-Saxon cemeteries*. Salisbury: Wessex Archaeology.

Fitzpatrick, A. 2001. Cross-Channel exchange, Hengistbury Head, and the end of hillforts. In J. Collis (ed.) *Society and settlement in Iron Age Europe*, 82–97. Sheffield: J.R. Collis.

Fitzpatrick, A. 2003. Roman amphorae in Iron Age Britain, *Journal of Roman Pottery Studies* 10, 10–25.

Gautier, S. and Annaert, R. 2006. Een woonerf uit de midden-ijzertijd onder de verkaveling Capelakker te Brecht-Overbroek (prov. Antwerpen). *Relicta* 2, 9–48.

Gerloff, S. 2004. Hallstatt fascination: 'Hallstatt' buckets, swords and chapes from Britain and Ireland. In H. Roche, E. Grogan, J. Bradley, J. Coles and B. Raftery (eds), *From megaliths to metals: Essays in honour of George Eogan*, 124–54. Oxford: Oxbow Books.

Giles, M. 2012. *A Forged Glamour. Landscape, Identity and Material Culture in the Iron Age.* Oxford: Windgather.

Gomez de Soto, J., Bourhis, J.-R., Ghesquière, E., Marcigny, C., Menez, Y., Rivallain, J. and Verron, G. 2009. Pour en finir avec le Bronze final? Les haches à douille de type armoricain en France. In M.-J. Roulière-Lambert, A. Daubigney, P.-Y. Milcent, M. Talon and J. Vital (eds) *De l'âge du Bronze à l'âge du Fer en Europe occidentale (Xe – VIIe siècle av. J.-C.). La moyenne vallée du Rhône aux âges du Fer*, 507–12. Dijon.

Green, C. and Peacock, D. 2011. The puddingstone industries in France and Britain (http://www.sal.org.uk/fundraising/research/puddingstone/).

Gruel, K. and Haselgrove, C. 2007. British potins abroad: A new find from central France and the Iron Age in southeast England. In C. Gosden, H. Hamerow, P. de Jersey and G. Lock (eds), *Communities and Connections. Essays in Honour of Barry Cunliffe*, 240–62. Oxford: Oxford University Press.

Guillaumet, J.-P. and Eugène, A. 2009. À propos de trois objets métalliques, témoins des relations entre le pays éduen et les Îles Britanniques. In G. Cooney, K. Becker, J. Coles, M. Ryan and S. Sievers (eds), *Relics of Old Decency: Archaeological studies in later prehistory*, 241–8. Dublin: Wordwell.

Hamilton, S. 2007. Cultural choices in the 'British Eastern Channel Area' in the late pre-Roman Iron Age. In C. Haselgrove and T. Moore (eds), *The Later Iron Age in Britain and Beyond*, 81–106. Oxford: Oxbow Books.

Hansen, L. and Meyer, C. 2006. Leichen im Kornsilo – nicht nur Fürstengräber am Glauberg. *Hessen Archäologie* 2005, 65–8.

Haselgrove, C. 1982. Wealth, prestige and power: The dynamics of late Iron Age political centralisation in south-east England. In C. Renfrew and S. Shennan (eds), *Ranking, Resource and Exchange. Aspects of the Archaeology of Early European Society*, 79–88. Cambridge: Cambridge University Press.

Haselgrove, C. 1995. Late Iron Age society in Britain and north-west Europe: Structural transformation or superficial change? In B. Arnold and D. Gibson (eds), *Celtic Chiefdom, Celtic State*, 81–7. Cambridge: Cambridge University Press.

Haselgrove, C. 1999. The development of Iron Age coinage in Belgic Gaul. *Numismatic Chronicle* 159, 111–68.

Haselgrove, C. 2001. Iron Age Britain and its European setting. In J. Collis (ed.), *Society and Settlement in Iron Age Europe*, 37–72. Sheffield: J.R. Collis.

Haselgrove, C. 2002. Contacts between Britain and the Continent during the Iron Age. In A. Lang and V. Salač (eds), *Fernkontakte in der Eisenzeit*, 282–97. Prague: Archäologisches Institut der Akademie der Wissenschaften der Tschechischen Republik.

Haselgrove, C. and Hingley, R. 2006. Iron deposition and its significance in pre-Roman Britain. In G. Bataille and J.-P. Guillaumet (eds), *Les dépôts métalliques au second âge du Fer en Europe tempérée*, 147–63. Glux-en-Glenne: Bibracte Centre Archéologique Européen.

Haselgrove, C., Vander Linden, M. and Webley, L. in prep. Modern borders and the later prehistory of northwest Europe. In R. Crellin, C. Fowler and R. Tipping (eds), *Prehistory without borders*. Oxford: Oxbow Books.

Hawkes, C. 1959. The ABC of the British Iron Age, *Antiquity* 33, 170–82.

Henderson, J. 2007. *The Atlantic Iron Age. Settlement and Identity in the First Millennium BC.* Abingdon: Routledge.

Hessing, W. 1993. Ondeugende Bataven en verdwaalde Friezinnen? Enkele gedachten over de onverbrande menselijke resten uit de ijzertijd en de Romeinse tijd in West- en Noord-Nederland. In E. Drenth, W. Hessing and E. Knol (eds), *Het tweede leven van onze doden*, Nederlandse Archeologische Rapporten 15, 17–40. Amersfoort.

Hill, J. D. 1995. The pre-Roman Iron Age in Britain and Ireland (ca. 800 B.C. to A.D. 100): An overview. *Journal of World Prehistory* 9, 47–98.

Hill, J. D., and Willis, S. 2013. Middle Bronze Age to the end of the pre-Roman Iron Age, *c* 1500 BC to AD 50. In J. Ransley and F. Sturt (eds), *People and the Sea: A maritime archaeological research agenda for England*, CBA Research Report 171, 75–92. York: Council for British Archaeology.

Hodson, F. 1964. Cultural grouping within the British pre-Roman Iron Age. *Proceedings of the Prehistoric Society* 30, 99–110.

Holman, D. 2005. Iron Age coinage and settlement in east Kent. *Britannia* 36, 1–54.

Hunter, F. 2005. The image of the warrior in the British Iron Age: Coin iconography in context. In C. Haselgrove and D. Wigg-Wolf (eds), *Iron Age Coinage and Ritual Practices*, 43-68. Mainz: Philipp von Zabern.

Hunter, F., and Carruthers, M. (eds). 2012. *Iron Age Scotland: ScARF Panel Report*, version 2. (http://www.scottishheritagehub.com/sites/default/files/u12/ScARF%20Iron%20Age%20Sept%20 2012.pdf)

James, S. 1999. *The Atlantic Celts: Ancient people or modern invention?* London: British Museum Press.

Jay, M., Haselgrove, C., Hamilton, D., Hill, J. D. and Dent, J. 2012. Chariots and context: New radiocarbon dates from Wetwang and the chronology of Iron Age burials and brooches in East Yorkshire. *Oxford Journal of Archaeology* 31, 161–89.

Jay, M., Montgomery, J., Nehlich, O., Towers, J. and Evans, J. 2013. British Iron Age chariot burials of the Arras culture: a multi-isotope approach to investigating mobility levels and subsistence practices. *World Archaeology* 45, 473–91.

Koch, J. T. 2013. Ha C1a ≠ PC ('The earliest Hallstatt Iron Age cannot equal Proto-Celtic'). In J. T. Koch and B. Cunliffe (eds) *Celtic from the West 2. Rethinking the Bronze Age and the Arrival of Indo-Europeans in Atlantic Europe*, 1–16. Oxford: Oxbow Books.

Kurz, G. 1995. *Keltische Hort- und Gewässerfunde in Mitteleuropa – Deponierungen der Latènezeit*. Stuttgart: Konrad Theiss.

Le Bihan, J.-P., and Méniel, P. 2002. Un dépôt d'ossements du premier âge du Fer sur l'île d'Ouessant: Déchets alimentaires ou restes de banquets. In P. Méniel and B. Lambot (eds), *Découvertes récentes de l'âge du Fer dans le massif des Ardennes et ses marges. Repas des vivants et nourriture pour les morts en Gaule. Actes du XXVe colloque international de l'Association Française pour l'Etude de l'Age du Fer*, 303–16. Bulletin de la Société Archéologique Champenoise 16.

Le Bihan, J.-P., Guillaumet, J.-P., Méniel, P., Roussot-Larroque, J. and Villard, J.-F. 2007. Du Bronze moyen à l'Antiquité, un lieu de culte inscrit dans la longue durée: Mez-Notariou – Ouessant. In P. Barral, A. Daubigny, C. Dunning, G. Kaenel and M.-J. Roulière-Lambert (eds), *L'âge du Fer dans l'arc jurassien et ses marges. Dépôts, lieux sacrés et territorialité à l'âge du Fer. Actes du XXIXe colloque international de l'Association française pour l'étude de l'âge du Fer (Bienne (Suisse), 5–8 mai 2005)*, 629–52. Besançon: Presses Universitaires de Franche-Comté.

Lefort, A. 2008. *Les relations trans-Manche à la fin de l'âge du Fer: Contributions et perspectives à travers l'étude du site d'Urville-Nacqueville (Manche)*. Mémoire de Master 2, Université de Bourgogne.

Lefort, A. 2010. *Opération de fouilles archéologiques sur l'estran d'Urville-Nacqueville. Rapport final d'opération 2010*. Université de Bourgogne.

Lefort, A. 2011. *Opération de fouilles archéologiques sur l'estran d'Urville-Nacqueville. Rapport final d'opération 2011*. Université de Bourgogne.

Macready, S. and Thompson, F. 1984. *Cross-Channel Trade between Gaul and Britain in the pre-Roman Iron Age*. London: Society of Antiquaries of London.

Malrain, F. and Pinard, E. 2006. *Les sites laténiens de la moyenne vallée de l'Oise du Ve au Ier s. avant notre ère*, Revue Archéologique de Picardie Numéro Spécial 23.

Madgwick, R., Mulville, J. and Stevens, R. 2012. Diversity in foddering strategy and herd management in late Bronze Age Britain: An isotope investigation of pigs and other fauna from two midden sites. *Environmental Archaeology* 17, 126–40.

Marcigny, C. and Talon, M. 2009. Sur les rives de la Manche. Qu'en est-il du passage de l'âge du Bronze à l'âge du Fer à partir des découvertes récentes? in M.-J. Roulière-Lambert, A. Daubigney, P.-Y. Milcent, M. Talon and J. Vital (eds), *De l'âge du Bronze à l'âge du Fer en France et en Europe occidentale (Xe – VIIe siècle av. J.-C.). La moyenne vallée du Rhône aux âges du Fer. Actes du XXXe colloque international de l'AFEAF, co-organisé avec l'APRAB (Saint-Romain-en-Gal, 26-28 mai 2006)*, 385–403. Dijon.

McKinley, J., Schuster, J. and Millard, A. 2013. Dead-sea connections. A Bronze Age and Iron Age ritual site on the Isle of Thanet. In J. T. Koch and B. Cunliffe (eds), *Celtic from the West 2. Rethinking the Bronze Age and the Arrival of Indo-Europeans in Atlantic Europe*, 157–83. Oxford: Oxbow.

Milcent, P.-Y. 2009. Le passage de l'âge du Bronze à l'âge du Fer en Gaule au miroir des élites sociales: Une crise au VIIIe siècle av. J.-C.?. In M.-J. Roulière-Lambert (ed.), *De l'âge du Bronze à l'âge du Fer en France et en Europe occidentale (Xe–VIIe siècle av. J.-C.). La moyenne vallée du Rhône aux âges du Fer. Actes du XXXe colloque international de l'AFEAF, co-organisé avec l'APRAB (Saint-Romain-en-Gal, 26–28 mai 2006)*, 453–76. Dijon.

Moore, T. and Armada, X.-L. (eds). 2012a. *Atlantic Europe in the First Millennium BC. Crossing the Divide*. Oxford: Oxford University Press.

Moore, T. and Armada, X.-L. 2012b. Crossing the divide: Opening a dialogue on approaches to western European first millennium BC studies. In T. Moore and L. Armada (eds), *Atlantic Europe in the First Millennium BC. Crossing the Divide*, 3–77. Oxford: Oxford University Press.

Morris, F.M. 2010. *North Sea and Channel Connectivity during the Late Iron Age and Roman Period (175/150 BC–AD 409)*, British Archaeological Report S2157. Oxford: Archaeopress.

O'Connor, B. 2007. Llyn Fawr metalwork in Britain: A review. In C. Haselgrove and R. Pope (eds), *The Earlier Iron Age in Britain and Beyond*, 64–79. Oxford: Oxbow Books.

Oudry-Braillon, S. 2009. Vers une géographie des gestes funéraires au second âge du Fer dans le Nord-Pas-de-Calais? *Revue Archéologique de Picardie* 2009 (3–4), 61–70.

Parcero Oubiña, C., and Cobas Fernández, I. 2004. Iron Age archaeology of the northwest Iberian peninsula, *e-Keltoi: Journal of Interdisciplinary Celtic Studies* 6, 1–72. (http://www4.uwm.edu/celtic/ekeltoi/volumes/vol6/)

Parfitt, K. 2012. Folkestone: Roman villa or Iron Age oppidum? *Current Archaeology* 262, 22–9.

Paris, P., Petit, C., Huault, V., Pradier, B. and Faggionato, J.-L. 2000. Le vase en sapropélite de Saint-Gatien-des-Bois (Latène D1, Calvados, Basse-Normandie). Témoin d'échange entre la Bretagne insulaire et la Gaule. In M. Truffeau-Libre and A. Jacques (eds), *La céramique en Gaule et Bretagne romaines: Commerce, contacts et romanisation*, 107–16. Nord-Ouest Archéologie 12.

Pommepuy, C. 1999. Le matériel de mouture de la vallée de l'Aisne de l'âge du Bronze à La Tène finale: Formes et matériaux. *Revue Archéologique de Picardie* 1999 (3–4), 115–41.

Roymans, N. 2007. On the latènisation of late Iron Age material culture in the Lower Rhine/Meuse area. In S. Möllers, W. Schlüter and S. Sievers (ed.), *Keltische Einflüsse im nördlichen Mitteleuropa während der mittleren und jüngeren vorrömischen Eisenzeit*, 311–25. Bonn: Rudolf Habelt.

Schulze-Forster, J. 2007. Die Burgen der Mittelgebirgszone. Eisenzeitliche Fluchtburgen, befestigte Siedlungen, Zentralorte oder Kultplätze?. In S. Möllers and B. Zehm (eds), *Rätsel Schnippenburg. Sagenhafte Funde aus der Keltenzeit*, 109–44. Bonn: Rudolf Habelt.

Sharples, N. 1990. Late Iron Age society and Continental trade in Dorset. In A. Duval, J.-P. Le Bihan and Y. Menez (eds), *Les Gaulois d'Armorique*, 299–304. Revue Archéologique de l'Ouest Supplément 3.

Sharples, N. 2010a. Review of Jon C. Henderson 'The Atlantic Iron Age'. *Antiquaries Journal* 90, 480–1.

Sharples, N. 2010b. *Social Relations in Later Prehistory. Wessex in the First Millennium BC*. Oxford: Oxford University Press.

Sharples, N. and Waddington, K. 2011. *The Excavations at Whitchurch 2006–2009. An Interim Report*. Cardiff: Cardiff Studies in Archaeology Specialist Report 31.

Taylor, J. 2001. The Isle of Portland: An Iron Age port-of-trade. *Oxford Journal of Archaeology* 20, 187–205.

Teichmüller, M. 1992. Organic petrology in the service of archaeology. *International Journal of Coal Geology* 20, 1–21.

Trott, K. and Tomalin, D. 2003. The maritime role of the island of Vectis in the British pre-Roman Iron Age. *International Journal of Nautical Archaeology* 32, 158–81.

Tuohy, T. 1999. *Prehistoric Combs of Antler and Bone*. British Archaeological Report 285. Oxford: British Archaeological Reports.

University of Reading 2012. Iron Age people introduced Mediterranean cuisine to Britain! Press release 18th July 2012 (http://www.reading.ac.uk/news-and-events/releases/PR456267.aspx)

Van de Noort, R. 2011. Crossing the divide in the first millennium BC: A study into the cultural biographies of boats. In T. Moore and L. Armada (eds), *Atlantic Europe in the First Millennium BC. Crossing the Divide*, 521–33. Oxford: Oxford University Press.

van der Sanden, W. 1996. *Through Nature to Eternity. The Bog Bodies of Northwest Europe*. Amsterdam: Batavian Lion International.

van Heeringen, R.M. 1987. The Iron Age in the western Netherlands II: Site catalogue and pottery description map sheet I. *Berichten van de Rijksdienst voor het Oudheidkundig Bodemonderzoek* 37, 39–121.

Vauterin, C.-C., Chanson, K., Zaour, N., Féret, L. and Le Forestier, S. 2011. La culture matérielle de l'âge du Fer: Un outil de réflexion sur les sites d'habitat de Basse-Normandie. In P. Barral, B. Dedet, F. Delrieu, P. Giraud, I. Le Goff, S. Marion and A. Villard-Le Tiec (eds), *L'âge du Fer en Basse-Normandie*, 203–29. Besançon: Presses Universitaires de Franche-Comté.

Villard-Le Tiec, A., Gomez de Soto, J. and Bouvet, J.-P. 2010. Pratiques funéraires du second âge du Fer en Gaule de l'Ouest (Bretagne, Pays de la Loire, Poitou-Charentes). In P. Barral, B. Dedet, F. Delrieu, P. Giraud, I. Le Goff, S. Marion and A. Villard-Le Tiec (eds), *Gestes funéraires en Gaule au second âge du Fer*, 85–106. Besançon: Presses Universitaires de Franche-Comté.

Webley, L. 2008. *Iron Age Households: structure and practice in western Denmark, 500 BC–AD 200*. Aarhus: Aarhus University Press.

Webley, L. forthcoming. Households and communities. In C. Haselgrove, P. Wells and K. Rebay-Salisbury (eds), *The Oxford Handbook to the European Iron Age*. Oxford: Oxford University Press.

Wefers, S. 2011. Still using your saddle quern? A compilation of the oldest known rotary querns in western Europe. In D. Williams and D. Peacock (eds), *Bread for the People: The archaeology of mills and milling*, British Archaeological Report S2274, 67–76.

Wilhelmi, K. 1977. Zur Funktion und Verbreitung dreieckiger Tongewichte der Eisenzeit. *Germania* 55, 180–4.

9

Connections and separation? Narratives of Iron Age art in Britain and its relationship with the Continent

Jody Joy

The well-known 1st century BC hoard from Broighter near Limavady, Northern Ireland contained amongst other things a beautifully decorated tubular torc and a model of a nine-benched-and-oared sailing boat. This fascinating collection of artefacts very visibly links Iron Age art and travel but these links or connections have rarely been joined up in scholarship. There is much discussion assessing possible imports (e.g. Stead 1984) and exports (e.g. Megaw 1963), or detailing stylistic links (or lack thereof) between Britain and the Continent (e.g. Stead 1996, Ch. 2), but little consideration of how objects may have come to Britain or what imports or similarities in art style with the Continent might tell us about continental connections.

The aim of this paper is to re-assert the analytical value of Iron Age art with continental connections by considering a number of case studies in detail. Whilst not attempting to present an exhaustive survey of new discoveries, where possible, new, or less well-known objects are discussed, especially discoveries made by metal detector users and recorded through the Portable Antiquities Scheme (www.finds.org.uk).

Artistic backdrop

Before turning to the case studies, the evidence and the main arguments that have been put forward in the literature will be summarised, starting in the period just before so-called Celtic art was first made and used.

Early imports
A small number of continental imports dating to the sixth and fifth centuries BC have been discovered (Meyer 1985), particularly in and around the River Thames. These include possible objects from the Mediterranean world and central Europe such as the cordoned bucket from the River Wey at Brooklands, Weybridge (Figure 9.1). Discussion of these objects by Harden (1950) and Harbison and Laing (1974), among others, has tended to concentrate on whether they are genuine imports or artefacts discarded by nineteenth century collectors, with most of these objects assessed as more recent imports into Britain.

A recent paper by Richard Bradley and Amy Smith (2007) examining a Greek cup found in the River Thames questions this conclusion. Bradley and Smith point out that many of these imports come from a restricted area in or close to the River Thames (*ibid.*, 32). 19th century collectors, they argue, could have dumped their unwanted objects anywhere in Britain. They also link deposition of these objects in the River Thames to the deposition of early Iron Age swords in the middle Thames area.

Celtic Art Styles or 'Stages'

So-called Celtic or La Tène art first appears in Europe during the middle of the fifth century BC (see Jacobsthal 1969 [1944]). Early examples are known from Britain after 400 BC but they are rare (Garrow & Gosden 2012, 28; Jope 2000). Celtic art from Britain has been classified many times (e.g. De

Figure 9.1. The Brooklands Bucket from Weybridge, Surrey (P&E 1907,0715.1) (© The Trustees of the British Museum).

Navarro 1952; Jope 2000; Stead 1985a; 1985b) but common to all of these classifications is the idea that initially designs follow those on the Continent before so-called 'insular' styles develop from around 300 BC (Macdonald 2007, 329–332; Stead 1996, Ch. 2).

The most enduring classificatory scheme developed by Stead (1985a; 1985b) recognises five distinct, sequential styles or 'stages' of art. The earliest art (Stage I), dating from the fifth century BC to the second half of the fourth century, consists of a small repertoire of motifs thought to derive from the Greek and Etruscan worlds, particularly the palmette. Examples from Britain decorated in this style include a sword handle from Fiskerton, Lincolnshire and a scabbard from Wisbech, Cambridgeshire. Perhaps the best-known example is the Cerrigydrudion headpiece from Clwyd. This has been recently re-dated to the beginning of the fourth century BC and possibly the latter half of the fifth, showing that it is the earliest dated example of Celtic art from Britain (Garrow *et al.* 2009, 107). This dating calls into question the traditional assumption that early art necessarily always follows developments on the Continent. Indeed, if early imports of Mediterranean objects are genuine, there is no reason why some early developments in art could not have originated in Britain. For example, while examining a particular style of motif found on La Tène I pottery from Chinnor, Oxfordshire, Timothy Champion (1977) draws comparisons with similar motifs that appear on imported Etruscan metal vessels found on the Continent. To date, none of these vessels have been discovered in Britain but Champion argued that a local potter must have been familiar with one of these objects, most probably he argues because some also found their way to Britain.

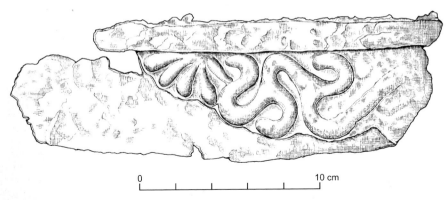

Figure 9.2. Decorated iron mount from cauldron SF 10, Chiseldon, Wiltshire (drawn by Craig Williams, © The Trustees of the British Museum).

Stage II of Stead's stylistic sequence is the 'Waldalgesheim' or 'Vegetal' Style. It dates to the later fourth and early third centuries BC and comprises flowing tendrils. The style is widely distributed from Hungary to England (Stead 1996, 22). Well-known examples include decorative friezes on the shield from Ratcliffe-on-Soar, Nottinghamshire (Watkin *et al.* 1996), which is very similar in its decorations to some Italian sword scabbards. To the examples from Britain we can add a decorative repoussé iron mount riveted to the upper section of a cauldron from Chiseldon, near Swindon, Wiltshire (Figure 9.2). This is part of a deposit of 17 cauldrons from a single large pit which has been radiocarbon dated to the fourth or third centuries BC (Joy & Baldwin forthcoming). The pit also contains two other cauldrons decorated in different styles but using the same manufacturing techniques. This evidence suggests the cauldron decorated with the Vegetal Style mount is not an import but was manufactured in Britain alongside the other cauldrons from the pit.

Stage III encompasses the broadly contemporary 'Plastic' and 'Sword' Styles, these objects are the last objects seen to be decorated in a similar fashion to continental Celtic art and date to the third and early second centuries BC (Garrow & Gosden 2012, 81). So-called dragon-pairs form part of the Sword Style, these are found on sword scabbards across Europe from Britain as far east as Romania (Stead 1996, 29; Wells 2012, 124–125). Few examples of Plastic Style art are known from Britain but recent finds show that the style was in use. In addition to the so-called Grotesque Torc from Snettisham, Norfolk can be added a copper-alloy pin from Ropely, Hampshire discovered by a metal detector user in October 2010 (Figure 9.3) and the copper-alloy head of a lynchpin from Cambridgeshire (Figure 9.4). Discovered sometime in the 1980s, unfortunately the exact findspot of the lynchpin was not recorded.

Despite these seemingly wide links, in style at least, between Britain and continental Europe, after around 300 BC Stead argues that there is a breakdown in the relationship with the Continent with the development of so-called insular art styles in Britain, which he labels Stages IV and V (Stead 1996, 29). Stage IV is seen as contemporary with Stage III, with Stage V starting before 200 BC but continuing to the Roman Conquest (Garrow & Gosden 2012, 81).

Figure 9.3. Decorated pin from Ropley, Hampshire (PAS No: HAMP-C319B7) (© The Trustees of the British Museum).

From the late second century BC and especially from 100 BC onwards, marked social changes such as the adoption of burials and the use of coinage occur in some areas of southern England and evidence for cross-Channel trade and the movement of peoples and ideas is also much more visible (Cunliffe 2009, 80; Morris 2010; Hill & Willis 2013, 75). For example, by the mid-first century BC Celtic art all but stops being deposited in southern England and is replaced in graves by imports and objects inspired by imports (Hunter 2006, 107). During the first two centuries AD art again takes on a different significance being made and used in unprecedented quantities, intimately linked to new identities created at the time of and on the frontiers of conquest (Davis & Gwilt 2008; Hunter 2008; Garrow & Gosden 2012; Joy 2014).

Problems with Stead's Stylistic Sequence
Philip Macdonald has recently interrogated the validity of Stead's classificatory scheme, questioning the chronological significance of his style sequence by highlighting objects ornamented with a number of different art styles (Macdonald 2007, 332–333). For example, he argues that while the terminal of the Clevedon torc is decorated with Stage V art, the collar of the terminal is ornamented in a way that is reminiscent of Stage II (*ibid.*, 332). Similarly, the Ratcliffe shield-boss discussed above is ornamented with Waldalgesheim Style (Stage II) friezes but the central boss is in the Sword Style (Stage III) (Stead 1996, 26). This evidence indicates that at each new stage, new motifs are added to the decorative repertoire and older styles or motifs are drawn upon and referenced in later work (see Garrow & Gosden 2012, 80). This clearly undermines the usefulness of Stead's art stages in terms of dating artefacts but it also opens up new avenues of enquiry, such as, questioning the motivations behind decorating objects with a mixture of art styles or stages.

Also of relevance to this paper is the contemporaneity of Stages III and IV; objects on the one hand that follow continental styles (Stage III) and the other, the first so-called insular style of art (Stage IV), are made and circulating in use at

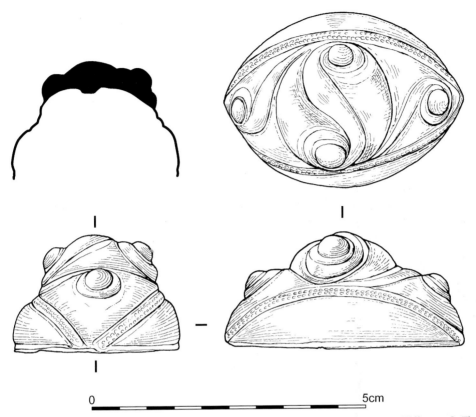

Figure 9.4. Copper-alloy head of a lynchpin (P&E 2013,8044.1) (drawn by Craig Williams, © The Trustees of the British Museum).

the same time. To blur the boundaries further, Stead himself draws on similarities between continental objects and 'insular' Stage IV objects. For example, coherencies are drawn between the Hungarian Sword Style and Stage IV objects such as the Witham shield and scabbard and the two shield bosses from the River Thames at Wandsworth (Stead 1996, 29–31).

Re-interpreting 'insular' art

The period when insular art styles are first in use (after 300 BC) also coincides with a time when very few discernible imports generally made it to Britain (see Hill & Willis 2013, 75) and these two pieces of evidence combined are used in the general narrative of Iron Age contacts with the Continent to argue that there are very few contacts with the Continent at this time (e.g. Cunliffe 2009, 84–86).

When a holistic approach to the evidence is adopted, evidence for continental connections can also be seen through the sharing of new technologies and artefact types (Webley, this volume). New strands of evidence support this argument. For example, it is also now possible to

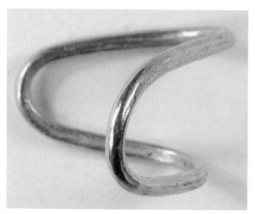

Figure 9.5. V-shaped finger ring from Biggleswade, Bedforshire (P&E 2011,8016.1) (© The Trustees of the British Museum).

consider other types of potential imported material culture such as v-shaped finger rings. These date from 400–200 BC and have a continental distribution centred around western Switzerland (Cunliffe 2005, 470, Figure 17.19). In addition to the well-known silver finger ring from Park Brow, West Sussex (Tait 1976, No. 458) can be added a number of recent gold finds by metal detector users. New finds include a ring found near Biggleswade, Bedfordshire (Figure 9.5) and a further possible ring from Yoxall, Staffordshire (PAS No: WMID-BCA708). In addition to a possible gold finger ring of a different type reportedly from the Queen's Barrow at Arras, East Riding (Jope 1995; Stead 1979, 86, Figure 34) and ribbon torcs (see below), these are amongst the only precious metal objects in circulation in Britain at this time. Mansel Spratling (in Tait 1976, 263) suggests Park Brow could be an Iron Age import as it is made of silver, which was otherwise very rarely used to manufacture objects in Britain at this time. Stead (1984, 62) defines the Park Brow finger ring as 'an unassociated stray find' as unfortunately its exact context was not recorded when it was excavated. The presence and wide distribution of the new finds of v-shaped finger rings add weight to the argument that they represent genuine finds dating to the Iron Age and, like the objects deposited in the Thames described above, makes it very unlikely that they were brought to this country by modern-day collectors.

The limited range of contexts Celtic art is found in before the late Iron Age is also frequently overlooked in the literature. As people were often not buried in archaeologically visible ways in Iron Age Britain, one of the contexts in which much of the art from the Continent derives is largely absent from the archaeological record (Champion 1977, 93). This means that outside of East Yorkshire (where there is a tradition for inhumation burials), before the late second century BC, when cremations first occur in south-east England and hoards become more common, deposition is restricted to watery contexts (primarily rivers), isolated or unusual burials, and fragmentary remains from settlements. Art objects may therefore have been far more common, they just weren't deposited in a manner which is archaeologically visible. It is also informative to question how much of the Celtic art from the Continent we would be aware of if the major regional burial traditions were not there, especially those objects dating earlier than 300 BC. For example, many of the objects listed in Jacobsthal's (1969 [1944]) catalogue of European Celtic art are either directly from, or are associated with graves.

Summary

In summary, the dominant interpretation that continental connections drop off around 300 BC can be challenged. Although Celtic art in Britain begins to diverge from the Continent

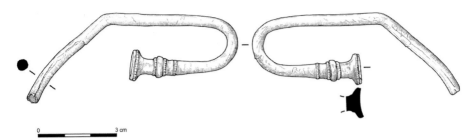

Figure 9.6. Torc fragment from Caister, Lincolnshire (PAS No: NLM-605352) (drawn by Craig Williams, © The Trustees of the British Museum).

at around this time, a small number of objects can be linked stylistically with continental material, implying that some form of contact whether through object exchange and/or the movement of people is still being maintained. The dominance in terms of the numbers of 'insular' style versus continental style art has probably masked this continuing pattern. Macdonald and others have shown that art styles or stages are not fixed, rather new styles add to the decorative repertoire. This means that art cannot be considered in isolation and other sources of evidence for continental connections such as new finds like v-shaped finger rings should also be sought. Nevertheless, the pattern of initial coherency in art styles with the Continent, with a slow shift to more insular styles, still holds and will be considered further in the discussion below.

How did imports get to Britain?

Like the cauldron mount from Chiseldon, many of the other objects discussed so far were made in Britain but show stylistic similarities with objects from the continent. A recently discovered example of a probable import from the continent is a gold torc found by a metal detector user at Caister, Lincolnshire (Figure 9.6). While it can be compared to similar gold examples from well-known continental deposits such as Waldalgesheim (Joachim 1995), bronze torcs of similar form are also typical of the Marne region during the beginning of the 4th century BC (e.g. Stead & Rigby 1999, nos. 1879 & 1796). A very similar gold torc was also discovered at Heerlen in the north-east corner of the Netherlands (Echt *et.al.* 2011).

Until recently there has been no joined up thinking between maritime and object specialists. In discussions of Celtic art objects they materialise in Britain with very little consideration of how they got here (Cunliffe 2009 is a notable exception). As Sean McGrail observes, "…the middle phase of many an ancient artefact's life … included an overseas voyage and thus … an important element in [the] prehistoric economic and social life [which is] not without interest to the most landlubberly of archaeologists" (McGrail 1993, 199).

A number of mechanisms by which objects arrived from the Continent have been put forward including as personal objects, gifts, war booty and by exchange, implying the movement of individuals, ideas or beliefs (Stead 1984, 43; Hunter 2006, 103; Morris 2010, 7–9). The journeys these objects undertook were probably also formed of a number of stages with crossing the Channel representing a small but major part of journeys probably also involving land and riverine travel as well as cabotage (see Cunliffe 2009, 88).

Work on Iron Age diets and site assemblages, for which evidence of fish is often conspicuously absent, indicates that for some groups there may have been a cultural prohibition on the consumption of food associated with water, including the sea (Willis 2007; Hill & Willis 2013, 82–83). Some people or groups probably did eat fish but the absence of fish remains on British Iron Age sites, and also across the North Sea in Belgium, has been demonstrated to be a real phenomenon and not a product of taphonomic processes (Dobney & Ervynck 2007, 409). One of the possible reasons for this could be that the sea had some form of wider social significance. Robert Van de Noort views the sea as having a potential otherworldly status of its own (Van de Noort 2011). Citing coins of Cunobelin and Verica that both depict Neptune, Steven Willis suggested that even if this is not intended to directly link Iron Age gods with the Roman pantheon, it does hint at the possibility that for people in the late Iron Age a sea god was important (Willis 2007, 120). The anthropologist Mary Helms (1988) observes that access to exotic objects and knowledge of how to use them are signs of prestige in traditional societies. It may be the case that the same was also true during the Iron Age with travel across the sea adding esteem, allure, or even supernatural associations to objects.

Going back to our imported objects from the River Thames region, they provide evidence for a limited maritime route connecting the Rhine region with the Thames (Cunliffe 2009, 84) with Britain at the very end of a Mediterranean and European network. Like swords and other prestige objects, these imports' lives ended with them being deposited in the River Thames. They were therefore adopted by and assimilated into local practices and belief systems (Bradley & Smith 2007). Perhaps part of the reason why they were selected for special deposition is the middle phase of their lives, as they had travelled from across the sea, acquiring further esteem and allure.

Exports and trade

Most of the very few identified examples of Celtic art exported from Britain date to the later Iron Age. These include, the vase-headed lynchpin from Blicquy, Hainaut, Belgium (Demarez & Leman-Delerive 2001), a mirror handle from the River Oise at Compiègne, north-east of Paris (Guillaumet & Schönfelder 2001), and a spouted vessel from Łęg Piekarski, from central Poland (Megaw 1963). Sadly, the provenance of the terret described in the British Museum register as originating from Fayum, Egypt cannot be proven. Indeed, the next item in the museum register with the same donor is also a terret from Bapchild, Kent, making a clerical error seem far more likely than an Egyptian terret.

Throughout much of the literature on continental contacts, especially for the late Iron Age, there is much preoccupation with identifying trade with the Roman world. Identified imports of objects and raw materials to Britain are seen to be traded in exchange for exports of equal economic value, 'a balance of trade' (see Fitzpatrick 1993, 235; 2001). As the examples above demonstrate, very few British exports have been hitherto identified and the general consensus in the literature is that these exports must have been archaeologically invisible items such as the slaves and war dogs mentioned by Strabo (Fitzpatrick 1993, 235–236; Hill & Willis 2013, 88). As Hill and Willis (2013, 87) stated, this stress on trade may be artificial and result from contemporary concerns with the importance of trade rather than mirroring what was happening during the Iron Age. An emphasis on trade is also driven by a wider idea, supported throughout the history of Iron Age research, that social change is driven by outside influences, be they Iron Age Europeans or Romans (see Fitzpatrick 1993, 235). As is outlined above, exchange of artefacts is also not necessarily direct. The occurrence of Roman or Greek goods in Britain, for example, does not necessarily imply direct contact (*ibid*.) and objects could have passed through many hands before they reached their final destination.

As will be highlighted in the case studies below and is argued by the title of this paper, rather than concentrating on trade and identifying imports and exports, we should instead examine objects that travel between Britain and the Continent from the perspective of the social connections they potentially manifest. We should also consider that the means by which these objects eventually reached their final destination is unlikely to have been direct and these objects could have passed through numerous hands and contexts.

Case studies

The case-studies presented here predominantly date to the later Iron Age. Torcs are preferentially selected as they seem to be an object type often specifically selected in the past for travel.

The Blair Drummond hoard

The Blair Drummond hoard (Figure 9.7), discovered by a metal detector user in 2009 and currently being researched by Fraser Hunter at the National Museum of Scotland, is a unique collection of objects showing wide-ranging continental connections (Hunter 2010a; 2010b; 2010c). Two ribbon torcs made from single strips of twisted gold with hooked terminals are part of a rare group of finds from Scotland and Ireland. Distinguished from Bronze Age ribbon torcs by their tight spiral twisting, these objects probably date from 300–50 BC (Warner 2004).

Two joining fragments comprising complicated hollow triplet nodules resembling a vertebral column make up half of a tubular torc. This torc is similar to examples found near Toulouse, southwest France. It is a technical masterpiece constructed solely by hammering-up metal sheet. Only half of this torc was buried and the surviving pieces were broken before they were put in the ground. The

Figure 9.7. The Blair Drummond hoard (© National Museum of Scotland).

link between Toulouse and Stirling is unlikely to have been direct and it is unclear whether the Stirling torc was made in south-west France or in Scotland. If the torc is not an import, it was made by a metalworker familiar with the methods and techniques of manufacture common in south-west France at the time.

The fourth torc in the hoard is unique. Superficially it resembles a British type constructed from twisted wires with loop terminals such as many of those found at Snettisham, Norfolk (Stead 1991) (see below) but the way it is manufactured is like nothing else from Iron Age Britain. The eight twisted wires of the neck-ring are looped to form the terminal and then the two ends of each wire twisted into eight pairs to form the core of the hoop. The terminals are embellished with twisted wire fragments and balls of gold, creating a raised decorative effect. This seems like an attempt to recreate the terminals of twisted wire torcs where raised decoration is created by lost wax casting. The metalworking techniques of filigree and granulation used on the Blair Drummond torc were not really used in Iron Age Europe, leading Hunter to suggest that the metalworker originated and/or was trained in the Mediterranean (Hunter 2010c). Through this torc and the fragmentary example with triplet nodules a connection with Mediterranean metalworking techniques can be made indicating wider interaction spheres than have hitherto been appreciated, especially from the perspective of the sometimes parochial world of British Iron Age scholarship. Unfortunately without further research it is difficult to establish where the torcs were made, if they were made for an individual from Stirling or if these objects were exchanged as gifts or for some other reason.

Investigation of the findspot has exposed a large, circular wooden structure which is 11m in diameter and thought to be contemporary with the hoard, which if this is the case was buried near the back of the structure. It has an east facing door and a central pit but other domestic evidence was not uncovered. This evidence, combined with the isolated, wet nature of the setting has led Hunter to interpret it tentatively as some form of shrine rather than a house. The hoard looks therefore to be a religious offering made within a special building sometime between 300–100 BC (*ibid.*).

The Blair Drummond hoard fits into a wider tradition of hoarding of torcs which contain a mixture of local and exotic material. Another gold hoard in Scotland from Netherurd contained torcs and torc fragments (Feachem 1958) which probably originate from East Anglia and 'bullet-shaped' coins from northern France (Hunter 1997, 515). A concentration of finds of 'bullet' coins in Dorset has led to suggestions that many of these coins reached Britain from France via a route between the Cotentin Peninsula and Dorset (Haselgrove 2009, 174), although it is far from certain how the coins in the Netherurd hoard reached Scotland. From further afield, other examples of these torc hoards include the 1st century BC Broighter hoard mentioned in the introduction. The location of the Broighter Hoard in a salt marsh, on the edge of a sea-lough periodically inundated by the sea, caused Warner (1991, 617) to suggest the hoard was some kind of offering to the sea.

Hoard A, Snettisham, Norfolk
Hoard A at Snettisham could also be included in this group. It comprises three complete, and the remains of a fourth, tubular torcs (Clarke 1954; Stead 1991). Hoard A is one of 14 or so hoards from this well-known site (Joy and Farley forthcoming). Many hoards at Snettisham contain nests of torcs. Others such as Hoard F contain fragmentary torcs, bracelets, rings and ingots. All told this is one of the largest assemblages of precious metal from anywhere in

prehistoric Europe. The reason Hoard A has been singled out from the rest of the assemblage is that the torcs in the hoard are unusual. Many of the torcs from Snettisham are made of twisted wires. This so-called 'Snettisham Type' of torc is thought to have been made and used in East Anglia. Fragments of tubular torc are also known from some of the other hoards, particularly Hoard F, but these are much smaller in size. The tubular torcs from Hoard A on the other hand are much larger and have a more international currency with similar examples known from the Continent such as at Mailly-le-Camp, France (Clarke 1954), the Saint Louis hoard from near Basel (Megaw & Megaw 2001, Figure 309), as well as the example already discussed from Broighter in Northern Ireland. Even if the tubular torcs from Snettisham were made in Norfolk, the inspiration of their design comes from elsewhere.

So how then do we account for the inclusion of this type of torc at Snettisham? Snettisham is located on higher ground on what once might have been a headland (Figure 9.8). Recent analysis by Stephen Willis (2007, 120–121) showed that a number of late Iron Age sites interpreted as shrines are also located on higher ground overlooking the point where freshwater meets the sea. Snettisham can be viewed as an early example of this phenomenon, overlooking the River Heacham. The location of Snettisham may therefore be the source of its significance. If Snettisham was some form of shrine or a site of significance for Iron Age beliefs, it would explain why so much material was deposited there (Hutcheson 2004, 89–90). The location of Snettisham could also be linked to close contacts with the Continent. The distribution of twisted wire 'Snettisham Type' torcs during the second and first centuries BC in Britain is very much centred on East Anglia, in particular north-west Norfolk, and the identity of the people from this region seems very much bound up with torcs (Hutcheson 2004, 2007; Davies 1996). The gold and other precious metals used to make the torcs are thought to have been sourced by melting down coins imported from the Continent (see Sharples 2010, 146–159). By siting their most important religious site close to the sea they may also have been referencing these contacts.

The Winchester hoard, Hampshire
In 2000 a metal detector user discovered an unusual collection of jewellery near Winchester, Hampshire (Hill *et al.* 2004) (Figure 9.9). The jewellery, which was probably deposited as a hoard (*ibid.*, 3), comprised two torcs or necklaces of unusual manufacture, four brooches (consisting of two pairs), two chains and two bracelets. We know that the two brooches within each pair were originally attached to one another by one of the two chains as one pair was discovered still linked by a chain. The torc necklaces are slightly different sizes causing Hill *et al.* (*ibid.*) to interpret the jewellery as a matching set perhaps for a man and a woman or a senior and junior. The torc necklaces are unique in terms of manufacture, form and the method by which the terminals are clasped. Fortunately the brooches, although unusual because they are gold, are of a well-known type that can be dated to *c.* 75 – 25 BC.

This is a remarkable discovery, but of particular importance for the arguments presented here are the necklace torcs and the properties of the gold used to make these objects. Analysis of the gold indicates that if it did come from Britain it was from a source otherwise not used, or that the gold was refined but owing to the low silver content, it is thought that the source of the gold is more likely to have been within the Mediterranean world (*ibid.* 5). The necklace torcs are made in a different manner from the Snettisham Type torcs discussed above. They were made by bending and threading fine wires through each other to create

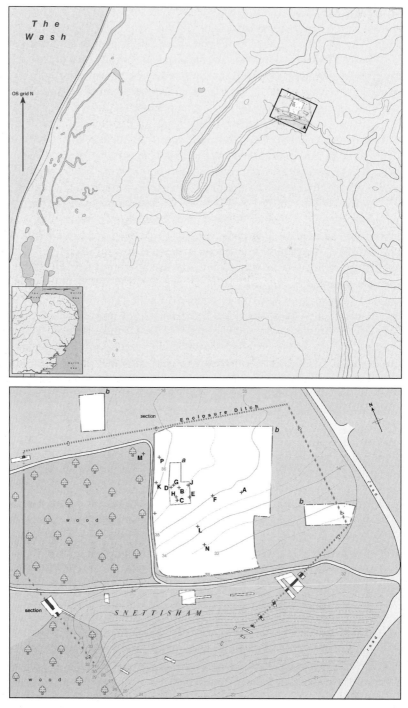

Figure 9.8. A map showing the location of the hoards found at Snettisham, Norfolk (drawn by Stephen Crummy, © The Trustees of the British Museum).

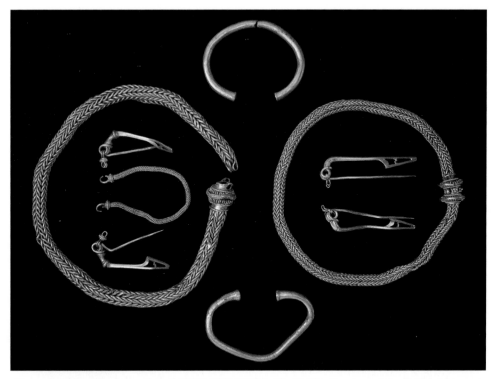

Figure 9.9. The Winchester hoard (P&E 2001,0901.1-10) (© The Trustees of the British Museum).

'loop-in-loop' chains, which were then linked together. This form of construction makes the necklace torcs far more flexible than the contemporary Snettisham Type or tubular torcs discussed above. This flexibility also necessitates the use of a clasp to secure the torc necklaces when worn, something that is not necessary with tubular or Snettisham Type torcs which are far more rigid. Like the source of the gold used to make these objects, the loop-in-loop technique and the form of the clasps used to make the torc necklaces is far closer to the technology and objects manufactured in the Mediterranean world at this time than they are to the techniques used to make similar objects in Britain, as is the use of filigree and granulation techniques to decorate the terminal clasps of the necklace torcs. Drawing all of this evidence together, the Winchester necklace torcs, like the torcs from the Blair Drummond hoard described above, may well have been made by craftspeople trained in the Mediterranean world (*ibid.* 16).

What then should we make of this remarkable discovery? How did these objects made by people working and/or trained in the Mediterranean world end up being deposited as a hoard of objects in a field in southern England, most probably sometime in the second half of the first century BC? Hill *et al.* (2004, 19) argue that the hoard probably represents a special commission for metalworkers trained in the Mediterranean world, requested to manufacture their own interpretation of a torc, an artefact typical of north Europe which may have been some kind of social symbol. It is impossible to ascertain who commissioned these objects and to unravel the complexity of their biographies before they were placed in the ground. Perhaps they belonged to a wealthy individual or couple who came to southern England in the mid-first century BC (Sharples 2010, 151). Alternatively, they could have been commissioned by one of the individuals who minted coinage declaring themselves as rulers or kings in southern England in the later first century BC (Hill *et al.* 2004, 19). The idea that they were some kind of diplomatic gift, perhaps from the Roman world has even been suggested (Creighton 2006, 42–44). What is clear is that the hoard represents increasingly close contact between southern England and parts of northern France in the second and first centuries BC and wider contact and knowledge of the Mediterranean world. What remains uncertain is the exact form of this contact and how this knowledge was gained and maintained. Was it via widely travelled individuals or did objects like the Winchester necklace torcs pass through numerous hands carrying their messages of a wider world with them?

Iron Age helmet, near Canterbury, Kent
Although not straightforwardly an 'art' object, a recent find of a late Iron Age helmet (Figure 9.10) and brooch made by a metal detector user in October 2012 near Canterbury, Kent, similarly demonstrates wider continental connections (Farley *et al.* 2014, 383). Subsequent investigation of the findspot by the Canterbury Archaeological Trust exposed a small, circular burial pit as well as cremated human bone and fragments of copper alloy. The helmet was placed in the grave upside down. The presence of the brooch probably indicates, like a number of other late Iron Age cremations from Kent, that the cremated bones were placed in a cloth or leather bag secured by the brooch (see Champion 2007, 127). The bag was then placed inside the helmet. Like the brooches from the Winchester Hoard the brooch can be dated to *c.* 75–25 BC (Farley *et al.* 2014, 383). Close parallels for the Canterbury helmet can be found on the Continent including a river find from Belleville near Lyon, a site find from the oppidum Vielle Toulouse and graves from Sigoyer, north of Marseille. All of these examples are from south-eastern France and date from the early-to-mid first century BC (*ibid.*).

This type of helmet has been attributed to both Roman and Gallic traditions of production but it does seem that the type is indigenous to Gaul, even if it was later adopted by the Romans during the Gallic wars. Context therefore is critical in interpreting these objects (*ibid.*). The helmets from Sigoyer have been interpreted as pre-Roman, whereas the helmet from Toulouse is seen to have belonged to a Roman auxiliary (*ibid.*).

The presence of a Gallic helmet dating to the mid-first century BC in a grave in Kent obviously invites speculation that this once belonged to a Roman auxiliary from one of Caesar's expeditions or possibly a native who took part in the Gallic wars. It is impossible to tie the helmet to historical events occurring in the mid-first century BC. Alongside Caesar's expeditions to Britain, was a wider military campaign on the Continent, which ultimately led to the incorporation of Gaul into the Roman Empire. The helmet is of a type which was used by Gauls and Romans, therefore there are many different ways it could have ended up in a grave in Kent. It is certainly possible that the helmet once belonged to a warrior from Britain or Gaul fighting as a mercenary against, or possibly even with, the Romans, who then brought the helmet to Britain. It could equally have been a gift or even an item acquired through trade but as Farley *et al.* (2014, 386) stress, even if the helmet were not directly associated with the Gallic wars, its military significance would not have been lost on the mourners at the grave side and its choice as a grave good is connected to some form of identity linked to military prowess, possibly that of the deceased or their kin.

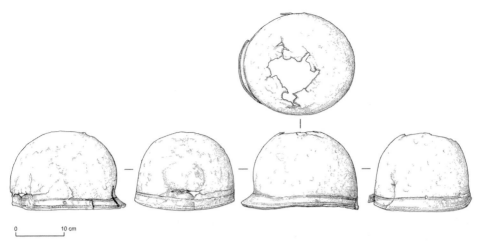

Figure 9.10. Helmet from near Canterbury, Kent (drawn by Craig Williams, © The Trustees of the British Museum).

Like the Winchester Hoard, the helmet highlights complicated connections with the Continent at this time of social upheaval in southern England, including the movement of people and the exchange of objects and ideas.

Discussion

'Insular' art

Returning to Stead's statement that British art 'pursued an independent course' after 300 BC (Stead 1996, 29), it has been shown that the dividing line is less stark than he claims. Connections between continental art and British art can continue to be made but the influence of continental decorative material is much less prevalent after the later third century BC in contrast to the predominance of the so-called insular styles. This means that although continental connections continue to be reflected in the art, a different social need develops which is manifested in the manufacture and use of insular art.

The identification of objects decorated in more than one art style mixing 'continental' and 'insular' raises a number of questions. Why would you draw upon older art styles and juxtapose old and new? One possibility is that it increases the complexity of the art, making it harder to 'read' and allowing many different interpretations to be made, depending on the viewer (Garrow & Gosden 2012, 80). Another interpretation could be that by incorporating familiar designs, new styles are made more palatable and seem less alien than they would otherwise appear. Alternatively, drawing on designs that may have once been linked to continental contacts and incorporating those decorative elements into new insular styles, may be a deliberate attempt to subvert those old linkages, replacing them with something new.

Vincent and Ruth Megaw (1993, 228) argue that the introduction of a new art style requires more than just copying from a handful of random imports. For example, the motifs on the pottery from Chinnor studied by Timothy Champion mentioned earlier were not widely adopted. If new styles are to be adopted widely and maintained, they have to be accepted and used by a dominant group within society: the impetus for this it is argued has to be continuing contact and social links between people. A different viewpoint, argued for in this paper, is that the reason Celtic art in Britain develops into new styles not seen on the Continent is not because of a cessation of continental contacts (these can be seen by the continuation of stylistic linkages and small numbers of imports such as v-shaped finger rings) but rather that the social reason for continuing links between continental and British art breaks down or becomes less important. In other words, art takes on a different significance in Britain and is used in different ways. Rather than being representative of wider contacts, over time, art in Britain becomes more focussed on the object and its uses. Art, particularly on sword-scabbards, has been interpreted by Melanie Giles (2008) as having apotropaic or protective qualities. Similarly, work on mirrors – incidentally also an object type largely peculiar to Britain – has demonstrated the link between the decoration and the reflective qualities of the mirror plate (Joy 2008; 2010, Ch. 4).

Imports?
When summarising his 1984 paper on continental imports Stead stated "very few imports can be identified, but the similarity of many British pieces to Continental material hints at the presence of imports which have not survived or which still await discovery" (Stead 1984, 63). The new finds reported in this paper, such as the v-shaped finger ring from Biggleswade, or the torc fragment from Caister, confirm Stead's assertion and add weight to Bradley and Smith's (2007) argument that many of these finds are genuine Iron Age imports rather than objects discarded by 19th century collectors as previously contested.

Despite the admittedly still relatively low number of examples known, recent discoveries show that Celtic art from Britain decorated in styles also used on the Continent form an important constituent of the known corpus. The number of Plastic Style objects now known from Britain, for example, is not incomparable to the known number of display shields, which have come to be seen as representative of middle Iron Age British Celtic art.

Continental connections
Debating whether these artefacts are imports or were made in Britain is argued to be less important than their potential to show continental connections. Following Stead (1984, 63), even if many of the artefacts decorated in these styles were made in Britain, their similarity to objects made and used on the Continent still requires explanation as it indicates linkages and connections to the Continent.

Objects from the Continent act to physically manifest continental connections and social relations but the nature and importance of these connections alters over time. For example, the exotic origins of early Continental imports may have been important in terms of their deposition in rivers and their incorporation into regional belief systems within Britain. On the other hand, it is clear that Britain was at the very end of a complicated exchange network. Continental connections in this instance could be limited to a knowledge that these objects originate from very far away without the need for direct personal contact or knowledge of the societies where these objects were made. By the fourth and third centuries BC, when stylistic similarities in Celtic art can be seen across huge expanses of Europe, the nature of connections with the Continent is likely to be very different. The extent to which art on the Continent is homogenous can be questioned with regional and temporal variations in form, decoration and depositional patterns clearly apparent (Wells 2012). Nevertheless, there are clear links in art style, object form and methods of manufacture.

It is likely that Celtic art objects were important in demonstrating kinship and in negotiations between groups being exchanged as gifts, or moving with people. Traditionally these objects, particularly art found on the Continent dating to the early La Tène period, have been seen to be related to elites but recent discoveries from non-elite contexts demonstrate that they were more widely distributed through society (Wells 2012, 206). This evidence fits more closely the contexts in which early La Tène art are found in Britain, where objects, especially those deposited in watery contexts, probably represent offerings made by communities rather than individuals in transactions between the living and the supernatural. Even when art has been found in graves, viewing these objects as signs of high-status and simply as the possessions of the deceased has been demonstrated to be far too simplistic, with the arrangement of objects in graves manifesting often complicated messages and meanings to the living as well as the dead (Garrow and Gosden 2012, Ch. 7, Giles 2012, Ch. 4–6; Wells 2012, Ch. 8).

It is argued that Celtic art during this period was vital in terms of maintaining links between societies. By manufacturing and decorating artefacts in similar ways objects were able to transgress social and geographical boundaries and facilitated different social transactions as all the protagonists involved were familiar with those objects. This does not mean that the objects had a universal meaning but rather that societies were able to incorporate those objects into their own social and belief systems but were at the same time able to easily exchange those objects precisely because they were familiar to other groups of people. Celtic art at this time therefore helped facilitate complicated social transactions between people aware of societies or groups on the Continent but contact was not sufficiently frequent to make such transactions easy.

Hill (1995, 88) has argued that distinct regionality in artefact form and style can develop because of a need to maintain regional differences when there are otherwise high levels of contact (see also Webley, this volume). Perhaps, contrary to traditional arguments, the development of so-called insular art styles in Britain from 300 BC occurred because there was no longer a social need to maintain links to the Continent through Celtic art, or those linkages became less important. Contacts were more commonplace and did not require transactions of complicated objects to facilitate social contact. Hence British Celtic art was instead made and used to participate in different social transactions relating to the decorated object and its function. Interestingly, as is shown by some of the case studies, when evidence for contact and exchange is at its highest during the later Iron Age, art objects such as the Winchester torcs are again seen to cross the Channel. Perhaps in a time of social upheaval complicated objects are again required to facilitate and manifest social connections.

Direct or indirect contact

It does not necessarily matter if contact is direct or staged, widely travelled people and artefacts create linkages and ties to the outside world manifested through and by the objects. Nevertheless, a number of mechanisms or forms of contact have been discussed that warrant further discussion. The case studies presented indicate that contact occurred in the form of the importation or exportation of objects, copying of Continental art styles and the use of manufacturing techniques more common on the Continent. There is no doubt that people travelled between Britain and the Continent throughout the Iron Age but the scale and significance of that movement is open to question and beyond the remits of this paper. The majority of objects imported from the Continent considered here are likely to have been moved or exchanged in a number of stages rather than representing direct travel from the location of manufacture to the location of deposition. This is an important point because as these objects were exchanged and passed between individuals they would have acquired complicated biographies, possibly blurring or confusing associations with the place where they were made and the people who made and used them. The process of copying objects is also interesting. In a number of cases objects like the cauldron decorated in the Vegetal Style from Chiseldon were made in Britain but were clearly inspired by a continental art style. Does this represent the work of a continental metalworker, copying from an imported object, or even someone who has travelled in Europe and returned to make artefacts in Britain? It is impossible to determine an answer to this question. Nevertheless, it was acceptable and indeed desirable to copy continental styles. Some of the possible motivations behind this have been discussed above, making it possible that these objects were designed with wider social transactions in mind. Another possibility is that by making artefacts in continental styles, wider social contacts were being referred to or referenced whether real, imagined or anticipated.

Conclusions

It is hoped that the continuing potential of Iron Age art to inform us of continental connections has been demonstrated. Past studies have concentrated too much on assessing whether objects are imports and art has sometimes been studied in isolation with little consideration of wider society.

By studying objects in detail from the perspective of the social connections they potentially manifest a number of issues have been raised. In many cases imports are incorporated into local practices, such as Hallstatt D objects deposited in watery locations or the Canterbury helmet which was placed in a Kentish cremation grave. Contact is not always direct and we need to consider in greater detail how objects moved in the middle phases of their lives and understand that many of these objects passed through numerous contexts and hands before they reached their ultimate destination. Finally, examples such as the Winchester torcs, which have been interpreted as diplomatic gifts, or associations with military activities highlighted by the example of the Canterbury helmet, demonstrate that we need to think about different kinds of relationship or exchange from the traditional idea of trade, particularly in the later Iron Age which is a time of social flux with greater movement of people and ideas.

Art and other artefacts play a central role in the often complicated and potentially dangerous contacts between groups. The small number of early Iron Age continental imports demonstrates limited links particularly between the Rhine region and the Thames. The continuity in style between British and continental early Celtic art demonstrate connections and linkages through technologies and art styles. So called 'insular' art dating from 300 BC may not necessarily represent a break in continental contact as previously argued. The development of insular art styles could in fact demonstrate that linkages have become more commonplace meaning that art that is coherent with the Continent was unnecessary or became less important. The prevalence of well-travelled objects such as torcs in the later Iron Age, a time of increasing continental contact and social change, demonstrates again the central role of objects in complicated social transactions.

Acknowledgements

I would like to thank Fraser Hunter, Mansel Spratling and the editors for their comments, help and advice, Julia Farley for allowing me to see her paper on the Canterbury Helmet prior to publication and Craig Williams for his excellent illustrations. All errors remain my own.

References

Bradley, R. and Smith, A. 2007. Questions of context: a Greek cup from the River Thames. In C. Gosden, H. Hamerow, P. De Jersey and G. Lock (eds), *Communities and connections, essays in honour of Barry Cunliffe*, 30–42. Oxford: Oxford University Press.

Champion, T. 1977. Some decorated Iron Age pottery from Chinnor. *The Antiquaries Journal* 57, 91–93.

Champion, T. 2007. Prehistoric Kent. In J. Williams (ed.) *The archaeology of Kent to AD 800*, 67–132. Rochester: Boydell Press.

Clarke, R. 1954. The early Iron Age treasure from Snettisham. *Proceedings of the Prehistoric Society* 20, 27–86.

Creighton, J. 2006. *Britannia: the creation of a Roman province*. London: Routledge.

Cunliffe, B. 2005. Iron Age communities in Britain: an account of England, Scotland and Wales from the seventh century BC until the Roman Conquest (4th Edition). London: Routledge.

Cunliffe, B. 2009. Looking forward: maritime contacts in the first millennium BC. In P. Clarke (ed.) *Bronze Age Connections: cultural contact in Prehistoric Europe*, 81–93. Oxford: Oxbow.

Davies, J. 1996. Where eagles dare: the Iron Age of Norfolk. *Proceedings of the Prehistoric Society* 62, 63–92.

Davis, M. and Gwilt, A. 2008. Material, style and identity in first century AD metalwork, with particular reference to the Severn Sisters hoard. In D. Garrow, C. Gosden and J. D. Hill (eds) *Rethinking Celtic art*, 146–184. Oxford: Oxbow.

Demarez, L. and Leman-Delerive, G. 2001. A linch-pin of British type found at Blicquy (Hainaut, Belgium). *The Antiquaries Journal* 81, 391–395.

De Navarro, J. 1952. The Celts in Britain and their art. In M. Charlesworth and M. Knowles (eds) *The Heritage of Early Britain*, 56–82. London: G. Bell and Sons Ltd.

Dobney, K. and Ervynck, A. 2007. To fish or not to fish? Evidence for the possible avoidance of fish consumption during the Iron Age around the North Sea. In C. Haselgrove and T. Moore (eds) *The Later Iron Age in Britain and Beyond*, 403–418. Oxford: Oxbow.

Echt, R., Marx, M., Megaw, V., Thiele, W.-R., Van Impe, L. and Verhart, L. 2011. An Iron Age gold torc from Heerlen (prov. Limburg/NL). *Archäologisches Korrespondenzblatt* 41, 31–49.

Farley, J., Parfitt, K. and Richardson, A. 2014. An Iron Age helmet burial from Bridge near Canterbury, Kent. *Proceedings of the Prehistoric Society* 80, 379–388.

Feachem, R. 1958. The "Cairnmuir" hoard from Netherurd, Peeblesshire. *Proceedings of the Society of Antiquaries of Scotland* 91, 112–16.

Fitzpatrick, A. 1993. Ethnicity and exchange: Germans, Celts and Romans in the late Iron Age. In C. Scarre and F. Healy (eds) *Trade and exchange in Prehistoric Europe*, 233–244. Oxford: Oxbow.

Fitzpatrick, A. 2001. Cross-channel exchange. Hengistbury Head, and the end of hillforts. In J. Collis (ed.) *Society and settlement in Iron Age Europe*, 82–97. Sheffield: J. R. Collis.

Garrow, D. and Gosden, C. 2012. *Technologies of Enchantment? Exploring Celtic Art: 400 BC to AD 100*. Oxford: Oxford University Press.

Garrow, D., Gosden, C., Hill, J. D. and Bronk Ramsey, C. 2009. Dating Celtic Art: a major radiocarbon dating programme of Iron Age and early Roman metalwork in Britain. *The Archaeological Journal* 166, 79–123.

Giles, M. 2008. Seeing red: the aesthetics of martial objects in the British and Irish Iron Age. In D. Garrow, C. Gosden and J. D. Hill (eds), *Rethinking Celtic Art*, 59–77. Oxford: Oxbow.

Giles, M. 2012. *A forged glamour: landscape, identity and material culture*. Oxford: Windgather Press.

Guillaumet, J. P. and M. Schönfelder. 2001. Un manche de miroir de type britannique provenant de Compiègne; un nouveau témoignage des contacts à travers la Manche. *Antiquités Nationales* 33, 125–8.

Harbison, P. and Laing, L. R. 1974. *Some Iron Age Mediterranean imports in England*. Oxford: British Archaeological Reports 5.

Harden, D. B. 1950. Italic and Etruscan finds from Britain. *Atti del Io congresso internazionale di preistoria e protoistoria mediterranea*, 315–324.

Haselgrove, C. 2009. Noughts and crosses: the archaeology of "globules-à-la-croix". In J. van Heesch and I. Heeren (eds), *Coinage in the Iron Age: essays in honour of Simone Scheers*, 173–86. London: Spink.

Helms, M. 1988. *Ulysses' Sail: an ethnographic odyssey of power, knowledge and geographical distance*. Princeton: Princeton University Press.

Hill, J. D. 1995. The pre-Roman Iron Age in Britain and Ireland (ca. 800 BC to AD 100): an overview. *Journal of World Prehistory* 9, 47–98.

Hill, J. D. and Willis, S. 2013. Middle Bronze Age to the end of the pre-Roman Iron Age, c 1500 BC to AD 50. In J. Ransley and F. Sturt (eds), *People and the Sea: a maritime archaeological research agenda for England*, 75–92. London: Council for British Archaeology.

Hill, J. D., Spence, A., La Niece, S. and Worrell, S. 2004. The Winchester hoard: a find of unique Iron Age gold jewellery from southern England. *The Antiquaries Journal* 84, 1–22.

Hunter, F. 1997. Iron Age coins in Scotland. *Proceedings of the Society of Antiquaries of Scotland* 127, 513–525.

Hunter, F. 2006. Art in later Iron Age society. In C. Haselgrove (ed.), *Celtes et Gaulois, l'Archéologie face à L'Histoire, 4: les mutations de la fin de l'âge du Fer. Actes de la table ronde de Cambridge: 7–8 juillet 2005*, 93–115. Glux-en-Glenne, Bibracte, Centre Archéologique Européen.

Hunter, F. 2008. Celtic Art in Roman Britain. In D. Garrow, C. Gosden and J. D. Hill (eds), *Rethinking Celtic Art*, 129–145. Oxford: Oxbow.

Hunter, F. 2010a. A unique Iron Age gold hoard found near Stirling. *Past* 65, 3–5.

Hunter, F. 2010b. Buried treasure: a major Iron Age gold hoard from the Stirling area. *The Forth Naturalist and Historian* 33, 61–4.

Hunter, F. 2010c. More torc. *The Searcher* 294, 27–28.

Hutcheson, N. 2004. *Later Iron Age Norfolk: metalwork, landscape and society*. Oxford: British Archaeological Reports, British Series 361.

Hutcheson, N. 2007. An archaeological investigation of later Iron Age Norfolk: analysing hoarding patterns across the landscape. In C. Haselgrove and T. Moore (eds) *The later Iron Age in Britain and Beyond*, 358–70. Oxford: Oxbow.

Jacobsthal, P. 1969 [1944]. *Early Celtic Art*. Oxford: Clarendon.

Joachim, H.-E. 1995. *Waldalgesheim, das Grab einer keltischen Fürsin*. Köln, Rheinland-Verlag GmbH.

Jope, E. M. 1995. A gold finger-ring found at Arras, gone missing long since. In B. Raftery (ed.) *Sights and sites of the Iron Age: essays on fieldwork and museum research presented to Ian Mathieson Stead*, 113–117. Oxford: Oxbow.

Jope, E. M. 2000. *Early Celtic Art in the British Isles*. Oxford: Clarendon.

Joy, J. 2008. Reflections on Celtic Art: a re-examination of mirror decoration. In D. Garrow, C. Gosden and J.D. Hill (eds), *Rethinking Celtic Art*, 78–99. Oxford: Oxbow.

Joy, J. 2010. *Iron Age mirrors: a biographical approach*. Oxford: British Archaeological Reports, British Series 518.

Joy, J. 2014. Brit-art: Celtic Art in Roman Britain and on its Frontiers. In C. Gosden, S. Crawford and K. Ulmschneider (eds) *Celtic art in Europe: Making Connections. Essays in Honour of Vincent Megaw on his 80th birthday*, 315–324. Oxford: Oxbow.

Joy, J. and Farley, J. forthcoming. *The Snettisham treasure*. London: British Museum.

Joy, J. and Baldwin, A. forthcoming. *The bubbling cauldron: the Iron Age cauldrons from Chiseldon, Wiltshire*. London: British Museum.

Macdonald, P. 2007. Perspectives on insular La Tène art. In C. Haselgrove and T. Moore (eds) *The Later Iron Age in Britain and beyond*, 329–338. Oxford: Oxbow.

McGrail, S. 1993. Prehistoric seafaring in the channel. In C. Scarre and F. Healy (eds) *Trade and exchange in prehistoric Europe*, 199–210. Oxford: Oxbow Monograph 33.

Megaw, J. V. S. 1963. A British bronze bowl if the Belgic Iron Age from Poland. *The Antiquaries Journal* 43, 219–232.

Megaw, J. V. S. and Megaw, M. R. 1993. Cheshire Cats, Mickey Mice, the new Europe and ancient Celtic Art. In C. Scarre and F. Healy (eds), *Trade and Exchange in Prehistoric Europe*, 199–210. Oxford: Oxbow Monograph 33.

Megaw, R. and Megaw, J. V. S. 2001. *Celtic art from its beginnings to the Book of Kells*. London: Thames & Hudson.

Meyer, M. 1985. Hallstatt imports in Britain. *Bulletin of the Institute of Archaeology London* 21–22, 69–84.

Morris, F. 2010. *North Sea and channel connectivity during the late Iron Age and Roman period (175/150BC – AD409)*. Oxford: British Archaeological Report International Series 2157.

Sharples, N. 2010. *Social relations in later prehistory: Wessex in the first millennium BC*. Oxford: Oxford University Press.

Stead, I. M. 1979. *The Arras culture*. York: Yorkshire Philosophical Society.

Stead, I. M. 1984. Some notes on imported metalwork in Iron Age Britain. In S. Macready and F. Thompson (eds), *Cross-channel trade between Gaul and Britain in the pre-Roman Iron Age*, 43–66. London: Society of Antiquaries Occasional Paper No. IV.

Stead, I. M. 1985a. *The Battersea Shield*. London: British Museum Press.

Stead, I. M. 1985b. *Celtic Art in Britain before the Roman Conquest*. London: British Museum Press.

Stead, I. M. 1991. The Snettisham treasure: excavations in 1990. *Antiquity* 65, 447–65.

Stead, I. M. 1996. *Celtic Art in Britain before the Roman Conquest* (2nd Edition). London: British Museum Press.

Stead, I. M and Rigby, V. 1999. *The Morel Collection: Iron Age antiquities from Champagne in the British Museum*. London: British Museum Press.

Tait, H. 1976. *Jewellery through 7,000 years*. London: British Museum Press.

Van de Noort, R. 2011. *North Sea archaeologies: a maritime biography, 10,000 BC – AD 1,500*. Oxford: Oxford University Press.

Warner, R. 1991. The Broighter hoard. In S. Moscati, O.-H. Frey, V. Kruta, B. Raftery and M. Szabó (eds) *The Celts*, 617. New York, Rizzoli.

Warner, R. 2004. Irish gold artefacts: observations from Hartmann's analytical data. In H. Roche, E. Grogan, J. Bradley, J. Coles and B. Raftery (eds) *From megaliths to metal: essays in honour of George Eogan*, 72–82. Oxford: Oxbow.

Watkin, J., Stead, I., Hook, D. and Palmer, S. 1996. A decorated shield-boss from the River Trent, near Ratcliffe-on-Soar. *The Antiquaries Journal* 76, 17–30.

Wells, P. 2012. *How ancient Europeans saw the world: vision, patterns and the shaping of the mind in prehistoric times*. Princeton: Princeton University Press.

Willis, S. 2007. Sea, coast, estuary, land, and culture in Iron Age Britain. In C. Haselgrove and T. Moore (eds) *The later Iron Age in Britain and Beyond*, 107–129. Oxford: Oxbow.

10

Continental Connections: concluding discussion

Fraser Sturt and Duncan Garrow

It is all too easy to fall into established tropes when considering the changing nature of continental connections – to discuss 'isolated islands' or 'hyper connected seaways'. Part of the trouble lies in the fact that, as with many other clichés, each of these extremes has proven to be true at different points in time: from the impact of changing palaeogeography on hominin habitation patterns in the Palaeolithic, through to more recent movement of goods and people across seaways. As such, the papers in this volume have made clear the need for a more subtle appreciation of movement, communication and interaction than stereotypical presumptions permit. This re-evaluation requires a careful consideration both of how we determine connectivity from archaeological remains and, just as significantly, of how we frame the topic and orientate ourselves in relation to it.

Interestingly, the majority of papers presented within this volume have given an account of the history of archaeology's engagement with the topic of continental connections in their particular period, demonstrating that this specific theoretical engagement has been as long lasting and varied as any other. Yet, there remains a palpable sense that each generation discovers similar (if not quite the same) issues afresh; crafting new visions of the means, motivation and significance of cross-Channel contact from changing patterns in the material record. While in part this may be explained by an ever-increasing evidence base and the development of new investigative techniques, the trend appears more complex and long lived than this. Clark (1966) described the seismic shift that he saw occurring in British archaeology with the move away from invasion-led narratives of change to a burgeoning sense of indigenous development. He directly related the 'neurosis' (1966, 172) of seeing invasion as the driver of change to the social conditions that the archaeologists espousing it operated in:

> "The insular torpor that oppressed British archaeology during the late Victorian and Edwardian eras can only be fully savoured by turning over the periodical literature of the period. At least the anxiety to trace invaders led British archaeologists after the War of 1914–18 themselves to invade the Continent, to scour museums, investigate field monuments and even, as Sir Mortimer Wheeler, Professor Frere, Mrs Cotton, Mr Case and others have done, to undertake excavations in France or, like Professor Hawkes, in Portugal" (Clark 1966, 173).

The impact of the culture historical work undertaken in the era Clark describes still has a significant legacy in terms of how we understand connectivity and communication today.

It placed an emphasis on relating the changing distributions of specific artefact types to the explicit movement of identifiable groups of people. However, as Clark (1966) pointed out, work of this kind was often driven by a desire to know how the advances made on the continent were transmitted to the British Isles in a unidirectional manner. From the vantage point that Clark's own historical and political situation provided, this was too simplistic and presumptive:

> "The imperial past made us citizens of the world and as such we have gained a sense of proportion that one trusts will always be retained. What is happening among the younger school of British archaeologists is a new attempt to re-examine the evidence so far as possible with an open mind" (Clark 1966, 173).

It is interesting to reflect on this statement within the context of this volume. Clark refers to a sense of proportion, recourse to evidence and dissatisfaction with previous accounts driving research forward. However, when looking at the works of Abercromby (1902), Childe (1929), Crawford (1936), Piggott (1954), Clark (1966) and Case (1969), or even Whittle (1977), O'Connor (1980), Thomas (1991), Sheridan (2000) and Whittle *et al.* (2011) it would be inaccurate to state that there is no sense of proportion, or lack of reference to evidence. However, a change in the nature of that sense of proportion and what evidence is thought to mean can clearly be seen. As discussed below, with changing social dynamics in the present come shifting understandings of how people in the past may have related to one another, and the scale at which that interaction could have occurred. Thus the 'proportion' or sense of scale that Clark (1966) refers to changes through time, as does how we construe 'interaction' to take place from material culture. Thus, the 'open mind' that Clark (*ibid.*, 173) identifies as a product of his historical moment can be seen as an on-going part of archaeological practice; as our understanding of the contemporary world changes, so too can our thoughts about the past.

It is for this reason that Clark stressed the importance of recognising the links between archaeological interpretation and the contemporary political firmament that archaeologists operate within. "Turning over the periodical literature of the period" (Clark 1966, 172) is not just useful with regard to understanding the peccadillos of culture history, but has relevance for reviewing our own positions. In light of this it is perhaps worthwhile casting our net wider than a review of archaeology's engagement with the topic if we wish to understand how our own ideas may be being shaped by the world we live in.

Mannin (2013) charts the difficulties of understanding contemporary political relations across Europe and the impact of history on them. He notes (*ibid.*, 81) that until recently the political and historical literature failed to take into account the impact that membership of the European Union had had on political and social life in Britain. This was born from the belief that Britain had an 'exceptional' and different relationship to the EU than other member states, in part due to its island nature. However, Mannin demonstrates (*ibid.*, 82), that when a broader view is taken of what is rendered as unique or exceptional within this national narrative of historical relations those 'exceptional' qualities begin to appear more mundane and widely shared across Europe. As Webley (this volume) argues, when the presumption of difference created by the presence of the English Channel, Irish and North Seas is removed, more interesting cross cutting histories of interconnection emerge.

For Mannin (2013) a strong national narrative of difference and separation had ridden over the convincing evidence for broader European consensus leading to changing legal and social practices. This study acts as a timely reminder that even when studying the very recent past our assumptions as to the nature of social interaction are heavily skewed by presumptions based on the impacts of geography on connectivity. It is thus perhaps unsurprising that we find it easiest to talk about archaeologies of similarity when Britain is joined to the continent and have focused on differences during periods of separation by water. However, this presumption needs to be strongly challenged to ensure it is robust.

Furthermore, to follow Clark's (1966) argument about the impact of contemporary experience on archaeological interpretation, we need to give some thought as to how recent innovations have changed the way we conceive of interaction. We now live in a constantly connected world where virtual networks rapidly form, spread and then decay at a global scale. We thus should not be surprised to see a rise in our interest regarding connectivity, alongside a growing contentment for the archaeological record to indicate dramatic changes in the nature of communication. We no longer expect continuity of practice or process, nor see a requirement for linear patterns of development.

It is for this reason that it is worth restating Hawkes's famous statement, that "every age gets the Stonehenge it deserves – or desires" (1967, 174). It seems to us that every age also gets the understanding of continental connections that it deserves, or (perhaps more significantly) desires. To this end we have identified five key themes that have emerged from the arguments made in the chapters presented here. These relate to: visibility, equifinality, ebbs and flows in connectivity, the nature of interaction, and scale/resolution. It is not our intention to argue that the material record is so weak that any interpretation can be placed upon it, but rather to suggest that it has a range of qualities that need to be recognised and considered when evaluating what questions we can reasonably ask of it.

Visibility

The archaeological record is notoriously fragmentary and challenging to work with (Lucas 2012). Any attempt to understand the changing nature of continental connections through prehistory has to confront the issue of visibility. As Wilkin and Vander Linden (this volume) note, due to its partial nature, the surviving material record should not be taken as an 'accurate' reflection of cross-Channel relations. It is quite possible that customs, ideas and knowledge were more significant in driving communication and created broader networks across the continent than robust material remains suggest. As such, material culture might better be viewed as one proxy for interaction that needs to be bolstered and considered in light of others (isotopic, DNA, environmental, etc.) to ensure that we are not overawed by, or over-dependant on, 'the lure of the tangible'.

In this light, as several papers within the volume note, the absence of material evidence for connectivity should not be taken as evidence of absence. This is especially important given the argument (made below and in several of the papers within the volume) that we are capable of interpreting the same evidence in different ways, to argue both for and against interaction. Thus, rather than viewing the visible evidence in a binary presence/absence fashion, we may be better placed to see it as a more subtle expression of contemporary conditions (discussed below), registering shifting degrees of interaction, rather than absolutes.

Equifinality

Related to the theme above, and perhaps the greatest of all challenges posed by research into prehistory, is the problem of equifinality; that the same end result can be achieved through different processes. This aspect of the archaeological record has sustained debate and disagreement in academic texts over the last century. For Childe (1925) and Piggott (1954), the appearance of new material forms directly attested to an 'invasion' of continental groups into the British Isles, while for Clark (1966) the same material spoke of indigenous developments. It would be disingenuous to depict these changes in interpretation as a linear progression through time, with ever improved and more accurate representations of the past emerging from them. This is because the processes which lie behind the deposition of the material remains we find today are hard to discern, resulting in an end product created by archaeological investigation which *is* equifinal in nature. A new vessel or lithic form may be the result of population movement, an exchange of ideas, or indeed both. As noted in our introduction to this volume and discussed by Anderson-Whymark and Garrow (this volume), the problems we face are further compounded by the fact that we have the ability to interpret both similarity *and* difference in material forms as indicators for both high and low levels of interaction. Thus our quanta for measuring difference may be the same as those used to express similarity.

Here we would like to contend that rather than seeing this as a negative statement, there is in fact a liberation to be found in recognising the equifinal nature of parts of the archaeological record, and the arguments we create from it. In so doing we can begin to consider the questions we ask of our data and how appropriate or answerable they may be. The papers in this volume have shown that from the Palaeolithic through to the Iron Age, connections with and across the continent existed, although as Warren (this volume) notes, the degree to which they were 'materially celebrated' may have varied. An appreciation of the history of archaeological thought demonstrates that we have interpreted distributions of material culture very differently through time. Today, perhaps again for reasons of historical conditions, we find ourselves more open to a 'blurred' reading of the data, where previously contradictory arguments can be held at the same time and both are seen to be valid. We can accept both movements of people and sharing of ideas, times of heightened communication along one axis and a waning along another. The equifinality of the record and our arguments may not be a failing, but an indication of the multiple processes and shifting nature of continental connections that occurred in the past. Scarre's contribution to this volume documents this well, with consideration of processes of transmission and translation, how practices and products may look similar, but on closer examination demonstrate subtle, yet significant, variation through time.

Making this step towards higher temporal resolution accounts and more detailed consideration of the material record may help us to highlight minor but significant differences in material form to help move discussion forward. However, we should not expect such changes to answer automatically our longest standing questions to do with the nature of interaction, as these largely relate to interpretive stances rather than innate and testable qualities of the archaeological record.

Ebbs and flows

With an increasing appreciation that the physical space over which we envisage communication to have occurred is differently textured, affording differing degrees of communication, comes the understanding that the nature of continental connections are unlikely to be fixed. Just as the physical geography of Europe has changed over the period considered in this volume, so too have its social structures and interaction patterns. As such, it seems more logical to conclude that patterns of interaction would ebb and flow both across space and through time rather than remain constant. Following the argument above, it would also appear to be the case that social contact and changes in material culture style did not always go hand-in-hand. Thus, as Webley argues (this volume), to fixate on a limited range of material culture alone as a marker for interaction will result in potentially misleading conclusions. This is not to say that changes in material form, or the movement of goods across the continent is not without significance; but it should not be seen as the sole indicator for the degree of connectivity occurring. As documented by Joy and Scarre's papers (this volume), the significance of these materials may change across space and through time, and thus may need to be studied in more detail than as a simple marker of shared ideas and practice. What emerges from this realisation, as Webley (this volume) asserts, is that the rewarding challenge lies in untangling the interplay between different sorts of regional and pan-regional relationships and how they may differentially express themselves. In many ways this can be seen as a continuation of Clark's (1966) desire to see the evidence looked at with an 'open mind'.

Interaction: spheres and arrows

This open mind and understanding of the equifinal nature of the material record directly plays into how we understand and represent communication and interaction. Cunliffe (2001; 2007; 2011; 2012) has given considerable consideration to this topic, arguing that our visualisation of the geography of Europe has shaped our presumptions about the insular nature of Britain and Ireland:

> "To understand these systems it is necessary to reverse our cognitive geography so as to see Britain not as an inward looking entity in its own right but as a series of maritime zones functioning as part of broader European regions, the sea linking rather than dividing" (Cunliffe 2007, 99).

In part, Cunliffe has achieved this through literally re-orienting his maps to provide a different view, with Britain seen to look into Europe rather than out into the Atlantic. Such representative devices do a lot more than make us pause for thought, and significantly help to address underlying assumptions. It is interesting to note that prior to widespread use of air travel and with maritime transportation dominant such statements were not required (see Crawford 1935) since knowledge of these waterborne thoroughfares was well established within the population. However, Cunliffe's work, along with other recent publications on the role of maritime transportation in prehistory (Westerdahl 1995; Callaghan and Scarre 2009; Garrow and Sturt 2011; Van de Noort 2011), document the need to re-familiarise ourselves with the affordances of this environment and what they may mean for communication.

Within the chapters of this volume we have seen direct consideration of how we discuss and visualise connectivity, from the use of arrows to indicate direction, timing and intensity through to use of geometric shapes to represent zones of interaction. Given the discussion above, we should not be surprised that we find these images both helpful and frustrating. The creation of boundaries along the edges of interaction zones always creates a division, no matter how soft, that some (with good reason) will choose to question. As discussed above, even the act of recognising bodies of water as features gives them a barrier-like status that is at times unhelpful. Arrows too are problematic, didactically suggesting directionality and tempo of movement, where more diffuse processes may be seen to be at play. However, there is something in both the presence of arrows and spheres within our depictions that is useful to recognise. As Whittle *et al.*'s (2011) work has shown, we can detect a 'grain' within the material record that when matched to radiocarbon dating can be given a temporal component. This naturally lends itself to abstract representation in lines and isochrones. However, those lines might best be seen as indicative vectors rather than direct representations of process. The presence of spheres or zones of interaction combat this unyielding nature of arrows to offer glimpses into more complex patterns of material and social interaction, yet still suffer from the difficulty of resolving exactly where the 'edges' may lie. Thus, we are perhaps best off viewing all of these representations as we do palaeogeographic renderings of space: they are all models with varying degrees of precision and accuracy, but all have something to offer in terms of explaining the shifting form of communication and connectivity through time.

Scale/resolution

Our final theme relates to scale and resolution: the scope of our investigations fundamentally shape what we infer and understand about the nature of connectivity. We have seen, especially in the papers by Joy, Scarre and Warren, that what can appear similar at a coarse grained spatio/temporal scale breaks down into something subtly different and more interesting on closer examination. In a similar way, Wilkins and Vander Linden's and Webley's papers demonstrate that where we choose to place the boundaries of our studies has a dramatic impact on how we interpret the material record. The presumption of the water as a barrier leads to presumptions about interaction, but so too does the homogenisation of continental Europe into a single undifferentiated whole.

It is interesting to note that while a number of the papers in this volume directly engaged with the impact of changing spatial scales, there was less direct consideration of changing frequencies of interaction. This enabled all of us to operate within a broadly binary system; considering communication verses lack of communication. However, sitting behind many of the arguments raised in the papers presented here are increasingly complex questions as to how changes in intensity and directionality of communication would impact on observed patterns.

Summary

Understanding the changing nature of continental connections is fraught with problems, from the equifinal nature of the archaeological record through to determining whether that record reflects increasing or decreasing interaction. However, as all of the papers in this volume have made clear, it remains a fruitful avenue for research. By engaging with this longstanding topic we are forced to confront the assumptions made in the past, alongside those that we make today. It requires that we engage with the same robust qualities of the material record that indicated to antiquarians and cultural historians that people and ideas ebbed and flowed across Europe in the past, while leaving the exact process by which that occurred obscured. Our sense of proportion may have changed since Clark (1966) commented on it, but it still requires an opening and questioning mind to recheck and redraw its boundaries.

References

Abercromby, J. 1902. The oldest Bronze Age ceramic type in Britain, its close analogies on the Rhine, its probable origin in central Europe. *Journal of the Royal Anthropological Institute* 32, 373–397.

Case, H. 1969. Neolithic explanations. *Antiquity* 43, 176–186.

Callaghan, R. and Scarre, C. 2009. Simulating the western seaways. *Oxford Journal of Archaeology* 28, 357–372.

Childe, V. G. 1925. *The Dawn of European Civilisation*. London: Keegan Paul.

Clark, J. G. 1966. The invasion hypothesis in British archaeology. *Antiquity* 40, 172–89.

Crawford, O. G. S. 1935. Western seaways. In L. Buxton (ed.), *Custom is King. Essays Presented to R. R. Marett on his Seventieth Birthday*. London: Hutchinson.

Cunliffe, B. 2001. *Facing the Ocean: the Atlantic and its Peoples*. Oxford: Oxford University Press.

Cunliffe, B. 2007. Continent cut off by fog: just how insular is Britain? *Scottish Archaeological Journal* 29, 99–112.

Cunliffe, B. 2011. *Europe Between the Oceans: 9000 BC–AD 1000*. Oxford: Oxford University Press.

Cunliffe, B. 2012. *Britain Begins*. Oxford: Oxford University Press.

Garrow, D. and Sturt, F. 2011. Grey waters bright with Neolithic argonauts? Maritime connections and the Mesolithic–Neolithic transition within the 'western seaways' of Britain, *c.* 5000–3500 BC. *Antiquity* 85, 59–72.

Lucas, G. 2012. *Understanding the Archaeological Record*. Cambridge: Cambridge University Press.

Mannin, M. 2013. Britain: Europeanization and the battle with history. In C. Bretherton and M. Mannin (eds), *The Europeanization of European Politics*, 81–94. Basingstoke: Palgrave Macmillan.

O'Connor, B. 1980. *Cross Channel Relations in the Later Bronze Age*. Oxford: British Archaeological Report International Series 91. Oxford: British Archaeological Reports.

Piggott, S. 1954. *The Neolithic cultures of the British Isles*. Cambridge: Cambridge University Press.

Sheridan, A. 2000. Achnacreebeag and its French connections: vive the 'auld' alliance. In J. Henderson (ed.) *The Prehistory and Early History of Atlantic Europe*, 1–16. British Archaeological Report S861. Oxford: Archaeopress.

Thomas, J. 2013. *The Birth of Neolithic Britain. An Interpretive Account*. Oxford: Oxford University Press.

Van de Noort, R. 2011. *North Sea Archaeologies: a Maritime Biography, 10,000 BC–AD 1,500*. Oxford: Oxford University Press.

Westerdahl, C. 1995. Traditional transport zones in relation to ship types. In O. Olsen, F. Rieck, J. Skamby Madsen (eds), *Shipshape. Essays for Ole Crumlin-Pedersen*, 213–230. Roskilde: Viking Ship Museum.

Whittle, A. 1977. *The Earlier Neolithic of southern England and its Continental Background*. British Archaeological Report S35. Oxford: British Archaeological Reports.

Whittle, A., Bayliss, A. and Healy, F. 2011. *Gathering Time: dating the early Neolithic enclosures of southern Britain and Ireland*. Oxford: Oxbow Books.